EAS

STARTING FROM SCRATCH

INSPIRED TO BE A JUMP JOCKEY

HENRIETTA KNIGHT

STARTING FROM SCRATCH

INSPIRED TO BE A JUMP JOCKEY

RACING POST

First published in Great Britain in 2019 by
Racing Post Books
27 Kingfisher Court, Hambridge Road, Newbury, Berkshire, RG14 5SJ

10 9 8 7 6 5 4 3 2 1

ISBN 978-1-83950-030-5

Designed by Fiona Pike
Cover designed by Samantha Creedon

Back cover images
(top left) Edward Whitaker/Racing Post
(top right) Edward Whitaker/Racing Post
(bottom left) Patrick McCann/Racing Post
(bottom right) cranhamphoto.com

Printed and bound in the UK by CPI Group (UK) Ltd, Croydon, CR0 4YY

www.racingpost.com/shop

Dedicated to
Terence Walter Biddlecombe
Champion National Hunt jockey
1964-65
1965-66
1968-69
Simply the best

Contents

Foreword by Sir Anthony McCoy OBE

As an ex-school mistress, I had expected Henrietta to give every jockey in this book marks out of ten, but fortunately she has concentrated on writing about her observations, rather than her likes and dislikes. I say fortunately because I never felt I quite fitted the mould of what Hen likes to see in a rider.

Thankfully, for me, her late husband Terry Biddlecombe enjoyed watching me ride Hen's horses a little more than she did. Having been the chief selector for the British Three-Day Event team, judged horses and riders at top shows and, of course, trained Best Mate to win three Cheltenham Gold Cups, she always leaned towards horsemen rather than jockeys.

My background was entirely in racing and I had no exposure to any other form of riding so probably fell short on some points of style.

What I did have, in abundance, was an unquestionable will to win. Something that is absolutely top of the list of qualities that you look for in any sportsman.

This book is about what has made each jockey tick and his or her background in the sport. Reading it during the winter nights will give you a lot of pleasure.

Appreciation

This book gives a unique insight into the finest sportsmen of all, the National Hunt jockeys, and who better to write it than Henrietta Knight given her vast knowledge and experience of the game and equestrian sports in general.

It gives the reader an in-depth look into jump jockeys' lives: how they started, their backgrounds, what drove them, their successes and their lows and highs, and what motivated them to be jockeys.

This book is a must-read, not just for National Hunt and racing enthusiasts, but for any sports fan and for anyone interested in human nature. These pages can be used to reminisce or serve as an inspiration. Sit back and enjoy the ride.

Yogi Breisner MBE

Introduction

Writing this book has been an enlightening experience and I have thoroughly enjoyed it. I have heard some fascinating stories, and the 14 months of research have enriched my life.

The early education of unraced horses has always been of great interest to me and, just as ways of training racehorses differ widely, I have also learned there is no fixed pathway to becoming a National Hunt jockey. Until I talked to those who have been, and in many cases still are, the backbone of the National Hunt game, I had not fully appreciated the complexity of their own early lives.

Good horses certainly help to make good jockeys, but often childhood experiences have played a major part. For those who started out without any horse connections, a simple interest in racing saw them benefit from lessons and admirably plough their own furrow. Others, brought up in horse environments, may have begun with an advantage, but did not necessarily turn out to be the best jockeys, and indeed in some cases were less receptive to instruction because they believed they already knew how to ride. Some jockeys exhibited star quality from day one – complete naturals, they were destined to be successful – but the best, while knowing they were good, still appreciated help. They were hard on themselves and analysed any weaknesses. They wanted to get even better, and left no stone unturned. These were the champions. I hope today's aspiring jockeys will derive encouragement from seeing how those before them started out.

National Hunt racing is a tough sport, and those who ride the horses have massive responsibilities. Obviously they are answerable to owners and trainers, but they are at the mercy of the racing press and public opinion as well, and need the temperament to withstand being constantly in the limelight. In the last century fewer race meetings and the absence of the internet and mobile phones meant the stress was lower; nowadays jockeys' lives are full-on every day, at times manic. No wonder some – even those at the top of their game – succumb to pressure. Fortunately mental anguish and associated health issues are at last receiving a better understanding.

Highs and lows happen in all sports but, having been married to a former champion jockey myself, I find it easier to understand the intensity of emotion that rules jockeys' lives, and the importance of confidence. Jump jockeys are a great bunch: not only do they ride to win races but they are also incredibly brave, and the majority become hooked on the adrenalin kick associated with race-riding and love the camaraderie of the weighing room. But they are not as tough as they sometimes think they are.

It was not easy to draw up a list of jockeys for this book, and it kept getting longer. Those interviewed represent a wide cross-section of the profession, not just the top rank, but I could write a second volume on the ones I've missed out, and I really regret some of the jockeys who have been omitted. I apologise to all those I've failed to include – in particular, the omissions from the north of England and Scotland. There were not enough days in the year to visit them all.

National Hunt jockeys will always be close to my heart, and I've appreciated the frankness and trust that have been afforded to me, as well as enjoying the great senses of humour. This book demonstrates my love for jump racing and my fascination for examining its grass roots. A big thank you to you all for your brilliant stories.

Henrietta Knight

Lockinge, August 2019

Marcus Armytage

In the 20th century it was always a tremendous achievement for an amateur jockey to win the Grand National. Fulke Walwyn won the race on Reynoldstown in 1936, but after Charlie Fenwick partnered Ben Nevis to victory in 1980 and Dick Saunders rode Grittar in 1982 no other amateur lifted the prize until Marcus Armytage steered Mr Frisk to victory in 1990. He rode an exceptionally good race and was a hugely popular winner.

Marcus was always an accomplished horseman, and horses were known to run sweetly for him. He comes from a powerful horse family: at East Ilsley in Berkshire his father Roddy trained plenty of good National Hunt horses, while his mother Sue, under her maiden name of Whitehead, was a top international show-jumper and rode for Dorothy Paget, with Scorchin one of her top horses. As a rider Marcus obviously inherited plenty of his mother's genes, as did his sister Gee, who was one and a half years younger and also turned out to be a first-class jump jockey.

Marcus and Gee both rode numerous ponies as children, starting off with a Shetland. Marcus then graduated to a bigger pony called Fairy, whom he took to the Fancy Dress class at the Old Berkshire Pony Club Show, but Gee refused to lead him up. Both children competed regularly at the local shows, and in particular spent many Sundays at Stocklands Equestrian Centre near Winchester. 'I often had four faults,' said Marcus, 'and Gee jumped clear round after clear round, so I had to wait for the whole of her class to finish, and for her to do the jump-off. I much preferred to go hunting.' This he did with the Old Berkshire Hunt and the Heythrop Hunt, where his grandmother, Pug Whitehead, managed Ted Marsh's horses. He loved his days with this pack, and spent many hours with the renowned huntsman Captain Ronnie Wallace. Marcus usually accompanied him when he went out hunting, and would be invited to ride up front to open any necessary gates.

Besides the horses the family kept a collection of animals: two tame foxes, as well as a pet badger notorious for using the downstairs lavatory – even sitting upon it like a human being. On one occasion Roddy rescued an injured mallard duck, and its presence in the yard encouraged hundreds of the species to fly in every evening for a good feed of grain.

Marcus always liked the idea of becoming a jockey, and rode his first racehorse at the age of 12. This horse, Royal William, never pulled, which was considered ideal for the young boy, who enjoyed taking it out on exercise with the main string. At that time the Armytage training facilities boasted one of the first all-weather gallops: 'It stretched up a hillside, and its surface was industrial sand, which one of the lads constantly went over with a magnet to remove dangerous pieces of metal.' There was also a tight schooling ring, surfaced with wood chippings, the edges piled high with soil. Around the ring telegraph poles were laid out, which the horses were taught to jump. 'It helped the jockeys as well as the racehorses – the obstacles demanded plenty of respect. The horses learned to pick up their feet.' Marcus and Gee loved jumping their ponies round the ring.

Before Marcus went to Eton, where his fellow pupils included David Cameron and Boris Johnson, he attended a boys' preparatory school at Scaitcliffe, but with both schools fully boarding he nearly gave up the idea of being a jockey. With very little time to ride in term time he could only partner the racehorses during the holidays, but his experience and love of racing continued to grow, and he remembers being allowed to ride the lovely grey horse Pioneer Spirit, one of his father's good chasers, back from the gallops after it had completed its work.

At the age of 16, on his father's advice, Marcus was granted an amateur jockeys' licence, but in the 1970s and 1980s, to qualify to ride against professionals an amateur had to have 15 rides in amateur races. Roddy bought a very slow horse, bred by the Queen, called Honours Even, which used to take off going to the start but in the race itself quickly stopped pulling and was painfully slow. This horse taught the young jockey a great deal, and Marcus had further rides on the mare, Chevalgan, in a series of amateur hurdle races. But the best tutor was Brown Jock, whom Marcus frequently rode at Windsor, a course close to his school. In 1981, with Marcus still only 16, Brown Jock provided him with his first win on a racecourse – at Plumpton on Easter Saturday. The horse was not first past the post, but was awarded the race after a stewards' inquiry. Marcus remembers going back into the weighing room and saying to the clerk of the scales, Charles Stebbing, 'I'm objecting.' When asked why he replied, 'Because my mother told me to.'

That weekend marked the turning point in his career. Shortly afterwards Marcus won a bumper race at Hereford on Tom Tailor in a three-way finish: he was in the middle between Paul Nicholls and Mark Caswell.

Marcus had a gap year after leaving Eton before enrolling at Cirencester Agricultural College, where he spent three enjoyable years and obtained a Diploma in Rural Estate Management. For the first six months of his gap year he had worked in Wensleydale on a dairy farm and ridden out for trainer Chris Thornton. The rest was spent with Dick Saunders in Northamptonshire schooling Dick's point-to-point horses – all valuable experience for race-riding.

During his time at Cirencester the majority of the racehorses Marcus rode were based at Ilsley with his father, but on several occasions during the holidays he went to David Barons' yard in the West Country, where in those days Paul Nicholls was riding most of the horses. Marcus remembers riding Seagram, who won the Grand National in 1991, for 20 minutes of steady cantering around a field that had been harrowed after harvest: 'He was such a strong puller that by the end my arms had virtually gone.'

It was during his college years that Marcus had his first race, at Windsor, against the professionals. In those days the weighing of jockeys was far less strictly policed, and there was plenty of low cunning from jockeys who were too heavy – my late husband Terry Biddlecombe always struggled with his weight, and had many tales to tell. Lead was often removed from weight cloths and girths were discreetly hidden in order to meet the correct weights. On the day in question, Marcus clearly remembers, he weighed out for his race and placed his saddle on the rails in the weighing room – only for John Francome to come in after riding a winner and put his own tiny saddle on top of Marcus's. He subsequently weighed in with the pad alone and, not surprisingly, was spot on the weight.

Marcus had the perfect grounding for a jockey and, although he remained an amateur because of his height and weight, he was well able to hold his own against the professionals. Known as Fluffy to his friends, he was always a natural horseman who found jumping fences easy. He had good balance, took advantage of his long legs and rode a sensible length. He sat in the right place on a horse's back, just behind the withers.

He went on to ride 100 winners under rules, including three at the Cheltenham Festival. He won the prestigious Whitbread Trophy at Sandown, and during the 1990s contested the famous Pardubice steeplechase in Czechoslovakia on three occasions, always riding a Czech-trained horse. Despite some falls it was a great experience for an amateur. As well as winning the Grand National, Marcus was Fegentri champion – the top amateur Flat-race rider in Europe – in the same year.

His association with Mr Frisk was remarkable. He had often noticed the horse being exercised in East Ilsley close to his father's yard, in the days when Kim Bailey trained in the same village. Indeed, everyone knew the horse, because Tracey, Kim's wife, would exercise him by leading him from her event horse. Marcus's wins on Mr Frisk in amateur races at Ascot, as well as winning a chase at Doncaster and finishing in third place in the Hennessy Gold Cup at Newbury, showed how well horse and jockey gelled. The fairy-tale Grand National victory confirmed the jockey's unflappable nature and inborn riding talent.

He retired to become racing correspondent for the *Daily Telegraph*, and by understanding the sport so well, together with the intelligence and education he brings to the task, makes what he writes for the paper both colourful and interesting. His contribution to racing, which he adores, cannot be overemphasised, yet had he followed his Eton schoolmates, he might easily have ended up as a politician.

Paul Barton

The strength and solidarity of Paul Barton was demonstrated to the full when he took on one of the most soul-searching and responsible jobs in racing. In 2013, he became head of the stewarding panel for Britain's racecourses, a position he held for four years following 22 years with the Jockey Club and ending with the British Horseracing Authority.

Yet, prior to his time in officialdom, Paul had been an extremely successful and popular National Hunt jockey, holding a licence for 15 years and riding more than 350 winners, including Peter Scot in the 1979 Welsh Grand National. Always trustworthy and dependable, with a level head – he was seldom swayed by outside influences – he was greatly respected by his fellow jockeys.

Born in February 1954 on the Isle of Wight, Paul is an only child. His paternal grandfather was a bare-knuckle boxer and knife sharpener; his mother came from a Welsh mining family. Later in his childhood, Paul's family moved to a council house in Rugby, where his mother and father took on a pub – and went on to run a number of pubs throughout the Midlands. As a child, Paul had little interest in riding, 'even though my dad liked racing'.

However, at the age of 11, he did get his first experience with horses when he went to Caroline Bradley's show-jumping yard in Pattishall, Northamptonshire. A top rider renowned for being a very strict taskmaster, Caroline obviously gave the young lad a good grounding. He never rode any horses while he was there, just did menial tasks in the yard, but even these he thoroughly enjoyed.

When Paul's mother and father moved to run a pub in Dudley, near Wolverhampton, there were ponies in the neighbouring fields, and on twilight evenings Paul and a friend would venture out and jump onto their backs. Ignorance was bliss – no bridles, no saddles, no hats – but it was fun and challenging. There were also some stables nearby, and the young would-be jockey would get riding lessons there in return for mucking out boxes. 'From day one, I always felt at home on a pony.'

When Paul was 14, and having changed schools many times to fit in with his parents' work, he went to see the careers officer, and was taken round factories, but did not like what he saw. By now he had his sights set on race-riding, even though his friends were already telling him he would grow too tall and too big to be a jockey – indeed, a doctor who measured him at the time estimated his final weight would be around 11st. Since Paul's mother was only 5ft 4in and his father 5ft 7in, plus Paul himself a mere 8st, he decided to defy the doctor's prophecy and wrote to a number of trainers whose names and addresses he had found in Raceform's *Horses in Training* booklet. There were no racing schools in those days.

Paul's first assignment in racing was a part-time job with Ron Mason near Rugby, a small trainer with predominantly Flat horses who proved to be a fantastic schoolmaster and gave the aspiring jockey plenty of help in his holidays. Paul lived in the hostel with the rest of the lads and began riding out on the racehorses as well as mucking out stables. Yet because he had accepted he would be too big to be a Flat-race jockey, he could not wait to leave school and move to a jumping yard.

He went back to his bible, *Horses in Training*, to find a National Hunt trainer with at least 30 horses, and ended up writing to Frank Cundell, Tim Forster and David Gandolfo. Through a horse called Choral Cluster, Paul's father had a connection with Gandolfo, which made him seem the most suitable thus, says Paul, 'I left school on the Friday, and began working for Gandy on the Monday.' When Paul arrived at the Downs Stables in Oxfordshire, Gandy's famous training establishment, he had never had a riding lesson and never jumped an obstacle – not even a pole on the ground. Yet he remained with his boss for 16 years.

Gandy never gave him a lesson, and when for the first time he was allowed to jump a horse over a hurdle he lost his balance, fell off and broke his arm. Subsequently he learned by copying the other jockeys, especially Bill Shoemark and Clive Candy, the yard's amateur rider, both of whom rode many winners for the trainer. During the early years Paul shared a room in the lads' hostel with Clive.

Some of Paul's early memories make one's hair stand on end. On one occasion he was very excited to be told he could ride the stable stalwart, Hopeful Lad, in a boys' race over hurdles. But he was soon brought down to earth when the horse was badly injured a few days before the planned outing. Instead of getting a ride on a racecourse, Paul was asked to lead his pal into a field where he was humanely put to sleep by the vet, after which he was buried in a pit close to the gallops. This good racehorse and great servant to the yard coming to such a sudden and sad ending brought home to the young jockey just how uncertain and tough life can be when you work with horses. It is a true saying – 'where there is livestock, there is always dead stock'.

Paul well remembers his 17th birthday, because he got on the scales and discovered he weighed 10½st. He promptly put himself on a fruit diet for four weeks and lost 14lb. At 18 he had his first ride in public on Scrabble at Devon and Exeter racecourse. He was overweight, riding at 9st 9lb, and unplaced, but a few weeks later rode Indigo Jones to victory at Folkestone for trainer John Webb. Paul Barton's innings with Gandy, which were longer than any other jockey, were remarkable. However, in the 1984-85 season he decided upon a change and moved on to John Edwards' yard in Herefordshire.

He continued to ride winners but on a cold, wet afternoon at Newbury racecourse in 1987 he decided to call it a day. His career had been one of admirable consistency and, although he had not figured among the top names in the jockeys' lists, he was a competent and brave rider with a good racing brain. He enjoyed his years in the saddle and always had a strong work ethic, but he admits he was not particularly ambitious. Nevertheless, he registered some notable wins, and from a jockey who had never ridden bareback – other than in the fields at Dudley – and had never taken part in pony races, show-jumping events, or been out hunting. It was a success story.

David Bass

David Bass's story is an unusual one. He was born in Bedford in 1988 to parents who were both musicians. His mother Rowena, a music teacher and a vicar, plays both the harp and the piano; his father Philip is a superb pianist who has given private music lessons for many years, as well as writing books for children. There were two girls as well as David, and the youngest, Elizabeth, plays the harp professionally and has appeared many times at the Proms. So where did David get his interest in horses?

When he was three the Bass family moved from Bedford to live at Ringstead in Northamptonshire, a small, rural village that was definitely more congenial for the children. Philip followed racing in his spare time, often going to nearby Towcester racecourse or the local point-to-points at Guilsborough, Dingley and Newton Bromswold. David would go with him, and initially got hooked on the idea of being a point-to-point rider when he grew up. He had a few riding lessons when he was six, but as football took over, his interest in horses waned. He always loved sport, and also enjoyed skateboarding, but his musical genes were strong too. He had lessons on the drums and, while still at secondary school in Kettering, started a band called Dood Linda, which means 'smashing sound' in Swahili.

When his full-time education ended in 2004, David's mother worried about what her son would do. He was offered a job at Moulton College to be an assistant greenkeeper on the golf course, but a day out with his father at Stratford racecourse put other thoughts into his head. He decided he would like a career in National Hunt racing and, when he heard about the British Racing School in Newmarket, he applied and was accepted on a nine-week course.

When he arrived at the school David barely knew how to ride a horse. Beforehand he had managed a few weeks at Clarissa Caroe's racing yard, where she had helped him on the ponies, but 'I was so green, I couldn't even tack up'. He loved his stay in Newmarket, learned plenty, and when he left he was placed at trainer Richard Phillips' establishment at Adlestrop near Stow-on-the-Wold. Richard Dunwoody did some coaching there, and taught the lads to look stylish on a horse Equicizer. Dunwoody had been one of David's pin-ups, but he found the lessons an anti-climax, while the trainer deflated his enthusiasm for the game by constantly telling him how badly he rode and that his hands needed cutting off and sending back to racing school.

Nevertheless, the young jockey spent two years with Richard Phillips and did a small amount of schooling, while finding jumping 'a very strange experience'. When he left he was told bluntly, 'You'll never make it as a rider. You're too heavy and you're too soft. You might get lucky one day in a point-to-point if all the other horses fall.' A spell at Sheila Crow's point-to-point academy near Shrewsbury only lasted six weeks: all he did was ride a few horses at home and then lead them up at the races.

At this point David's fortunes changed. He answered an advertisement in the *Horse and Hound*, which began: 'Lad or Lass wanting point-to-point rides'. The sender was none other than the notorious trainer Johnny 'Mad' Manners.

Adjectives to describe this unique character and his unorthodox methods are hard to find. It was not unusual to see a selection of Manners' cattle, having escaped from their fields, roaming around the streets of Highworth, the small country town in Wiltshire close to Common Farm, where he combined farming, training and the management of his resident stallions. Yet he did help a number of aspiring jockeys and sent out many winners, both on the point-to-point circuit and in hunter chases. Indeed, he won the Fox Hunters' Chase at Aintree twice, in 1994 with Killeshin and in 1998 with Cavalero.

David Bass was 18 when he moved to Johnny Manners' farm and, despite having done very little jumping, he rode in his first point-to-point ten days later. He also remembers having to calve a cow and help to cover mares on only his first day.

He spent two valuable years with the Highworth trainer and was given more than a hundred point-to-point rides, which yielded 15 winners. Man From Highworth was particularly good to him, and he won the Coronation Cup at Larkhill as well as riding him in the Cheltenham Foxhunter Chase. In April 2009, when claiming 7lb, he won a novice chase at Towcester, which was David's first win under rules.

In September 2009, on the advice of Felix de Giles, the rider moved to Nicky Henderson's yard in Lambourn and took out a conditional jockeys' licence. In November he won a hurdle race at Sandown on Scots Dragoon, and the following spring took the Swinton Hurdle at Haydock on Eradicate as well as the Mares' Final at Newbury on Ryde Back. It was a dream start. He benefited enormously from his experiences in the leading trainer's yard, especially when working horses on the gallops and schooling them alongside top National Hunt jockeys. With his 3lb claim, David even rode Sprinter Sacre to victory in the horse's first novice chase over two miles at Doncaster.

Unfortunately, when David lost his claim the rides became less plentiful. 'I was not good enough,' he says frankly, 'and I had not shown enough improvement.' Therefore, he moved from Seven Barrows to ride out for Kim Bailey, for whom he has had a number of winners. He also partnered Ben Pauling's first winner as a trainer when Raven's Tower won at Plumpton in November 2013, which helped him get the ride on Barters Hill, who won the Grade 1 Challow Hurdle at Newbury in December 2015, and on Willoughby Court at the Cheltenham Festival in 2017, where he was victorious in the prestigious Neptune Investment Management Novices' Hurdle, another Grade 1 race.

From an inauspicious start, David Bass's career as a National Hunt jockey has progressed in leaps and bounds. Indeed, in 2016, when riding The Last Samuri, he was second in the Aintree Grand National – it would have been the fulfilment of a dream if the horse had lasted home up the long run-in.

David Bass has never show-jumped, never pony-raced and never hunted. Although he received help from Johnny Manners, Mick Fitzgerald and Yogi Breisner, he learned about jumping through trial and error. 'I came into race-riding to have a connection with racing, not through a love of horses, but good horses teach riders, and I've been fortunate to have ridden a number of class animals.'

David is a determined jockey and rides in a positive way, but the lack of early practice as a child has meant he has never found the jumping side that easy. He does not always sit deep into his horses and, unlike the top riders, he does not always see strides into the fences. Yet horses run for him, and they appear to share his enthusiasm. He is extremely popular among his fellow jockeys and is sure to ride many more winners.

Mattie Batchelor

'Batch', as Mattie Batchelor is often known, is one of the most popular jockeys in Britain. Born in Brighton in 1976, where his mother was his primary school's dinner lady, he had his first riding lesson on a family holiday to Ireland and greatly enjoyed the experience. Back in England, he then met a girl whose brother rode out for the trainer Charlie Moore at his stables close to Brighton racecourse. Mattie managed to find his way to the yard, and a couple of employees gave him some riding lessons on an old pony, Klute, who was stabled alongside the racehorses. After a few months he was allowed to accompany the other horses up to the gallops.

Charlie Moore's facilities were basic but effective. He trained plenty of winners, and Mattie gained valuable experience watching how the horses were prepared. When he was 16 he was given the leg-up on an old thoroughbred called John's Wager who had a brilliant temperament, and he learned to canter him on the gallops. He only rode out once a day, however, because there were no more suitable horses for him to ride. The only time he was told that he could ride another, the filly took off with him and collided with a lamp post. Mattie fell off, and the next day limped into school to sit his leaving exam feeling bruised and sore.

As Batch's riding improved, he went for a few months to Gary Moore, Charlie's son, who was at that time training in Epsom. It was an eye-opener to see the famous gallops. Afterwards, when back in Brighton, his father took him to the old racecourse at Lewes to ride out for Ray Goldstein, 'the Iron Man', who taught him how to jump horses and allowed him to school over hurdles.

In 1996 Mattie had his first ride for Charlie Moore, at Windsor in a conditional jockeys' handicap hurdle. The horse was unplaced, but the experience was priceless, and in 1997 he rode his first winner over hurdles, Nahrawali, also for Charlie and again at Windsor. In 1998, shortly after Gary had taken over the reins at his father's yard in Brighton, Batch was given two completely different kinds of race-rides on the same day. Lift Boy carried a light weight to win a five-furlong sprint at Lingfield, and Be Surprised was responsible for Mattie's first spin over fences in a handicap chase, once more at Windsor. They finished fifth.

Mattie rode out for the Moore family for many years, and it was convenient for him to carry on living at home. But as well as going racing there were plenty of jobs around the yard, in particular levelling out the divots on the home-made all-weather gallop, a tiring assignment as the surface needed to be forked back by hand. On certain days, if the temperature was high and the sun was shining, he could not face raking the woodchips that were mixed with manure from the stables, and instead he and his accomplice Ian Mongan would wander off to watch the nearby cricket matches.

In March 1999, Dave Roberts, Mattie Batchelor's agent, told me that his jockey would be a suitable partner for the mare I trained called Heart, who was due to run in a hurdle race at Newbury. She needed a few pounds to be taken off her back. In consultation with her owner, Shirley Brasher, it was decided to give this promising young rider a chance, and he duly won, beating Richard Dunwoody.

The win at Newbury marked the beginning of Mattie's ventures beyond the confines of Brighton, and from then on he began riding out in the Lambourn area and broadening his horizons in the racing world. With his quick wit and enthusiasm, he was an immediate hit. He enjoyed life and was often to be seen playing football for the jockey teams in and around Lambourn.

John Francome became one of Mattie's major supporters, and gave him valuable advice on his jumping technique. Batch rode plenty of winners for well-established trainers, in particular Oliver Sherwood, but did not forget the smaller Sussex yards, and regularly rode out for Anna Newton-Smith, John Bridger, John Ffitch-Heyes and Tom McGovern. Plumpton and Fontwell were his favourite tracks, and for several seasons he was the leading jockey at Plumpton.

At the turn of the century, Mattie Batchelor forged an important link with Mark Bradstock at Letcombe Bassett near Wantage, which led to him winning the 2m5f novices' handicap chase at the Cheltenham Festival in 2005 on King Harald and then, in 2011, the prestigious Hennessy Gold Cup at Newbury on Carruthers. Batch's wins are always popular, and his beaming smile has become his feature. In June 2017, he registered the 300th success of his career at Les Landes racecourse in Jersey – indeed, over the years he has made many successful sorties to Jersey, as well as to Norway.

Batch also became an internet sensation with his Wocket Woy series on social media, which he created with fellow jockey Marc Goldstein, with whom he rode out on wet cold mornings on the South Downs. 'It started on the gallops,' explains Marc – known in the films as the Pwoducer. 'Mattie messes about every day anyway, and one morning I just decided to film it.' The two jockeys use Sheena West's racehorses for their amusing clips on daily happenings behind the scenes in a racing yard. The weekly show has led to invitations to attend many prestigious equestrian events including the Horse of the Year Show.

Batch's cheeky manner and sense of fun have lifted many spirits, and when he won Channel 4's *Come Dine With Me* contest in 2013 he demonstrated yet another of his inborn talents. He is a fine chef and, when riding out at West Lockinge Farm, caused plenty of amusement bedecked in a striped apron when serving up cooked breakfasts. Mattie Batchelor will go down as one of racing's star entertainers and has done plenty for the sport. He has brought it home to the public, and not only is he an accomplished jockey but he is also extremely popular and knowledgeable.

Frank Berry

Ten-times Irish jump racing champion, Frank Berry is one of the legends of National Hunt racing, and his win in the 1972 Cheltenham Gold Cup on Glencaraig Lady, superbly called by the late Sir Peter O'Sullevan, was a famous victory.

Frank was born in Granard, Co Longford, in September 1950. It is not a county renowned for its horse ties, but Frank came from a hunting family. His father, also called Frank, farmed and had cattle, and as a child the young Frank had 'a cracking little pony' who jumped at the RDS (Royal Dublin Society) horse show in the 14.2hh class. His neighbour and great friend Eddie Macken, a horseman of outstanding ability and style whose prowess in the show-jumping world was universally acclaimed, used to help Frank with his riding.

Frank enjoyed riding his ponies, but was not that competitive. He was small in stature and very light, thus when one of his best friends became an apprentice on the Curragh he was happy to do the same, and left school at 14 to become apprenticed to Michael Hurley, who had around 30 horses in his yard. At 16, Frank had his first ride for his trainer at Leopardstown on Shoe Sha – and the horse duly won. However, there were not many horses in the trainer's care and Frank only had a few more winners during his first year, but as time went on he had many successes, especially after his 17th birthday.

By the time he was 18, Frank was struggling with his weight, but fortunately this did not stop him riding the quirky but talented Giolla Mear in several races after the horse's usual rider, Paddy Power, had suffered a broken leg when the colt had been difficult to pull up after a race and had gone through a barrier. Frank duly won the Desmond Stakes at the Curragh on him. Towards the end of the season, he was victorious on the same horse in the 1968 Irish St Leger.

At the end of that year, with his weight rapidly rising, Frank moved to work for Francis Flood at Grangecon in Co Wicklow. The trainer had learned his trade from Paddy Sleator and been amateur champion jockey himself six times. He only trained 30 horses, but he had a number of good ones and Frank stayed with this highly respected horseman for 19 seasons, where he did plenty of schooling and was given invaluable help with his riding. Frank changed his licence from the Flat to a conditional one for National Hunt racing, and became the yard's claiming jockey. He loved the jumping aspect, and it brought back memories of his show-jumping days as a child. He was a natural rider over an obstacle and had a great eye for a fence.

In 1971 Frank rode the Fortina mare Glencaraig Lady into fifth place in the King George VI Chase at Kempton, before winning the Cheltenham Gold Cup three months later. Prior to the blue riband she only had two runs in the new season, which has become the popular way with a number of the good horses today. Bobsline was another of the Flood stars, and in 1984 Frank won the Arkle Chase at Cheltenham on him. He also rode for other trainers, and in particular registered many successes for Brian Lusk, who hailed from Northern Ireland and trained Skymas to win the Champion Chase at the Cheltenham Festival in 1976 and 1977.

One of Frank Berry's greatest friends was Tommy Carberry, another top jockey, and in 1975 both men tied for the Irish jockeys' championship. Frank subsequently won the title seven more times in his own right, and shared it twice more.

In 1988, he had a bad fall at Roscommon and, though he did not want to retire, on doctors' advice he was forced to hang up his boots at the age of 38. He stayed on for a few months as assistant to Francis Flood, but then took out a trainers' licence in his own right and successfully trained for ten seasons. After training Laura's Beau for the leading owner JP McManus to finish third in the 1992 Aintree Grand National, his link with JP became stronger and, when he handed in his training licence, he was immediately signed up to manage the McManus string of racehorses.

Nowadays, Frank plays a vital role in JP's racing empire, and the trust between the two of them is well known. He has a good eye for a horse, and is brilliant with the jockeys who ride for his boss. He gives them advice and confidence, and they listen to him. His two sons Fran and Alan have also successfully made inroads in racing. The former as a top Flat-race jockey and the latter as right-hand man to Jonjo O'Neill.

A quiet man with a depth of knowledge, Frank does not waste words – to have a conversation with him is a privilege. 'How many fish would still be alive if they'd learned to keep their mouths shut?' his boss JP McManus once remarked.

From a limited horse background, to becoming a champion in the saddle, Frank is an inspiration to the jockeys of today. He has a fine, gentlemanly approach to life, and an undisputed prestigious position in National Hunt racing.

Rachael Blackmore

A breath of fresh air in National Hunt racing, Rachael Blackmore has set the sport alive with her outstanding achievements. Gone are the days when the suffragettes stole the limelight and Emily Davison threw herself to her death beneath the King's horse in the 1913 Epsom Derby. Rachael has shown that lady riders can hold their own against the top men, and is an inspiration to those attempting to follow in her footsteps. In the 2018-19 Irish National Hunt season she had more rides than any of her contemporaries.

Rachael's home is Mortlestown Castle, near Killenaule in Co Tipperary. Born in 1989, she was riding ponies from an early age on the family farm. Her father bred both half-breds and thoroughbreds and has always enjoyed hunting and eventing, while her mother Eimir took her Connemara pony to compete in the amateur riders class at the 2017 RDS horse show.

As a child, Rachael Blackmore was involved in every type of pony activity – the Tipperary Hunt Pony Club, local rallies and shows, hunting and eventing – and had a number of good ponies. She won the British Pony Club Show-jumping Championships on her horse Fiddles, while her event horse, Oakengrove Rainbow, was a good mare and went to the one-star event at Tattersalls when the rider was barely 17.

Rachael has always been a fearless rider, and nothing ever fazed her as a child. When she was seven she would go hunting on her 12.2hh pony, Bubbles, who had been bought from Liz Grant, mother of Mark, and pulled hard. Before venturing out with the hounds Rachael would ride her around the stubble field or on a neighbour's gallop to settle her. 'My dad would put a big knot in my reins to help me hold her, I would wedge my hands on the knot and let her on – it was similar to bridging one's reins. I used to just sit there and hang on. But despite being hot-headed she was an incredibly cool pony, and she loved jumping.'

Another of Rachael's ponies, Tommy, was 13.2hh and a near-thoroughbred. He was extremely fast, and she rode him in the Pony Club Mounted Games classes at the RDS horse show. She also took him to a couple of pony races, and remembers beating Paul Townend on only her second time out. Paul was top of the league when it came to pony racing, and it was a feat for anybody to relegate him into second place.

It was after the pony races that Rachael began to get more interested in racing, and she remembers the excitement of taking part in a sweepstake at her friend's house for the Grand National. When she left school at 17 and went to Dublin and then to Limerick to study science, she continued with her riding and rode out on the point-to-point horses at the local trainer Aidan Kennedy's Co Tipperary yard.

With the Kennedy family, Rachael sat on many different horses and learned a vast amount about racing. She was even given the chance to ride in point-to-points and remembers finishing third in her first race on Arbour Hill at Castletown Geoghegan in 2009. She loved the point-to-points but, due to barely weighing 9st, she had to carry a lot of lead to make the weights up to 12st.

Rachael had no wins for Aidan Kennedy, but was given a number of outside rides, including Luska Lad for JJ 'Shark' Hanlon and Klassy for Sam Curling: both horses were victorious three times, and she ended up with 11 point-to-point winners. During her years in college, she rode out for Pat Doyle at Holycross near Thurles as well as for Shark near Bagenalstown in Co Carlow. The top jockeys Davy Russell and Derek O'Connor rode a number of the Doyle horses at home, and to school alongside such renowned experts taught Rachael a priceless amount. She maintains that it was a fantastic opportunity to be able to watch them and be helped by them.

Rachael had seven wins on the track as an amateur, and rode her first winner under rules in 2011 when Stowaway Pearl, trained by Shark Hanlon, was successful in a ladies' handicap hurdle at Thurles. She then decided to make race-riding her career and she turned professional in March 2015 at the age of 26. Once again it was Shark who provided her with her initial success when Most Honourable won at Clonmel in September 2015. Her riding ability was quickly recognised, and in the 2016-17 season she won the conditional jockeys' championship with 32 winners, a major achievement since no other female jockey had ever won it.

Rachael's rise to the top of her profession has been a revelation. In April 2019 she ended her season in Ireland with 90 winners, and was second in the championship behind Paul Townend. A Plus Tard was her first Cheltenham Festival winner in March 2019 when landing the Close Brothers Novices' Handicap Chase, and she then gained her first Grade 1 success when partnering Minella Indo to win the Albert Bartlett Novices' Hurdle, becoming the first lady jockey to register a Grade 1 winner over hurdles at the festival. The trainer of both horses, Henry de Bromhead, has been one of her greatest promoters.

Every top athlete needs a helping hand for back-up and advice, and as well as her amazingly supportive parents Rachael has been fortunate from an early age to have mixed with experienced people across the horse world – Nicky Cassidy, who evented for Ireland and rode in the Olympics, was an enormous help to her during her teenage years. Yet, ultimately, it is the individual that counts, and Rachael is an extremely talented rider who has an uncanny understanding with the horses she rides: they jump for her and they run for her.

People's lives are what they make them, and Rachael has made the best of all that has been offered to her. She is deservedly reaping the rewards. She is level-headed and unflappable on the big occasions, and always 100 per cent focused on racing. If hard work and dedication are the requisites in the tough life of a National Hunt jockey, then Rachael possesses both. She has already set new records, and looks assured of more successes.

Sean and James Bowen

When looking back over Sean and James Bowen's childhoods, it is hard to separate the two brothers, even though there are three and a half years between them. Sean was born in September 1997 and James in March 2001. Both are now outstanding National Hunt jockeys, and from the very beginning their lives revolved around ponies and horses within the admirably hard-working, down-to-earth family residing near Fishguard within the heart of Pembrokeshire.

Their father, Peter, the son of a horse dealer and nowadays a successful trainer, has himself always been involved with horses, and from an early age helped his own father with the breaking in of youngsters. 'It makes one aware of what horses can do and how they can behave.' The boys' mother Karen, is the daughter of the famous showman Bill Bryan and rode at all the major county shows. Sean and James could not have a stronger pedigree. They both wanted to be jockeys right from the start.

The Bowen boys rode ponies from an early age, coming home from school to ride them and have races up their father's gallop. 'We used to time each other from the bottom of the hill to the top,' says James. 'Our 12.2hh pony, Striker, was slow and lazy but we all rode him. He taught us a lot. Our cousins Peter and Josh used to bring over their ponies in the holidays and we raced against them. The best thing was that we often swapped ponies, so we didn't just get used to riding our own.'

In their childhood days the Bowen boys' riding was always linked to racing: no horse shows and very little hunting; all the boys were interested in was speed – 'we even rode our ponies in racing saddles'. Yes, they were Pony Club members, because in Britain pony racing requires certain qualifications. 'We had to take our ponies out hunting on four occasions each year and attend four Pony Club race rallies as well – but we didn't like the idea of shows and we did no show-jumping.' Both boys began pony racing before they were 12, and had several top ponies. 'Push The Button, the 13.2hh pony, who is now 16, was very good, and our thoroughbred pony Cudlick Verona, whom Dad bought semi-broken, won the Pony Racing Championships on several occasions and is still racing today.' James spent two years on Cudlick Verona. Their parents spent a lot of time and money making sure James and Sean had good ponies for the pony racing circuit. 'It was a massive cost, and they gave up everything to take us round the country.'

Once the Bowen boys were established in the pony races in England and Wales and had won races, Peter felt some experience on the Irish pony racing tracks would further sharpen them up. Thus they spent several summers with Gordon Elliott and rode Irish ponies on the Irish circuit at places like Dingle, which certainly opened their eyes. Sean had a winner in Ireland when he was barely 15.

In the Bowen household school was way down the list of priorities. The children occasionally attended Fishguard School, but neither of them enjoyed sitting at a desk, and a lot of their education was conducted at home. By the time they left school at 14 they were already riding out racehorses in the mornings and late afternoons.

Point-to-pointing was next on the agenda, but neither child had done much jumping. 'I had only ever jumped over Dad's hurdles when I played around with the ponies,' Sean recalls, 'but I remember being taken to a local point-to-point course to school with Mickey, my older brother, who was preparing Iron Man to run in a race. I was put on an old schoolmaster and told to sit upsides him. It was quite scary, as I'd never jumped a chase fence, and we went quite fast. In my first point-to-point I rode National Action, but I got overexcited and began firing him into the fences. He went longer and longer and stood off way too far from each fence. I was eventually catapulted into the air and ended up sitting on the ground. My pride was rock bottom afterwards because I thought I could ride.'

After Sean's initial hiccup both brothers did extremely well with their point-to-point careers. At 16 Sean was the novice rider champion with ten winners, mostly on horses for David Brace, but James went a step further when, also as a 16-year-old, he won the championship with 30 winners, setting an all-time record. Brother Mickey did a fantastic job by training the majority of the horses he rode.

In October 2014, after the point-to-point dinner at Stratford, Sean was approached by Paul Nicholls to join his yard at Ditcheat as his conditional jockey. He subsequently spent 18 months there and at the end of the 2014-15 season was champion conditional rider. He gained an enormous amount of experience from riding top-class horses and racing on Grade 1 tracks, and in April 2015 he won the bet365 Gold Cup Chase at Sandown on Just A Par for his boss. He was also successful in the Grand Sefton Chase in December 2016 over the Grand National fences at Aintree – but when he won his second bet365 Gold Cup in 2017 on Henllan Harri the horse was trained by his father. Sean's first winner under rules had been for Bernard Llewellyn in 2014, when Kosmina Bay won an amateur riders' hands-and-heels handicap hurdle at Uttoxeter.

James Bowen mirrored his brother's successful start to his career as a top National Hunt jockey by joining Nicky Henderson's yard in the autumn of 2017. He had already had some winners under rules, the first being Curious Carlos at Cartmel on May 27, and it took him less than a year to ride 75 winners and lose his claim. He too won the conditional jockeys' championship at the end of the 2017-18 National Hunt season. By winning the Welsh National on Raz De Maree in January 2018 for Gavin Cromwell he became the first 16-year-old to win the race and the horse, at 13, the oldest winner since the Second World War. More big winners flowed for James in the spring of 2018 and he won the prestigious Lanzarote Hurdle at Kempton on the Nicky Henderson-trained William Henry.

The careers of Sean and James Bowen are fascinating success stories. Nothing is ever too much trouble for their parents if there are races to be won, and they seem to have passed on this attribute to all three of their sons. Both jockeys have first-class manners and an uncanny way with horses. Like their astute father, Peter, the boys know the form of the horses they ride as well as the capabilities of those they race against. Both lads have good hands, and ride sensible, tactical races without ever appearing to get flustered. They do not over-pressurise their horses and push them out of their strides, which is probably why they jump consistently well.

To date, neither of the Bowen brothers has had a Cheltenham Festival winner, though in March 2018 Shantou Flyer was beaten only a neck by Coo Star Sivola in the Ultima Handicap Chase. James considers this to have been his most infuriating race of the year and says he has watched it many times since. But Yogi Breisner, the jumping guru who tirelessly works on the correct balance of the riders, and has given both James and Sean plenty of help with their jumping, told James that 'what you think to be instinctively right at the time is normally correct', and he now feels he did not do anything wrong. It is surely just a matter of time before the Bowen festival hoodoo is lifted.

Graham Bradley

Graham Bradley will go down as one of National Hunt racing's most talented and stylish jockeys, but also as the one who caused an unparalleled stir in 2002 by openly admitting to tipping winners for financial gain.

Three years after retiring from race-riding, 'Brad' gave evidence at the trial of his former weighing-room colleague Barrie Wright. 'I was just trying to help an old mate out,' he said. But in his evidence he admitted having had a punter to whom he passed on the names of horses he expected to win. As a result, he was 'warned off' for five years – effectively excluded by the authorities from all premises connected to horseracing such as racecourses and trainers' yards. 'Giving privileged information to someone who gambled was stupid,' reflected rueful Brad. 'I was giving someone winners and accepting money for it.' Thus, the former jockey was forced into racing exile, and for a man who loved the sport and was gifted with racehorses it was a very harsh penalty, and one that would damage his reputation.

During his 23 years as a jockey, Graham Bradley rode 750 winners, which included most of the prestigious National Hunt races. Not only did he partner Bregawn to victory in the 1983 Cheltenham Gold Cup, but he also won the Hennessy Gold Cup at Newbury twice (Bregawn in 1982 and Suny Bay in 1997), the Champion Hurdle on Collier Bay (1996), the King George VI Chase at Kempton on Wayward Lad (1985), the Welsh Grand National twice, with Righthand Man (1984) and Stearsby (1986), and the Aintree Hurdle in 1993 on Morley Street. He also won the Irish Grand National on Rhyme 'N' Reason in 1985. His ride on Morley Street was, in the words of AP McCoy, 'absolute perfection'.

Brad was a brilliant judge of a horse's ability. Not only did he have unbelievable balance, he also had superb hands, which encouraged horses to gallop and jump. 'As an amateur I used to ride too short, but I learned from this and corrected my style. Riding short caused my hands to be too tense. When I joined the Dickinsons in 1979 and became professional, I dropped my irons. I could relax my hands and make them lighter.'

Graham Bradley was born in Wetherby in 1960. It was a close-knit family, but his adored mother died of cancer when he was only 14. His father, Norman, was a trainer, primarily for Jack Hanson at Crackhill Farm, Sicklinghall, and the young Bradley always wanted to be a jockey, even though he did not sit on a racehorse until he was 14. Unlike many jump jockeys he was never interested in show-jumping. Indeed, he barely jumped an obstacle until he went to WA Stephenson's yard as a 19-year-old. 'When I was at school, I wanted to be a Flat jockey,' says Brad, 'and it's one of my big regrets that I was never the slightest bit interested in going hunting or jumping ponies. It was never going to be easy for my dad to make a jockey out of me, but he had plenty of patience and carefully plotted my career.'

When he was about 12 his father put him on an overgrown pony of Mrs Hanson's and lunged him on a large circle, but he kept losing his irons and nearly falling off, complaining that the pony was trotting too fast. He was never allowed to canter on the lunge, and indeed later on never rode a canter on any of Mrs Hanson's racehorses. Riding out with the racing string on the roads was as far as he went. Fortunately, he overcame his early fears by joining a local riding school close to the A1 near Wetherby racecourse, and it was around the same time that he first got to ride at a racecourse on one of the riding school horses, even though it was only in the car park.

Before joining the Stephenson establishment at Crawleas in County Durham upon the recommendation of Tommy Stack, who famously rode Red Rum to victory in the Grand National in 1977, Brad rode out and worked for Tommy Shedden, who trained at Grange Park, Wetherby. 'At the time, I was being educated at Wetherby High School, and at weekends I would cycle the four miles to Tommy's, where I was paid £1 for a day's work on the Saturday and 50p for every Sunday.'

In 1977 and 1978 he had a few rides in races – mostly on the Flat – but they were unsuccessful forays. His first ride in public was on Sweet Slievenamon for Steve Nesbitt at Redcar. He divided his summer holidays between riding out for Michael Jarvis in Newmarket, where on a couple of occasions he rode work upsides the legendary Lester Piggott – 'What a man to try to copy' – and for Eric Collingwood at Middleham, both highly respected yards.

When Graham joined the WA Stephenson workforce in 1977, all was not rosy: the master trainer did not take an immediate shine to the young lad, whom he christened 'Pretty Boy'. Brad witnessed many of the customary treatments dished out to young stable lads in those days. 'There was a big muckheap at the yard. New lads would be stripped naked and buried up to their necks. If they dug themselves out they'd then be strung up to the beams in the barn in a large haynet.' The main problem for Brad was that WA never saw him schooling or riding work because he rarely went up the gallops, leaving this to his trusted ex-jockey head lad Kit Stobbs. 'He only ever saw me ride out from the yard once, and did not like what he saw. The only time he came on the gallops I got run away with on a lunatic horse called Supermacado.' But the ambitious young jockey did plenty of schooling over the obstacles in WA's field below the house. The row of five telegraph poles was famous, and the horses certainly learned to respect them.

There were 16 jockeys at Crawleas when Brad arrived there, and after two years his progress was minimal. 'By 1979 I'd earned a total of £60.89 from my rides in races and I'd had no winners.' His move to the Dickinsons' yard at Harewood came as no surprise. Brad's father got him the job there, even though the response Norman got from 'the Boss', as everyone called Tony Dickinson, was, 'We've got four jockeys in the yard and six youngsters already, and I don't want to take on another. But seeing as it's your son I'll take him on as a paid lad.'

It was the best placing any father could have come up with, and with the whole Dickinson team behind him – Monica, 'Mrs D', and

Michael, 'Bud' – the aspiring National Hunt jockey fell on his feet and was given the most incredible opportunities. Here were class horses and true horsemen. The Dickinson training of racehorses took on another dimension, and it did not take long before Brad's natural riding ability was recognised.

❝ Because there were so many horses to be schooled, the senior riders did all the work over fences and the conditionals would put them over poles and hurdles. Michael watched everything and missed nothing. There were plenty of bollockings about riding too short, but these were never bellowed across the schooling ground as some trainers like to do. Michael would take you to one side on the way home and point out exactly what you had done wrong. The criticism was always constructive, and he soon realised that I could hold everything and had good hands. ❞

Brad's first winner was for Tony Dickinson – he had turned professional (conditional) towards the end of 1979. In March 1980 he rode Talon to victory over hurdles at Sedgefield. In the 1980-81 season he was champion conditional with 38 winners. Not bad for a boy who WA Stephenson had predicted would get 'no rides from the Dickinson establishment'. Despite the help he had from Michael Dickinson and jockey Robert Earnshaw, who was 'absolutely magic at putting horses over fences', Graham Bradley had very few lessons during his years as a jockey, but he attributes some of his success to the instruction he received from Yogi Breisner.

Brad was always a brilliant judge of pace, and his ability to read a race enabled him to be in the right place at the right time. This ability was undoubtedly inborn. Race-riding, he maintains, is all about confidence, and balance, rhythm and timing are of the utmost importance. 'Michael Dickinson always told me, "Never make up ground in a race when you are going uphill or downhill – or on a bend. Only make up your ground on the level."' Brad never forgot these words of wisdom.

When Graham Bradley retired from race-riding with a winner at Wetherby, Ontheboil, in 1999, there were numerous tributes. AP McCoy said he regarded him as a legend and a great friend, while John Francome said that no jockey was more stylish or more generous with his knowledge, never once turning away a youngster seeking advice.

Brad's downfall was probably due to his inborn determination to make money, a side to his nature that meant he was often on the wrong side of the officials, and his visits to the BHA's headquarters in London were frequent. Nevertheless Brad's friends have always stood by him, even though his actions have raised plenty of eyebrows in racing and lost him a considerable amount of credibility within the sport.

Graham Bradley's ability as a jockey, however, has never been disputed. When he was in top form, his riding was pure poetry, and he set an enviable example to the National Hunt jockeys of today. When he rode me winners I felt privileged to have him on my horses.

Jonathan Burke

Johnny Burke was always pony mad. Before he got his first pony, Captain Brownie, a naughty 13hh crossbred, he would ride his hobby horses around the yard and make little jumps for them. But that first pony taught him a massive amount – 'I had so many falls off him. He was very naughty.' He also did plenty of show-jumping on his other pony, Willow, who was very talented and performed really well. Sometimes he would go hunting with the Conna Harriers and this helped his riding even more. It sharpened him up and improved his balance.

Johnny was reared in Co Cork in a busy, horse-orientated yard: his father Liam Burke, who has always been involved in racing, used to ride work for Phonsie O'Brien and Mouse Morris, and habitually bought and sold horses, primarily point-to-pointers. Currently he is training at Winacre near Mallow, and in 2008 he was responsible for the winner of the Irish Arkle Chase, Thyne Again. Earlier he had trained a number of point-to-point horses for Paul Barber, Paul Nicholls' landlord and principal owner, including Valley Henry.

Johnny's mother died when he was only five, but the Burkes' neighbours loved the cheeky little boy and fed him well – in fact they gave him so many cakes and pies that he became too heavy to take part in pony races. When he was 12, and already weighing 10st, Paul Barber told him he was obese and would never make a jockey. But when he took his life seriously the weight fell off him, and he had a few rides on the Flat – indeed, the horse he rode in the Irish Cesarewitch in 2017, Benkei, only carried 9st 8lb.

During his childhood, the top jockey Davy Condon lived close by, and encouraged Johnny to ride every day before school. On Saturdays Davy would take him to ride out at Willie Mullins' yard, where Paul Townend also gave him valuable advice, and by the age of 16 he had a licence to ride in bumper races. In March 2012 there was a point-to-point day at Cork racecourse, and he won one of the bumper races on Trendy Gift. The following year he had 60 rides in point-to-points and five winners.

At 17 Jonathan finished school and began to ride out once a week at Noel Meade's in Co Meath as well as two or three times weekly for Willie Mullins. He got his driving licence and his own car. In 2014 he partnered Very Much So for Willie to win the Land Rover Bumper at Punchestown. A month later, on the advice of Ted Walsh, Davy Condon and Paul Townend, he turned professional, though he continued to ride out regularly for his father. He was then helped by a brilliant agent, Garry Cribbin, who managed to get him a number of top-race rides. His first winner as a conditional jockey was for Adrian Maguire on Golden Kite, who won the Connacht National in 2014.

It was after this first big win that Johnny moved to Henry de Bromhead. He had a good winner for the Potts family, trained by Jim Dreaper, and got signed on to ride 70 per cent of their horses, but not the novices. He won a big race on Sizing Europe at Gowran Park in 2014, and the Galway Plate on Shanahan's Turn in 2015. He also won the Midlands National in 2015 for Jim Dreaper on Goonyella. Like his father Tom, who trained Arkle, Jim Dreaper has an exceptional way with horses, and taught Johnny a lot. 'If a horse makes a mistake at a fence,' he used to say, 'you should pat him on the neck to restore his confidence.' What a refreshing view. How many jockeys would punish their mounts for making an error by pointlessly resorting to the whip?

In 2015 Johnny Burke was champion conditional jockey in Ireland having won a novice chase on Sizing John for Henry de Bromhead and a two-mile hurdle on Apple's Jade for Willie Mullins at Leopardstown at the big Christmas meeting.

It was after these sparkling successes, however, that injuries began to take their toll. In 2016 he suffered a bad fall at home when schooling for his father. The horse he was riding did a somersault over a fence, leaving him with crushed vertebrae and he was unable to ride for five months. He was back in July, but then in December a broken leg meant a further two months off, and in 2017 another five and a half months on the sidelines following a fall at Navan where he chipped a bone in his shoulder and tore all the ligaments off the joint. It was a disastrous year for him. During his time out of the saddle, however, Johnny did commentaries at many of the Cork point-to-point tracks, and was by all accounts brilliant in that role.

When back in action he was offered a full-time job in England at Charlie Longsdon's yard – Barry Geraghty and Davy Russell had recommended him – and his name began reappearing on the racecards at British race meetings. It took him a while to adjust, he says: due to the smaller fields and quicker ground many of the races are run at a faster pace than they are on the other side of the Irish Sea. There is 'no let-up in the tempo', and many of the home straights on English courses are long: 'Once one turns for home, a jockey has to kick on.' Also, in Britain, Johnny has found there is a far greater emphasis on jockeys' fitness. He still follows the Irish form closely and loves returning to Ireland to ride winners in his homeland, but he has done well since his move to England and is now associated with a number of high-profile training yards.

Nina Carberry

Nina Carberry was undoubtedly one of the most talented lady jockeys to have ridden under National Hunt rules. She comes from a family steeped in racing history: her father Tommy was a brilliant rider and was five-times champion Irish National Hunt jockey. He won the Grand National in 1975 and two Cheltenham Gold Cups in 1970 and 1971 on L'Escargot, as well as the 1975 Gold Cup on Ten Up and the 1980 Gold Cup on the later-to-be-disqualified Tied Cottage. Nina's grandfather Dan Moore was also champion jockey on five occasions in Ireland and then became a champion trainer. Her second brother of five, Paul, was also a fine jockey – some would say the best horseman ever seen – and she has always looked up to him and modelled her riding style on his.

Attractive, outgoing and with a lovely manner, she no longer holds her amateur jockeys' licence, although she continues to partner high-class young thoroughbreds on a daily basis when riding out for champion Flat trainer Aidan O'Brien.

The first pony Nina rode in Ashbourne, Co Meath, where she grew up, was Jack, a Shetland. He was an old mine pony and lived until he was 35. He taught her a lot about balance because he would stop so quickly, even in canter, that unless his rider was sitting in the right place it was over his head that the jockey would go. Jack had a straight shoulder and a short neck. He had to have a crupper attached to the saddle so that it did not go forward. It took all of Nina's skill to master the art of riding Jack, but he was a great little jumper and, when her brothers were riding racehorses and schooling them over a line of fences, they would put up a little pole for him beside each fence. 'I learned to bridge my reins when I was four years old.' She was already competitive – determined to keep up with her brothers.

In due course the pony-mad child progressed from her Shetland to ride bigger animals and Catkin, who was chestnut and 13.2hh, was passed down to her from her cousin. On this pony Nina did some eventing and participated in numerous Pony Club activities. An early memory of hers is riding her event horse Benjamin Barclay Brown in a tetrathlon, during which, as well as the running, swimming and shooting, all the contestants had to negotiate a cross-country course. Part of the test was to open and shut a gate, but as they were walking up to it, her horse must have thought he had to jump it, and took charge. Despite her attempts to stop him he half-jumped it and then went over backwards on top of his rider, giving her the first taste of concussion, although there would be many more occasions when she was knocked out while racing and schooling horses.

Hunting was a childhood passion, and she did plenty of it with the Ward Union Hunt. Her brother Paul is still hunting mad. When Nina was only ten she would get Paul's hunters ready for him so he could spend a few hours out hunting before going racing. Nina had two brilliant Connemara hunting ponies that she shared with her younger brothers. They were tremendous schoolmasters. Negotiating the massive drains (ditches) further helped her with her balance, and she developed exceptionally good hands and judgement. If a rider holds on to a horse's head tightly it cannot stretch its neck over a ditch and it invariably fails to make the landing bank. A long rein and sitting in the right place behind a horse's shoulders and withers are paramount.

Nina also rode in plenty of pony races, and had a number of wins. She loved every minute of it. Her mother, Pamela, would take her daughter all over Ireland for them. She remembers her first ever ride, in a consolation charity race at Navan organised by Barry Geraghty's father: when the chance ride came up she was wearing jeans, but borrowed a helmet and ended up winning. Paul Townend, Tom Queally and Paddy Flood were all competing at the same time and Nina rode in these races for three years – on some weekends a jockey could have four or five rides in a day. 'They make one streetwise and sharp,' she says. 'One has to be aware of what is happening on either side, and the pony races taught me to look after my feet, because if I went too close to the rails I would strike the railings with my toes and it would really hurt!'

A bright child with a sharp brain, Nina was a natural sportswoman – when at school she had excelled at basketball and was picked to represent Ireland. After a year at college, point-to-points were next on her agenda and she had her first ride when she was 17. This was in Northern Ireland for Liam Lennon and she was placed third. Her first winner was in 2003 on Mountpill Lad, in the ladies' open race at Loughrea for John Paul Brennan. That same year she had her first ride for Enda Bolger at Kilfeacle in Co Tipperary and was second on Shady Lad. It was a chance ride because the trainer had misread the entry form and entered the horse in what he believed to be a men's open race, and Nina was the only girl rider available.

That day at Kilfeacle marked the beginning of a long and successful partnership with the renowned cross-country trainer. She spent many days schooling for him at Howardstown in Co Limerick, and says he was a brilliant teacher. John Thomas McNamara was also riding for Enda, and Nina says that she learned a huge amount from him. Her first win for the Bolger yard was on Good Step in the La Touche Cup at Punchestown, but there were many more, and her association with the JP McManus horses in the cross-country races at Cheltenham as well as at Punchestown became legendary. It was aboard Josies Orders for JP and Enda that she notched her final winner at the Punchestown festival in 2018.

It was not only in the cross-country races that she excelled. Her first win at Cheltenham was in 2005 on Dabiroun for Paul Nolan in the Fred Winter Juvenile Handicap Hurdle. In 2015 and 2016 Nina won the Foxhunter Chase at the Cheltenham Festival aboard On The Fringe, as well as taking the Aintree Fox Hunters' on the same horse, also in 2015.

Nina Carberry ended up with 412 wins as an amateur rider under National Hunt rules, and Enda Bolger considers her to have been one of the finest riders over a fence he has ever seen – with the exception of John Francome, who remains his hero.

Now that she is married to Ted Walsh, Ruby's brother, and they have two daughters, Rosie and Holly, one assumes the children will grow up with all the same natural instincts for riding. There will certainly be no shortage of good ponies or expert tuition from a mother who was at the top of her game.

Paul Carberry

Paul Carberry was always destined to be a jump jockey, and became one of the most naturally gifted and talented National Hunt jockeys the sport has ever seen, with exceptional balance and supreme artistry in the saddle. He had the apparent ability to persuade horses to do anything he wanted. His love for riding has never left him and his passion for hunting endures. As well, he now has a new interest in show-jumping. Family apart, horses are Paul's life, they are the centre of his universe.

Trainer Noel Meade once said that Paul,

> Would never punish or mistreat a horse or ask it to do anything that it was not capable of doing. He has always been at his most comfortable when riding and less at ease when surrounded by people, which is why he has often appeared shy when in a crowd.

Yet close friends have often witnessed the other side to Paul Carberry – his quick wit and sharp sense of humour. This side, coupled with a streak of devilment, has often taken him into deep water and been responsible for a number of well-documented brushes with authority. He seems to enjoy being different: a trait that has always set him apart from his contemporaries.

Paul was born in February 1974, near Ratoath, in Co Meath. He was Tommy and Pamela's second child – his brother Thomas was a year older, Mark came next, and then there was a longer gap to Philip, Nina and Peterjon. The Carberry children were brought up in the countryside and 'there was nothing else I ever wanted to do bar ride horses'. Paul's first pony was Jack – the same pony that was handed down to Nina and Philip a few years later. Then came Spiddal, Buckly Boy and Minnie. The ponies would go show-jumping as well as hunting.

Paul hated school, had no interest in learning and never completed any homework – 'I would ride the ponies and horses until it was dark and told to come back into the house.' At 15 he was sent to America to spend three months with the trainer Michael Smithwick in Maryland. 'Dad had sold a horse to him and I was allowed to travel over with it. It was my first time on a plane, and we travelled from Shannon to JFK on a cargo flight. I remember sitting up in the cockpit for most of the journey. It was great!' He learned a lot about jumping racehorses during his time in the USA. 'The horses were taught to relax and jump properly. I also watched a couple of rodeos, and noted how the cowboys balanced themselves with long legs wrapped around the wild horses. It taught me to ride with longer leathers when I got home to Ireland.'

Paul finally left school when he was 16, having already got a taste for race-riding in a couple of point-to-points, and the very next day he had his first winner when Joseph Knibb won in Bray. The horse carried 12st 7lb, but Paul, with his small, light frame, weighed only 7st. He carried over five stone of lead.

In spring 1990 Pamela and Tommy decided to send Paul to serve his apprenticeship in a Flat racing yard. He signed up with Jim Bolger's establishment for £60 a week on a three-year contract. Always one of the top Flat trainers in the country, Bolger has a strict work ethic. His assistant in 1990 was Aidan O'Brien, and the young jockeys there at the same time included AP McCoy and Seamie Heffernan. The stable jockey was Christy Roche. It was an impressive line-up of talent. Paul had never been one to take discipline and the regime was not easy for him to accept, but he did complete his apprenticeship despite taking part in a number of pranks. On one occasion, AP, Paul and Calvin McCormack took three bridles from Jim Bolger's yard and caught three horses in a farmer's field, which they proceeded to ride bareback for a spin over hedges and walls in the adjacent countryside – but Paul had a fall, hit his head on a wall, and had to be carried back to his digs semi-conscious.

Many top jockeys have seen their careers take off at Coolcullen, and the riding experience Paul gained there was priceless.

❧ Jim Bolger would always give you a chance if he thought you were up for the job, but it was not plain sailing. Jim and I rarely saw eye to eye. He had his way of doing things and I had mine, but he did give me a number of rides on the Flat, and I had my first winner for the master trainer when Petronelli won at Leopardstown in August 1990. But, looking back, I was just fairly bored by the Flat-race regime, and all I wanted to do was to jump horses. I always saw my time there as a stepping stone. ❞

Tommy Carberry was responsible for his son's move to Noel Meade's yard in the summer of 1992. He had known the trainer for many years and they were good friends and this move significantly marked Paul's transition from the Flat into National Hunt racing. Apart from two years in England (1995-1997) when Paul was retained by Robert Ogden, the two men were closely involved in jump racing for 15 years. They had many significant winners and, despite a few differences of opinion, largely due to Paul's issues with alcohol, they remain the best of friends.

As a jockey Paul had 14 winners at the Cheltenham Festival and numerous Grade 1 successes, with horses such as Harchibald, Pandorama, Solwhit, Sausalito Bay, Florida Pearl, Beef Or Salmon, Harbour Pilot and Bobbyjo all giving him big-race victories. In 1999 the latter, trained by his father, won the Grand National. In his excitement at the victory, Paul hung from the rafters in the old Aintree winner's enclosure.

Paul Carberry's career as a National Hunt jockey had a premature ending in 2016 due to a serious leg fracture but he still maintains that hunting was always his first love: 'If hunting had been a professional sport I would have given up race-riding.' Even when he was racing, Paul tried to hunt twice weekly with the Ward Union, and often spent an hour or two with the hounds before driving to the racecourses.

In his days as a jump jockey Paul Carberry turned many heads, and most of his fellow riders idolised him. All the young jockeys wanted to look like him on a horse, but nobody could copy his style. 'He was the ultimate jockey of his era,' says Davy Russell. 'He simply took racing to another level.' He was always utterly fearless, with incredible balance and beautiful hands. He never mistreated his horses and seldom resorted to the whip. 'When a horse came off the bridle for Paul, it would rarely go any faster if he hit it,' says Noel Meade. 'The horse had already given him its best.' Aspiring young jockeys should watch videos of Paul Carberry riding and marvel at his race tactics. They would learn plenty. His style was pure poetry. He has horses in his veins and his children are already following in his footsteps. They appear to be fearless.

David Casey

David Casey grew up in the town of Waterford, where his father managed an insurance company. Though none of his three sisters had any interest in riding, he was always keen on sport, especially soccer, and when he was seven he had basic lessons at a local riding school. Although he enjoyed sitting on the ponies he knew nothing about racing, even though he would watch it on television at weekends.

At the riding school he learned to walk, trot and canter, but never jumped even a low pole, yet when he was 15, and his time at school was drawing towards an end, he remembers having a talk with the careers adviser and, on the back of a bet with one of his mates whom he told that he was going to sign up for the Racing Apprentice School in Kildare, he announced that he wanted to be a jockey. Lengthy discussions with his parents ensued before he joined the centre in 1991 and rapidly became hooked on racing. He soon moved on to the Equitation School at the Curragh Camp, run by the Army, where there were a number of retired show-jumpers but no racehorses. It was a useful start, because on those experienced horses he had his first jumping lessons.

When his course finished he was sent to Tony Redmond, who had also been reared in Co Waterford and was a knowledgeable horseman and a much-respected Curragh trainer. David sat on his first racehorse and stayed for nearly two years. The boss insisted on a high standard of stable management and there were strict rules. David was apprenticed to him and was given nine rides on the Flat – he was very light and weighed barely 6½st. On his first ride, he carried 7st 8lb.

He thoroughly enjoyed his days on the Curragh, even though there were a few hairy moments – on one occasion, riding a big ex-point-to-point horse by King's Ride he remembers being run away with on the old schooling ground. 'It literally took off with me and jumped the concrete railings at the end of the gallops onto the verge beside the road. Being so light, I was catapulted into orbit, but fortunately escaped serious injuries.'

When Tony Redmond retired, David moved to Michael Hourigan's yard in Co Limerick. Many good jockeys have graduated from this establishment, and Timmy Murphy, Peter Henley and Kevin O'Brien were all there when David arrived. Paul Moloney signed on just before David left. David had done precious little jumping on the Curragh, but here there was a lot of schooling and it was a brilliant place for lads to learn. Even though conditions were spartan, the work was tough and David had no rides while he was with Michael, he values the time he spent there.

In 1994, David changed to Willie Mullins' yard at Closutton in Co Carlow and was given several rides on Native Baby, on whom he finished second on two occasions in bumper races. He instantly fitted into his new surroundings, but little did he realise how significant this move to the champion trainer would prove. At the end of January 1995 he rode his first winner when If You Say Yes won a claiming hurdle at Tramore. 'It was a shocking day – very wet and snowing.' By April he had ridden six winners, and the following season (1995-96) was crowned champion conditional jockey, an outstanding achievement for a rider who had barely jumped an obstacle as a child. It demonstrates his determination to succeed and daily jumping does not rate highly in the maestro's list of priorities. Practice was minimal.

At the same time, David had also been riding for Charlie Swan and Arthur Moore, and it was through the latter that he was introduced to Oliver Sherwood. Although the Mullins base had become like home, in 2000 David moved to England to Sherwood's for a taste of racing across the Irish Sea. He notched up some good wins, in particular on Cenkos, and lived with AP McCoy in Baydon. The two became good friends, but David never forgets the silence when he beat AP a short head at Sandown in the William Hill Hurdle after riding Copeland to victory for Martin Pipe.

His short stay in England was educational and successful, but he always knew he would return to Ireland, and in 2002 he left the 'travelling circus', as he called his journeys around England, to return to Willie Mullins. The Closutton trainer was expanding his operation rapidly, and it was not long before David was presented with a number of appetising rides. His first big winner for Mullins was as a 3lb claimer on Mystical City in the 1996 Galway Hurdle – although it was a valuable handicap he had been able to claim his allowance thanks to Willie managing to get the rules altered the day before the festival.

David Casey won numerous highly prestigious races, including the Irish Hennessy Gold Cup (twice), the Thyestes Chase (twice), the French Champion Hurdle (twice), the Galway Plate, the Galway Hurdle and the RSA Chase at the Cheltenham Festival. He was beaten only a short head in the Cheltenham Gold Cup in 2014 when Lord Windermere prevailed over On His Own.

When he retired with a winner on Long Dog at Listowel in September 2015 he had ridden 776 winners, including four in France and two in Australia. His rise had been meteoric, and throughout his career he had been a model of consistency. Nowadays David holds an enviable position at Willie Mullins' yard as the trainer's right-hand man, where his horsemanship and extensive racing knowledge are undoubtedly invaluable.

Bob Champion MBE

Robert 'Bob' Champion, who was awarded an MBE in 1982, is a thoroughly admirable man. Not only did he partner Aldaniti, owned by the Embiricos family, to a fairy-tale win in the 1981 Grand National following his recovery from testicular cancer, but he has also raised over £15 million via the Bob Champion Cancer Trust to enable further research into the disease. In 1984, the moving story of his triumph over adversity was made into the film *Champions*, with John Hurt taking the leading role.

The hallmarks of Bob Champion's career as a National Hunt jockey were determination and dedication. He exhibited incredible bravery, not only dealing with his life-threatening illness but also riding in races. His tough yet happy upbringing, it would seem, undoubtedly helped him to cope with life and mirrored his future in the racing world.

Bob Champion was born in 1948 at Guisborough in the North Riding of Yorkshire. His parents lived at the Cleveland Hunt Kennels where his father, also called Bob, was the professional huntsman. Indeed, the Champion family is renowned for having been represented by seven generations of huntsmen: 'Uncle Nimrod was famous in the Ledbury country, and Uncle Jack hunted the Old Surrey and Burstow Hunt.'

Bob's father, an extremely popular man and greatly respected, brought up his son to have a strong work ethic, and ensured he was good-mannered and mixed well with people from all generations. His mother was strict but practical, and a big influence on her son's early life. She loved the country life and enjoyed the hunting too. Her own father had farmed at Bushley Park, near Tewkesbury in Gloucestershire. Bob and his sister Mary rode ponies from an early age and spent many days out hunting. Even when he was at secondary school he managed to hunt three days a week, his mother writing numerous letters to his teachers saying her son was suffering from 'flu'. When he won the Grand National, his history teacher Ian McKenzie, who had always supported his pupil, appeared in the unsaddling enclosure to congratulate him. 'Surprisingly I got good marks in my history exams. It was great to meet him again after so many years.'

During his teenage years Bob regularly accompanied his father to the local racecourses with the hunt knacker van, and any fatalities were taken back to Cleveland Kennels. 'We went to York, Catterick, Redcar, Ripon and Teesside Park. I loved watching the racing and I longed to ride racehorses. When I was questioned by the careers officer at school as to what I wanted to do when I left, I told him I wanted to be a jockey.'

When Bob was 12, Jim Fairgrieve, who was Bob Champion snr's best friend, took him under his wing at Peter Cazalet's famous racing stables at Fairlawne in Kent. Jim was the head lad, and his stable management was first class. Bob rode out every day and thoroughly enjoyed his time there, but was not allowed a full-time post on leaving school because it would have been hard for the man in charge to have applied the necessary pressure to his best friend's son. So Bob went to work in a hunting yard in Gloucestershire. He went hunting with the Avon Vale and rode in a number of point-to-points, in particular at Larkhill and Badbury Rings. When the top amateur rider John Daniels was injured, Bob rode several horses for Lucy Jones and had some good winners.

In 1966 Bob was accepted by Toby Balding to work in his yard at Fyfield in Hampshire, with the prospect of rides in amateur races, but on the very first day he broke his leg. When Bob was legged up on a horse just brought in from a summer at grass it attempted to buck him off before rearing over backwards. After a week or so with the leg in plaster, the farrier was persuaded to make Bob a special wide stirrup so the young jockey could resume riding. All went well until the local doctor came to ride out one Saturday morning and spotted the irregularity: no more riding for three months. To add insult to injury, in 1969 the jockey broke his other leg in exactly the same way off another horse also in Toby's yard who misbehaved when returning to training. Horses are often cold-backed and feral when they come in from the fields, but for the same scenario to befall Bob twice was bizarre.

Bob's first winner on a racecourse came in February 1969 on Altercation, in a novice chase at Plumpton. The horse had run seven times and fallen seven times, and no jockey wanted to ride it. It started at 250-1. It then ran three more times, and fell every time, after which it was retired. The young rider had a good innings as an amateur and rode eight winners in two weeks, but in those days wins like this were deemed unacceptable by the Jockey Club, which gave little support to those in the unpaid ranks and forbade them from continuing as amateurs as soon as they started winning races, forcing them to turn professional. Similar rulings would certainly have put an end to the careers of many of the current amateurs in Ireland, some of whom ride more winners than the professionals yet remain as amateurs indefinitely.

At Fyfield, Bob Champion's mentor was Eddie Harty, a fantastic horseman and a fine rider, with whom he shared many of the rides in the Balding yard. In the year that Eddie rode Highland Wedding to win the Grand National, Bob won the Eider Chase at Newcastle on the same horse.

Despite spending many months with Toby, who will go down in racing history as one of the best producers of top jockeys – Adrian Maguire and AP McCoy being two of his most famous graduates – Bob did not stay at the Hampshire yard throughout his riding career. In the 1970s he went freelance and rode winners for Jim Old, Patrick Haslam and Ken Cundell, and also spent time with Monty Stevens at Lucknam Park near Bath, who had a small string of racehorses and in his heyday produced the fast sprinter Raffingora. He was a skilful man, but sadly died young.

Monty's main interest was pigeon racing, and Bob remembers an occasion when one of the pigeons was flying about in the kitchen.

'This pigeon won't go back in the coop with its friends,' he told his boss.

Monty went out to his shed, picked up his 12-bore gun and shot it. If a single pigeon stepped out of line, he declared, it would lead all the others astray and they'd be no good for racing.

How often does this happen with racehorses? If one horse misbehaves and upsets the string it is a disturbing influence. Animals are creatures of habit, and bad habits are often copied. If horses are crib-biters or wind-suckers, the vice is invariably catching.

During these freelance years Bob Champion made several visits to America, and he strongly recommends young jockeys to get practice riding in other countries. Over the years, a number of top jockeys have improved themselves by spending summers in France, Sweden, Norway and the USA. Bob was rewarded for his overseas visits with 20 winners in the States, on horses produced by leading trainers such as Jonathan Sheppard and Burley Cocks.

It made me a far better jockey. It sharpened me up. The horses are trained to one fifth of a second on the gallops: it is slick timing, and one has to be on the ball at all times. Jump races in America at racecourses like Saratoga and Fair Hill are run at a quick pace – some of the novice chases are run over a distance of 1m6f. The horses best suited to this type of racing are seven-furlong sprinters. There is no place for the old-fashioned jump-bred horses from Ireland. They don't have the speed and are built too heavily for the quick, underfoot conditions.

Following the sad demise of Monty Stevens, Bob was invited to ride as stable jockey for Josh Gifford, a relationship that yielded many winners, with jockey and trainer developing a good understanding. Not only did Bob win the Grand National after his months of chemotherapy, but he had also previously won the Hennessy Gold Cup at Newbury in 1978 on Approaching, as well as the SGB Chase at Ascot in 1980 on Henry Bishop. In all, Bob won 503 races as a National Hunt jockey, and at the time he was diagnosed with cancer was lying in third place in the jockeys' championship. 'I was fit and riding well – I had even ridden a winner the day before my bad news.'

Bob has always been an optimist and an exceedingly hard worker. As a rider he was fearless and always enjoyed a challenge – those days hunting certainly taught him to look after himself from a young age – and during the dark days of hospital treatment his courage knew no bounds. He has set a great example to fellow sportsmen and cancer sufferers alike, and these days his tireless work helping others fight the disease and cope with the stress that comes with it is immeasurable. He has touched the hearts of millions.

Harry Cobden

Harry's mother was leading him around on his cousin's miniature Shetland when he was barely two years old. He had been born in Yeovil in November 1998 and by the time he was three he had his own old Shetland pony that was adept at knocking him off when it walked under the big bird table in the garden. Later he had a 12hh Welsh Mountain pony called Archie that seemed to enjoy dropping his riders, and Harry won the Tumblers' Club prize at the local Pony Club rallies for falling off more than any other child. The boys mostly rode bareback at home, and Harry remembers riding in their orchard and getting caught up in the branches of a tree. The pony carried on, but Harry was left behind. When he got older he would ride his 14.2hh pony Noah with only a head collar on him and gallop bareback round the fields. All this riding without a saddle did wonders for his balance. As John Francome says, it's the best way for a child to learn to ride.

The 700-acre Cobden farm near Yeovil in Somerset – 400 acres are rented – is predominantly grass, and when Harry was growing up there were always plenty of sheep and cattle to be seen. His great-grandfather, Toby, ran an abattoir in Langport, so Harry grew up to accept the ups and downs of animal husbandry. He still enjoys farming, and as a teenager was hands-on whenever needed, but his days out hunting were always his favourite. The hedges jumped in the Blackmore and Sparkford Vale county are notoriously big, but Harry loved the challenge.

When he was nine, Harry got his first introduction to trainer Ron Hodges, who would prove a major influence in his formative racing years. Ron watched Harry ride his 13.2hh pony Pimms, and in the evenings gave the child lessons on his gallops. The Hodges only lived five minutes away, and in the holidays Harry would cycle to the yard every day.

Harry was mad keen to ride in a pony race, but on the first occasion he was left standing at flagfall and finished last. It soon became apparent that Pimms would not be fast enough to race, and so his parents, realising how competitive their son was, paid £8,000 for the 13.2hh thoroughbred show pony Minfield Millionaire's Delight. This beautiful pony came from Kent and proved a real success, winning 16 times. The boy often missed days at school to ride in pony races. When he was 13 he rode racehorses at Paul Nicholls' yard at Ditcheat, and was even allowed to school Kauto Stone over hurdles. Megan Nicholls is the same age as Harry, and they rode together in the pony races.

Harry left school on his 16th birthday without having taken a single GCSE – 'I was not even qualified to work in McDonalds, as you need a C in English and Maths to do that' – yet he considers November 5, 2016, to be one of the best days of his life. He was sent to Anthony and Rachael Honeyball's racing yard at Potwell Farm, near Beaminster, and rode out for them most days, except Wednesdays when his mother drove him to David Brace's stables near Bridgend. At those two yards he received valuable jumping experience. 'At 14, I used to be too far behind my horses – probably due to sitting back over the hedges when out hunting. Then, at 16, I started getting in front of the movement. I had a lot to learn, but I had help from top people and rode plenty of different horses.'

While working in the Honeyballs' yard, Harry was becoming increasingly keen on point-to-pointing, and bought two pointers from David Brace, Cock Of The Rock and Silver Token. Between them they won 11 races in the 2015 season. His first winner on a racetrack was El Mondo for the Honeyballs in the spring of 2015 in a two-mile hunter chase at Leicester. Harry loved those days out, and rode at most of the local courses, which included Badbury Rings, Larkhill, Little Windsor and Milborne St Andrew. He ended up with 16 point-to-point wins and several hunter chase successes, and was champion novice rider. Admittedly he had good horses and plenty of help, but he rode them well and was quickly noticed by the experts.

In July 2015, when Harry had been with Anthony Honeyball for seven months, he was offered a conditional jockey's job at Paul

Nicholls'. There were plenty of opportunities in the champion trainer's establishment, so he moved to Ditcheat and duly turned professional.

The champion trainer is renowned for being a hard taskmaster and tough on his riders, and 'I found the first season quite difficult,' admits Harry. 'To start with, I was given a lot of high-profile rides at the big meetings, and I rode a good few winners, but then when I began riding horses with high weights in 20-runner handicaps, life was not that straightforward, and the successes did not come easily.' Harry rode many more horses in his second season with Paul Nicholls, and at the end of the 2016-17 season ended up champion conditional jockey. In his third year he notched up 50 winners for Colin Tizzard as well. He has ridden a number of top horses for Venn Farm, including Cue Card in the 2017 Betfair Chase at Haydock.

At the age of 20 Harry Cobden has already ridden class horses for the Nicholls yard and, having been promoted to first jockey at Ditcheat in the spring of 2018, and despite a serious fall at Market Rasen shortly after his appointment when he broke the C2 vertebra in his neck, he has not looked back. In his short career as a professional jockey he has already had more than 300 winners, and his win on Clan Des Obeaux in the 2018 King George VI Chase at Kempton on Boxing Day was a massive feather in his cap. To date, he has had eight Grade 1 wins as well as two Cheltenham Festival victories.

As Harry gains confidence and experience as one of the country's leading National Hunt jockeys his style is visibly changing. He already sits more quietly on the horses he rides and allows the fences to come to him, rather than vigorously riding them on the approaches. He has learned a lot through watching others, especially when jumping out hunting and following the likes of Rupert Nuttall, a former jockey and always a supreme horseman.

Despite leaving school at 16, Harry Cobden is highly intelligent and has an excellent business mind. Having bought 15 acres of land adjoining his parents' farm with the proceeds from his early race-riding successes, he is developing the shoots he runs from the woodlands on them. Buying and rearing pheasant chicks each summer and then planning the shooting days for the winter months take up plenty of his time, and offers a welcome diversion from the intensity of National Hunt racing. It is essential for top sportsmen to have outside interests in order to freshen their minds and release tensions. As Marcus Armytage has said,

Harry Cobden's talent, combined with a devil-may-care attitude, shrewd business mind, strong work ethic and a touch of arrogance, suggests he may well last the trip at Paul Nicholls' yard, when the shelf life of the incumbents since Ruby Walsh has tended to be short, and on occasions, not overly sweet.

Jamie Codd

A number of Irish jockeys who call themselves amateurs are certainly way above the professionals in ability, and JJ – Jamie – Codd is undoubtedly one of the most talented on the National Hunt circuit. His record at the top National Hunt festivals such as Cheltenham, Punchestown, Leopardstown and Fairyhouse is outstanding, and it is hardly surprising he is in great demand for the big meetings.

Jamie's father always had point-to-point horses and kept broodmares alongside his dairy cows at Mayglass, Co Wexford, and was a successful rider himself, especially in hunter chases, famously partnering Philipintown Hero to many victories. Jamie's brother William, who sadly died in 2018, was also an exceptional rider, riding numerous winners as an amateur.

Jamie and William and their sister Lisa spent many happy days in the Killinick Pony Club, did plenty of show-jumping and loved jumping the ponies over cross-country courses as well. At 16, Jamie represented Ireland at the Weston Park Pony Eventing Championships in Britain. He enjoyed eventing, and his best result was when he was victorious in a two-star event in Killarney, but above all he loved hunting, which has proved the making of so many National Hunt jockeys. His days with the Killinick Harriers over varied Irish countryside – banks, ditches and rails – taught him a vast amount and helped to develop his excellent light hands. Pony racing did not appeal, but he did take part in a few tetrathlons.

At 16, Jamie rode in his first point-to-point, and his first winner was Eyze for Mags Mullins at Bramblestown in October 2001. In November 2018 he rode his 900th point-to-point winner at Loughanmore in Northern Ireland and at 18 he joined Willie Mullins' yard, where he rode as an amateur for five years. Within two years he had ridden more than 50 winners under National Hunt rules. His first winner was for Willie Mullins when he was successful on Killultagh Thunder at Leopardstown in December 2001.

Horses jump for Jamie, especially in steeplechases, and he must have a brilliant clock in his head because he always has them in the right place at the right time in a race. Indeed, when he won the Champion Bumper at the Cheltenham Festival in 2017 on Fayonagh, he missed the start and was literally last away from the tapes, but still managed to get the mare's head in front when it mattered.

Jamie Codd is undoubtedly one of the finest amateur riders of his generation and he was champion in Ireland in the 2016-17 season. His first Grade 1 winner, Shaneshill, had been for Willie Mullins at the Punchestown festival in 2014, but he has now had nine Cheltenham Festival winners, comprising the Kim Muir four times, the National Hunt Chase twice, the Champion Bumper twice and the Cross Country Chase. Jamie combines riding in races with his work for Tattersalls (Ireland) as an agent at their National Hunt sales at either Cheltenham or Fairyhouse. He has countless admirers and is sure to continue to grace the winner's enclosure for many more years.

Aidan Coleman

In the summer of 2006, Irish trainer John Joseph Murphy contacted Terry Biddlecombe and I to say that he had a 17-year-old rider in his yard who he thought was ready for a move to England. John believed in his ability and he knew the boy was hungry to learn more.

Thus in July, Aidan Coleman arrived at West Lockinge Farm. It was the first time he had been away from home and he was a quiet, shy person, but it was soon clear he had a sharp mind – he seemed to live on his computer and was mad about racing. He stayed with us for 15 months, and learned a huge amount from Terry, who watched him daily on the gallops. He had done virtually no jumping in Ireland, except on his ponies and a few horses trained by Pat Doyle in Holycross, and we gave him plenty of tuition. Unfortunately, there were few opportunities for him to ride in races from my yard since the horses we trained were unsuitable for an inexperienced 17-year-old. Therefore we advised him to move to Venetia Williams' yard, and from there his career took off.

Having been born in 1988 Aidan did not ride properly until he was 12, when his parents, both schoolteachers, bought him a pony, Bubbles, and kept it in a small field beside their house. He grew up in the quiet rural community of Innishannon in Co Cork, and was close to his elder brother Kevin, who was always interested in racing and had become a jockey.

John Murphy's yard at Highfort in Upton is close to Innishannon, and he has a large number of racehorses, ranging from point-to-pointers and jumpers to youngsters for the Flat. He has also owned many good show-jumpers, and had learned his trade with Iris Kellett and later with Harvey Smith. In 2006, he trained Newmill to win the Queen Mother Champion Chase at Cheltenham. Aidan started visiting John's yard and the trainer taught him to ride his racehorses. He was always impressed by the boy's natural ability and enthusiasm.

At 13, Aidan had his first rides in pony races and was an immediate success: he was quick-thinking and extremely competitive. His biggest supporters were the McSweeney brothers, but he also rode a number of ponies for Eric Tyner. Although these were called pony races, the children were often mounted on horses, and whereas in England there is seldom the opportunity for a child to have more than one race per day, in Ireland five or six rides are the norm. As a result the young riders learn an unbelievable amount from partnering a variety of horses, most of them thoroughbreds who have probably raced on the track. Aidan ended up with more than 100 winners on the pony-race circuit, with Jack Doyle, Paddy Merrigan, Philip Enright and Martin Harley his most renowned opponents.

Since being taken on by Venetia Williams, for whose yard he rode many winners, Aidan Coleman has quietly worked his way up the ladder. His Grade 1 win at Cheltenham in the 2019 Stayers' Hurdle on Paisley Park was undoubtedly a big feather in his cap. He has consistently had winners for top trainers, especially for Jonjo O'Neill, and in 2016 was given the number-one position in John Ferguson's jump string. Nowadays, he is closely linked to Olly Murphy, a young trainer who looks set for a bright future. In June 2019, Aidan celebrated his 1,000th winner under National Hunt rules.

Davy Condon

To be forced into retirement at 31 was a cruel blow for Davy Condon. During his short riding career, this fine horseman had already notched up 398 winners.

Davy's mother is a Townend by birth, and her brother is the father of champion jockey Paul Townend. His father was a good amateur rider who was successful in many point-to-points. Unsurprisingly, Davy always wanted to be a jockey, and rode ponies from his earliest years. He regularly hunted with the Conna Harriers in Co Waterford on his 14.2hh pony Max, who was a real challenge to ride. From the age of five he was learning about balance, and he soon developed a fine eye for a fence.

At 12, Davy began to get rides in pony races, even though his father was against the idea of his son riding in these tough contests. Mark Walsh, Nina Carberry and Tom Queally were some of his opponents. The Condons' neighbour, trainer Liam Burke, took Davy to the meetings, and Davy Russell also helped him with his riding. He ended up with 45 winners between the flags, most of them on locally trained ponies. Jockey Johnny Burke became a good friend, even though he was a lot younger. The two of them used to race each other on their bikes when they were children and, says Johnny, 'We always carried proper racing whips and thrashed the wheels of our bicycles.'

Davy Condon left school at 15 to join Willie Mullins as an apprentice jockey on the Flat. In August 2001 he rode his first winner under rules on Slaney Boy at Tramore – in those early years he weighed less than 7st. He ended up with 111 Flat winners, but loved the jumping game. At Willie's yard, Ruby Walsh was the principal jockey, but he was also riding for Paul Nicholls in England, and with David Casey taking many of Ruby's rides on Saturdays, Davy Condon slotted himself into the pecking order just behind.

Thanks to Willie Mullins, the 2006-07 season saw Davy make a significant impact in National Hunt racing. He rode Homer Wells to win the big Listed prize at Gowran Park, the Thyestes Chase, and then partnered the 40-1 shot Ebaziyan to win the Supreme Novices' Hurdle at the Cheltenham Festival.

In 2008 Davy moved to Nicky Richards' yard at Greystoke in Cumbria, from where he won the Peterborough Chase on Monet's Garden and the Scottish Champion Hurdle on Noble Alan, but he only stayed in England for a year before returning to Ireland to join Noel Meade's stable, where for a while, due to the suspension of Paul Carberry, he found himself principal jockey. He rode a number of good horses for Noel, registering Grade 1 victories with Pandorama, Hollo Ladies and Go Native. In 2009 the latter won the Fighting Fifth Hurdle at Newcastle. While based in Co Meath, Davy also rode horses for Gordon Elliott and had his second Cheltenham Festival winner when Flaxen Flare was victorious in the 2013 Fred Winter Juvenile Handicap Hurdle.

All the more heartbreaking, then, for a rider who could possibly have been a future champion, to have his career brought to an end at the fourth-last fence in the 2015 Grand National when Portrait King's fall left him with a serious spinal injury. Yet despite weeks in hospital and a long convalescence, Davy has bounced back and although being unable to race-ride, he remains a valuable work-rider at Gordon Elliott's establishment, and one of his right-hand men. Davy still has a bright future ahead of him in the racing world.

Bryan Cooper

These days life is not as easy for Bryan Cooper as it was when he was first jockey for Michael O'Leary's prestigious Gigginstown House Stud. It could even be said that his future as a leading National Hunt jockey hangs in the balance, despite having a number of top-class wins to his name, including the 2016 Cheltenham Gold Cup, which he landed on Don Cossack.

Bryan always wanted to be a jockey, and on the very day he was born his parents won a pony in a raffle at a local show. Snowy became their son's first pony, and Bryan even rode her out with his father's string of racehorses. Nowadays, Tom Cooper has over 40 horses in training at Tralee, Co Kerry, and has had two Cheltenham Festival winners already: Forpadydeplasterer, whom Barry Geraghty rode in 2009 to win the Arkle Chase, and Total Enjoyment, who won the Champion Bumper in 2004 when ridden by Jim Culloty.

As a child Bryan would sit for hours on the back of the sofa pretending to be a jockey, riding a finish with his whip. He took Snowy to a few gymkhanas, but when he outgrew her it was the bigger ponies that he show-jumped, winning numerous classes and competing at the RDS horse show, and jumping in the Irish team at the European Show Jumping Championships at Fontainebleau.

He got his first taste of race-riding at 12 when he had a season of pony racing. He rode in the 12.2hh, 13.2hh and 14.2hh races against Danny Mullins and Paul Townend and he had several good wins. Then, during his school holidays, he would go to Dessie Hughes' yard on the Curragh where he rode out and learned proper stable management. The trainer was a first-class teacher, and Bryan has joyful memories of those summer months at Osborne Lodge.

When Bryan left school he worked for Kevin Prendergast on the Curragh and got his apprentice licence whilst there. He rode his first winner on the Flat at 16 for Eoin Doyle, on Dusty Trail at Tramore in a mile-and-a-half handicap. He never rode in any point-to-points, but had close on 60 rides on the Flat. At 15 he had been 8st 4lb, but his weight was going up and he was fast becoming too heavy to be a Flat jockey.

In 2009, Bryan returned to Dessie Hughes to ride in National Hunt races, and on only his second ride over obstacles rode a winner, Rossdara, for his father in a Clonmel maiden hurdle. He was then off for a while with a broken wrist, but came back with a flourish and rode three winners for Dessie in the space of ten days. In the 2010-11 season he won the conditional jockeys' championship, and also won his first Listed race when Coscorrig was victorious at Fairyhouse.

The teenage Cooper had another exceptional season in 2011-12 and finished with 36 wins, including a Grade 1 victory on Benefficient for Tony Martin at Leopardstown. In the 2012-13 season the racing world really took note of Bryan Cooper when he had three wins at the Cheltenham Festival on Benefficient (JLT Novices' Chase), Our Conor (Triumph Hurdle) and Ted Veale (County Hurdle).

Bryan stayed with Dessie Hughes for five years, until in January 2014 it was announced that he would take over the position of retained jockey for the Gigginstown House Stud from Davy Russell. It was a surprise appointment, but one which offered a great opportunity. He had some wonderful rides for the O'Learys, and visited the yards of many top trainers – in those days Gordon Elliott, Henry de Bromhead, Mouse Morris, Edward O'Grady and Paul Nolan were all supported by Gigginstown. In July 2017, however, Eddie O'Leary announced that Bryan would no longer be retained by his connections.

Despite having lost a top job in National Hunt racing, Bryan Cooper has not given up on his quest to ride winners and be associated with top-class horses. Davy Russell has demonstrated his riding skills without depending solely on Gigginstown horses, and Bryan still gets a few rides from his former employers, but life is undoubtedly tougher these days and he needs to obtain support from more leading trainers. Jockeys only seem to get the cream rides if they are closely attached to a big yard and Bryan has yet to find the yard that suits him. He remains a neat, stylish jockey, and if fortune goes the right way he could regain a high position on the jockeys' ladder.

Jim Crowley

Although a top Flat-race jockey and British champion in 2016, Jim Crowley has deep roots in jump racing. As a National Hunt jockey in the late 1990s and early part of the 2000s he rode more than 300 winners, though mostly in the north of England at lower-grade tracks. He never had a winner at Cheltenham, but was successful in the Lanzarote Hurdle at Kempton in 2005 when riding Crossbow Creek for Mark Rimell, and he had a number of wins abroad.

Indeed, he travelled a number of times to Czechoslovakia, in particular to Pardubice, where he had seven winners, although not in the big steeplechase. Towards the end of his career he partnered Registana, who was Czech-trained and a terrific mare. At one point, in 2004, it looked like she might lower the colours of Spot Thedifference, trained by Enda Bolger, in one of the Cheltenham cross-country races, but for running out. Jim won on her at Merano, a racecourse nestled under the Alps and by all accounts extremely beautiful. In 2004 he also won the Gran Premio Chase there on Masini, whom he later rode in the Grand Steeple Chase de Paris at Auteuil, but the year after his landmark victory, when he again rode in the big race, he jumped a wrong fence. According to Marcus Armytage in the *Daily Telegraph*,

> Jim was wearing a smart new pair of Gucci shoes and, after it had rained all night, he decided that walking the course would ruin them. In the race he planned to follow the leaders until he got to the last, quicken past them and win the huge pot. However, the leader fell, and Crowley had no option but to take up the running going to the second-last where, faced with a choice of three obstacles, he took the wrong one and was disqualified.

Jim was fined more than the price of his new Guccis and banned for 21 days, although the Italians failed to inform the British authorities and the ban was never enforced. 'They cost me a lot of money, those bloody shoes.'

Jim was born in Ascot, and the family house overlooked the racecourse. His father had ridden as a Flat-race jockey in Ireland, and his mother kept a number of point-to-point horses. As an only child, he had a wonderful upbringing and was always surrounded by horses and ponies – 'I could ride before I could walk.' He attended many horse shows and rode native ponies – Shetlands plus Welsh As and Bs at the top county shows, and qualified for both Olympia and the Horse of the Year Show. He thoroughly enjoyed the showing days, which also included working hunter classes and competing in Shetland Pony Grand Nationals – but he was also fascinated by racing, and well remembers leading up horses for his mother at the point-to-points at Tweseldown. He loved the hunting too – in those days point-to-point horses had to get properly qualified and go out hunting – and he spent many enjoyable days with Mr Goshen's hounds and the Staff College and Sandhurst foxhounds.

Jim had such a yearning to ride racehorses that at 15 he went to Con Horgan's yard near Maidenhead, where he got even more smitten by the racing bug, and then moved to Guy Harwood's establishment at Coombelands near Pulborough in Sussex. Granted his amateur licence he rode in several point-to-points before getting his first winner over jumps in 1997 for Dave Thom at Worcester when he partnered Captain Marmalade in a handicap hurdle. He had never even schooled a horse over hurdles, but with his show-jumping and hunting background he quickly adjusted to jumping obstacles at a faster pace.

After being placed second in a hunter chase at Wetherby in 1998, Jim was approached by Harvey Smith and asked if he'd like to join his and Sue's yard. After some deliberation he decided to move up north, and stayed at Craiglands Farm near Bingley for the next four years. Being part of Harvey's 'School of Life' was an incredible experience for the young jockey, as well as a real eye-opener. The methods were a long way from those at Coombelands, and at times totally unorthodox, but Harvey is a real horseman. He understands horses, and his show-jumping days mean he excels at teaching them to jump. Jim also rode out for Mary Reveley, another master trainer.

In the summer of 2005 Jim moved back south and began to have a number of rides on the Flat. He already had close links with Guy Harwood's daughter Lucinda, and he started riding out for Amanda Harwood. He was still light, and in 2006 won the Jockey Club Cup for Rod Millman at Newmarket on Hawridge Prince. Since then his rise to fame in Flat racing has been meteoric.

Riding on the Flat is obviously different from the days when he held a jump jockeys' licence, and he admits he still misses the camaraderie in National Hunt racing – 'it's much warmer in the jumps weighing room'. But whereas National Hunt racing is a sport, he concedes that Flat racing, with the millions of pounds of horseflesh at stake, is a business.

❢ Tony Hind is my agent on the Flat and books my rides. When Richard Hughes retired and there was a possible opening for championship honours I called Tony and he asked me to state my ambitions, but when I told him I'd be happy to finish off a season in the top three he told me that was not good enough – 'You either want to be champion or you don't.' Thus he helped to drive me to get championship honours in 2016, and my job with Sheikh Hamdan has been unbelievable. When you're a kid and you see those famous blue-and-white silks you dream of wearing them one day. The job with the sheikh has taken my career to another level. ❢

When Jim won the coveted Flat jockeys' title, he broke the record for the number of winners in a month. He had 46, beating both Fred Archer and Sir Gordon Richards, who had 45 apiece.

Given the differences between Flat racing and National Hunt it is fascinating to see how a well-established jump jockey can successfully transfer to the other code and achieve champion status. He has been fortunate to have ridden in races all over the world, and had winners in Australia, Dubai, India and even in St Moritz on the frozen lake. But Jim Crowley is a deep thinker who fully understands the highs and lows of sport. His marriage to Lucinda Harwood has been a huge plus, and through his three lovely children, Alice, Bella and Sam, he relives his own childhood days with ponies and still attends pony shows whenever he can.

Jim Culloty

Jim Culloty will forever be remembered for partnering Best Mate to three Cheltenham Gold Cups in 2002, 2003 and 2004. But his record doesn't stop there: his 394 wins included an Aintree Grand National on Bindaree in 2002, an Irish Grand National on Timbera in 2003, and the King George VI Chase at Kempton on Edredon Bleu in 2003. All this and he comes from a family without a significant connection to horseracing.

Jim is one of eight children, all of whom bar himself have attended university. Their father came from a well-educated family, and his children obviously inherited his intelligence. Jim's sister, Maria, is the mother of Oisin Murphy, the rising star in the Flat racing world who could easily have been an academic himself had he not chosen to ride horses. Jim's father did, however, have shares in a few racehorses and was an ardent follower of the sport. Jim himself enjoyed watching racing on television, but preferred hurling to football, which is surprising for a Kerry man given the county's strong ties with Gaelic football.

Jim sat on a friend's pony when he was ten and rode bareback. He subsequently went to the Killarney riding school with his brother Mike. They saved up to buy a pony of their own by setting up a little sandwich stall on the main road that passed their house and because it was on the way to the football ground there was plenty of trade, but they kept an Alsatian beside them just in case of trouble. When they had made enough money the boys went to Puck Fair at Killorglin and bought a pony for £350.

There was massive excitement when they took it home, and it was kept in a field owned by their Uncle Frank, who ran a well-known men's outfitters in Killarney. The pony proved a big hit. It was 13.3hh, and the boys would ride it after school and at weekends. Later, two small stables were built at the bottom of their garden, and the pony was joined by a point-to-pointer that Jim's father had formerly part-owned in Co Kilkenny. For the first time in his life the future jockey could ride a thoroughbred. However, his riding was confined to hacking along country lanes or cantering in fields: there were no gymkhanas in the area, as Co Kerry has no tradition of equestrian sports.

During his school holidays, Jim spent time with John Kennedy near Gowran Park in Co Kilkenny. He rode racehorses and greatly enjoyed himself. Then, for a couple of summer holidays, he was sent to John Jenkins' yard at Royston in Hertfordshire. An established trainer and former jockey, John is an extremely knowledgeable man who has always run a busy establishment, but in the 1980s the stable staff did not welcome new arrivals with open arms. Jim was subjected to the set rituals for new staff who were stripped naked – lads and girls – covered in hoof oil or grease, and rolled in the sand in the indoor school. They were then tied to the old-fashioned horse walker, where they would be left to jog round for several hours. Nowadays, such behaviour would never be tolerated and the staff would be in serious trouble with the authorities, but in Jim's days it was accepted as the norm.

Jim did well at school, passing his leaving certificate and applying for a place at university, but he was always more preoccupied with horseracing than intellectual studies, and unbeknown to his parents he answered an advertisement in the *Sporting Life* for a vacancy for a lad to ride in point-to-points. After persuading his father that it was the right move, he headed to England to ride for David Bloomfield on Bodmin Moor in Cornwall.

There were around 12 point-to-pointers in the yard – mostly homebred horses – and Jim worked long hours with little assistance, but enjoyed the challenge and rapidly learned how to jump horses over hurdles and small schooling fences. He rode in a number of West Country point-to-points and had four winners in his first season, which demonstrated his ability.

After a season at Bodmin, Jim met Philip Scholfield, Nick's father, who was a top rider and he helped Jim to take his career a step further by putting the young lad in touch with Jackie Retter, who held a training licence near Exeter. Mick Fitzgerald had ridden for her in his early years, and now the trainer was looking for another rising star. At 18, Jim made the move, obtained his amateur licence and had his first winner under rules for Jackie when Karicleigh Boy won a bumper at Exeter in January 1994. He continued to ride in point-to-points as well and clocked up 20 more winners. In 1993 he was crowned champion novice point-to-point rider. He also had further rides on the track, and in particular rode winners for the Messer-Bennetts family in Wadebridge.

After being attached to Jackie Retter for two years, Jim started looking for a move to a bigger yard. He wanted to be based further upcountry. Mick Fitzgerald advised him to apply for a job with me and Terry Biddlecombe. Our regular jockey Jason Titley was struggling with his weight, and Jim found it easy to do under 10st. On Mick's advice, Terry watched Jim's riding on a racing channel, and liked the way he kept his horses balanced as well as maintaining an even contact with their mouths. We decided to give him a try, and at the end of 1994 Jim moved to Oxfordshire. In 1997 he became the stable jockey at West Lockinge Farm, a position he held for eight years, and he rode many good horses for my owners. His patient agent, Chris Broad, found him plenty of outside rides as well, and in his first season, 1995-96, he rode 44 winners and captured the amateur riders' championship.

Having been champion jockey three times in his heyday, Terry was respected by the young rider who listened to him, and he acquired many race-riding skills from him, but Jim did not readily take criticism from me, and his unpunctuality and slapdash approach to stable management often saw him on the receiving end of my tongue. Yet his cheek and casual approach to life sometimes worked to his advantage – the owners loved him – and he became a valued member of our team. Above all, he was reliable on the racecourse and ice-cool under pressure. He was at his best when the chips were down. When he rode Best Mate in those Cheltenham Gold Cups he was totally focused and listened to everything Terry told him to do. I always kept out of any discussions and stayed well out of the way. What would I have known about riding around Cheltenham? Grandstand jockeys are the worst.

From the day when Jim Culloty as an amateur won the Warwick National on Full Of Oats in January 1996 to the moment in July 2005 at Market Rasen when he told me he would be hanging up his boots, I can look back on many memorable racing days. Best Mate put my name on the map, and Jim Culloty rode him. I will always be grateful to my jockey for the part he played.

After retiring, Jim's immediate successes as a trainer were remarkable. By producing Lord Windermere to follow in Best Mate's footsteps and win the Gold Cup on Prestbury's hallowed turf in 2014, he delivered a fairy-tale result. However, Jim did not have much luck afterwards, and his departure from training in 2017 came as no surprise. Whether he will continue to be connected to National Hunt racing remains to be seen, but his three children – Art, Eliza and Hugh – can certainly grow up proud of their father's achievements.

Hywel Davies

Having finished his studies at 19, Hywel Davies hitch-hiked with his best friend to France for a holiday. He remembers lying on a beach in Toulon and saying to his mate, 'When I get back, I'm going into racing.' This was exactly what happened.

Hywel and his brothers Geraint and Dyfrig rode regularly as children – their father, a farrier, was a popular figure in Wales. The future jockey competed on a number of famous show ponies for Gillian Cuff and won prizes at all the big shows, including the Royal Welsh. His showing jodhpurs were tightly fitted around his thin legs to show off the ponies to their best advantage. 'Mrs Cuff's daughter, Rosemary, used to stitch me into them. She liked them to be really tight and cling to me.'

After the show ponies, Hywel moved on to jumping ponies, and rode everything that was presented to him. He had an excellent nerve. In particular he did well with Cuffs's 14.1hh pony Copper Pride and jumped successfully at Hickstead and at the Horse of the Year Show. He loved riding the Grade-A ponies; he had a natural eye for a fence and could see a stride.

After this excellent start to his career in the show-jumping world, Hywel turned his attentions to point-to-pointing. He had to wait until his 16th birthday to get a licence, but then, just like James Bowen some years later, had a successful time on the Welsh point-to-point circuit. He also went to college in Aberystwyth and gained an OND degree.

Hywel had a lot going for him when it came to a career in the saddle. The young Hywel spent his summers with Roddy Armytage in East Ilsley in Berkshire, where he got the taste for riding out racehorses in a disciplined manner, and then rang three top National Hunt trainers to see if they would employ him. Fred Winter said no, and that he was full up. David Nicholson had too many jockeys on his list too, but Josh Gifford, although he already had six jockeys riding out for him, said, 'Come down and I'll have a look at you.' Hywel travelled to Findon on a Sunday and started riding out the following morning. Immediately feeling at home, he stayed with Josh for three seasons, after which he went back to Roddy Armytage as first jockey.

> Roddy had an oval all-weather ring on wood chippings. It was dug out deeply with high edges, and had four telegraph poles placed across the track. The horses really learned how to jump properly and pick up their legs. It was a brilliant system – they went short or long and on both reins.

On one occasion he remembers schooling 30 horses in a morning.

After his early successes in the saddle, Hywel then joined Tim Forster's yard and rode for him as first jockey for eight years. He has some amazing stories to tell about this renowned pessimist, but had some great days there and some high-profile wins, including Last Suspect at 50-1 in the 1985 Grand National, which was an amazing achievement. 'Only a Welshman could have conned Last Suspect into galloping around Aintree for 4½ miles,' said John Francome, who is half-Welsh himself on his mother's side.

'When you are a jockey,' says Hywel himself,

> There is more than one way to do the job. There are numerous different styles – no two jockeys could have been greater opposites than Jeff King and John Francome. Legs are a great advantage to a jump jockey, and the best ride by feel and instinct, both of which are probably bred into them, although can be improved through practice.

As well as the Grand National, Hywel won the 1989 Hennessy Gold Cup on Ghofar, the Champion Chase at Cheltenham on Barnbrook Again in 1990, and the Whitbread Gold Cup on Topsham Bay in 1992. He was a tough, strong jockey: the year before his Grand National victory he survived a shocking fall at Doncaster when he actually stopped breathing, but was revived by the ambulance men. Hywel, who now gains a lot of pleasure from watching his own son, James, ride winners on the track, had 762 wins as a National Hunt jockey.

Nico de Boinville

Nicolai (Nico) de Boinville has a different outlook on racing to many past and present National Hunt jockeys. Despite enjoying winners, he does not chase numbers, in marked contrast to the likes of AP McCoy and Richard Johnson. Nico lives for the big days. He considers himself at his best when under pressure and in the full gaze of the public. Outwardly unmoved when dealing with the media, he thrives on being in the limelight on stars such as Altior. External factors never faze him.

Nico loves a challenge, and he loves class horses – ones who demonstrate the best qualities of the thoroughbred breed – and certainly there is no substitute for the beauty and movement of a true champion. Good horses make good riders, and their superiority is indelibly printed in the minds of true horsemen. Much of this can undoubtedly be traced back to his childhood. He successfully rode show ponies at all the major horse shows, and in 1998 was the winner of the Search for a Star competition at the Horse of the Year Show.

Nico spent his childhood in Hampshire. His mother Shaunagh did plenty of riding herself as a child, her father was Master of the Vine and Craven Hunt, and her sister Phillippa, who is married to the trainer Patrick Chamings, did a considerable amount of eventing and represented the Craven Pony Club in many competitions. Nico rode ponies from an early age with his sister and younger brother, and particularly enjoyed the show circuit under the watchful eye of Richard and Marjorie Ramsey, who lived close by and produced many top-class ponies for the young boy to ride. 'Nico was really into the showing,' remembers Richard,

But was also good at dressage. He had a lovely black 13.2hh pony called Rosslyn Loyalty whom, aged 13, he rode to win his class at the Pony Club Dressage Championships against children of all ages, and he was placed third overall under three List 1 judges. He was unflustered and the pony gave a brilliant display. **9**

Richard further recalls that Nico would 'ride anything and everything. He was a determined child and always to be relied upon under pressure.'

Nico went to boarding school near Reading, but was often allowed out to ride and compete on his event horse. Having been accepted for university in Newcastle with the intention of reading politics, he took a gap year and wrote to the English-born trainer Richard Gibson, who then trained in Chantilly. Nico spent seven months there, finding France strange at first, and quite lonely, having not learned the language at school, but there were over 60 horses in the yard, including that now much-sought-after sire of jumpers, Doctor Dino.

The trainer paid great attention to detail, and Nico was up every morning before 5.30 helping with the feeding and learning about horses' legs – did they feel normal, or were there any abnormalities? He was fascinated by the training methods, and took out his amateur licence. Nico often spent his afternoons watching the racing on courses such as Longchamp and Saint-Cloud, and had two rides on the Flat at Fontainebleau, where he finished second and third, but got a stern lecture from his boss for not contacting him afterwards. After a race jockeys should always talk to the trainer.

When he returned to England he spent his mornings riding out for Patrick Chamings and Andrew Balding, and in August 2009 he had his first winner on Western Roots, who landed an amateur Flat race at Newbury for the Kingsclere trainer. In the spring Nico's first ride in a point-to-point had been less successful: he had fallen off at the first fence at Barbury Castle when the horse had virtually jumped the obstacle from a standstill.

University life did not suit Nico. He stayed at Newcastle just six weeks, and left in November to coincide with the Open meeting at Cheltenham. 'I just did not want to be there, even though I did manage to ride out for Howard Johnson, who was at that time training horses like Inglis Drever and Tidal Bay.' He resumed his riding out at the Chamings yard, and trained a point-to-point horse of his own from home. This was Baodai, and he successfully won on him as well as enjoying a ride in a hunter chase. Several people now offered him horses on the point-to-point circuit, and his ability began to get noticed. He rode 25 winners. It was then that he wrote another of his letters – this time to Nicky Henderson. It was to prove the turning point in his life.

In September 2009, at England's top jumping yard at Seven Barrows, Nico started his first proper job. He began as a stable lad, but his natural talents were soon recognised by Corky Browne, a key figure in the Henderson yard and head lad extraordinaire. A legend in racing, Corky knows more about training than most people in the sport – he retired only in 2019, aged 77.

His stable management, veterinary knowledge, handling of horses and way with people were always exceptional. In the summer Nico would help Corky to break in horses, and in 2013 he was the very first person to sit on Altior, no doubt sowing the seeds for the trust the pair of them have developed in each other during the horse's rise to stardom as a chaser of unbelievable merit.

In 2012, during his time with Nicky and while still an amateur, Nico took part in the Fegentri series of Flat races, whereby amateur riders from different countries compete across Europe. There was plenty of travelling and it was a great experience for an enthusiastic young jockey. In 1990 Marcus Armytage had won the overall title, but in Nico's year, 2012, no single rider stood out, though he had a lot of fun. Rachel King, who now lives in Australia, and Niall Kelly from Ireland were two of his opponents.

Nico de Boinville's early years with Nicky Henderson were slow going. He did very little schooling over the hurdles and fences and had virtually no rides under rules, but in February 2012 he finally had his first winner, on Barbers Shop, owned by the Queen, in a hunter chase at Fakenham. He won a similar race on the same horse at Fontwell, but was unplaced in the Foxhunter Chase at the Cheltenham Festival. This was Nico's first experience of the big stage, however, and his first ride at the prestigious meeting.

Yet despite these wins, Nico still did not get as many rides as he had hoped. He remembers thinking, 'I'd be much better off in France trying my luck over there.' At that time he had no aspirations to be a top professional jockey: he just wanted as many winners as possible as an amateur. But when he told his boss that he was about to leave he received a cool reception, and in November 2012 he was given a ride at the big Hennessy meeting at Newbury, and finished second. The following weekend he rode Petit Robin to victory at Sandown on Tingle Creek day. The race was televised, his riding ability was noticed, and it was a major breakthrough.

Nico worries that young lads today want to be jockeys without learning to ride properly with a proper length of leg. Today, everyone is in a hurry and the riders perch on their horses with short stirrups. They never develop balance. Many, he believes, have no basic education in riding and no proper jumping practice, and the British Racing School, in his opinion, further complicates matters by encouraging them to be jockeys although many of them will never make it. Young people, he says, need to be taught in far greater depth, how to look after and care for horses.

Nico does not particularly like summer jump racing either, even though he accepts that it has a place in the calendar. The immediate and long-term damage it does to horses upsets him from a welfare point of view, while excessive watering ruins the ground on the racecourses for the rest of the year. It prevents the roots from going deep into the soil and it seriously disturbs the underlying structure of the grass. He would be more than happy to see changes in England, at least for the habitually dry months of June and July, and to have race-free weeks.

Despite being a brave horseman, Nico de Boinville is also extremely sensitive: indeed, losing his mother two weeks before winning the Champion Chase on Sprinter Sacre hit him hard. Nico sees fantastic strides into a fence, no doubt learned from those early years in the Pony Club and Yogi Breisner has high praise for his natural skills. 'He sits into his horses and has soft hands, which gives his mounts confidence and helps to engage their hindquarters so that they can propel themselves from behind.'

His rise up the ranks of National Hunt racing has been a revelation, and his winning rides at the big festival meetings – Cheltenham, Aintree and Punchestown – have been copybook. With his coolness under pressure and his quiet style of riding he looks set for many more years at the top level, hopefully on more National Hunt stars – although Sprinter Sacre, Might Bite and Altior have already been exceptional partners for him. His wide equine interests mean that he will not necessarily confine himself to thoroughbreds in future years, and he is married to Serena, whose family is famous for its involvement in the Connemara pony world. When he eventually retires, Nico's future could turn out to be as unusual as the man himself.

Michael Dickinson

Michael William Dickinson seems to have more energy than is stored in a nuclear bomb. From the beginning, he was driven to succeed in every aspect of his chosen life in racing. His pursuit of perfection is legendary. He has had a remarkable career both as a National Hunt jockey and as a trainer, and his natural ability, enquiring mind and tireless work ethic have meant he has scaled heights that no others are likely to equal.

Michael's father, Tony, was himself a natural with horses. A horse dealer by trade, he ran a first-rate livery yard in Gisburn, Yorkshire, where Michael was born in 1950, and he had a great eye [...] nters, show-jumpers and event [...] upplied horses to the masters [...]s. He was also responsible for [...] rse, Lochinvar, to Major Derek [...] ng racehorse trainer. Tony was [...] ny days out hunting, primarily

[...] other, was also a good rider. [...] le family, she was a leading [...] Cup at the Royal Lancashire [...] en Elizabeth Cup at the Royal [...] lso a successful point-to-point [...] behind Michael's equestrian [...] orking relentlessly hard was as

[...] sters all rode ponies and were [...] y Club, attending a number [...] the Pony Club camps in the [...] ing Michael enjoyed most, and [...] r he wanted to go.

❝ It was fantastic country, all grass, and we would jump at least fifty obstacles every day – mostly walls and timber. In my school holidays I would hunt three days a week, and the foundations for my riding in races stems from my days out hunting. My 14.2hh pony Parkgate was outstanding. I did a small amount of show-jumping as well, but I was not very good at it. I wish I had done more. It is the best start for any aspiring National Hunt jockey. ❞

When he was 17, Michael had a two-week crash course at Holmes Chapel in Cheshire with Edy Goldmann, the brilliant riding instructor who had coached Sheila Willcox, the renowned Badminton three-day-event winner. It was at about the same time that he began riding in point-to-points. He started off by riding horses for the local master of hounds, John Henderson, and managed to finish fourth twice but the next year he had 18 rides and won six races. He had built chase fences at home and been taught how to school thoroughbreds at speed, and despite his height he was determined to ride on the track.

'When I was 17, I weighed 11st 10lb and stood 6ft 2in,' he recalls. 'I was considered too tall and too heavy to be a jockey but, later on, my regular riding weight was 10st 7lb, and on one occasion I did 10st 4lb. I got myself into shape by dieting, working hard, sitting in saunas and doing late-night runs in a plastic sweatsuit.'

When he left school, Michael went to Frenchie Nicholson, who trained close to Cheltenham racecourse and was renowned for making jockeys. In his riding days Frenchie had been a top National Hunt jockey, and in 1942 won the Cheltenham Gold Cup on Medoc II. His son David, 'The Duke', was a top National Hunt jockey himself who subsequently began his own training career at Condicote near Stow-on-the-Wold. Michael went there, as he puts it, for the maestro 'to toughen me up'. He spent a year living in Gloucestershire and enjoyed his days riding racehorses on Frenchie's sand gallops and hacking up Cleeve Hill behind the racecourse. He remembers schooling over hurdles with Pat Eddery and Tony Murray, who later became top Flat jockeys but began their careers in a jumping yard. While in the south, Michael had two rides under rules in hurdle races, one of which, Battle Hymn, was owned by Lord Vestey. It was a backward, slow horse but helped him to get started.

By 1968 Tony Dickinson had taken out his own training licence at Gisburn with six racehorses, four of which were sellers – horses of lesser quality best suited to running in selling races. Michael's first winner as a jockey was at Chepstow in March 1968 on South Rock, a horse trained by his father. Tony turned out a number of winners from his small string, and when he moved to train on a bigger scale at Harewood in Yorkshire, Michael went with him as the amateur jockey. He had plenty of success and was a big asset to his parents' increasingly powerful yard. Michael particularly enjoyed riding first-time-out novice chasers, because he had schooled them at home – he trusted them and he knew they could jump correctly. Indeed, the Dickinsons' record in these races was phenomenal.

Michael always enjoyed books about racing, and in his early race-riding days remembers reading John Hislop's masterpiece *Steeplechasing* at least ten times. It was his bible. He has spent the majority of his life studying the finer points of racing, and as a jockey was never happy to rest upon his laurels, but was forever looking for ways to improve his style and technique. At the end of the 1970-71 National Hunt season Michael was champion amateur rider.

Michael Dickinson's contribution to National Hunt racing cannot be over-emphasised. Not only was he a fine amateur rider whose festival wins on Gay Spartan (Sun Alliance Chase), Fascinating Forties (National Hunt Chase), Rainbow Valley (Kim Muir), The Chisler (National Hunt Handicap Chase) and Broncho II (Mildmay of Flete Chase) were outstanding, but as a professional he won the prestigious Benson & Hedges Handicap Chase on Dorlesa at Sandown in 1974. During his years as a jockey he rode a total of 378 winners, including five at the Cheltenham Festival.

Then he turned to training himself, and the precedent he set in training five horses to fill the first five places in the 1983 Cheltenham

Gold Cup will never be repeated. Many have termed him a mad genius, but his energy and enthusiasm know no bounds and he is always happy to give advice.

Nowadays, as he continues his training career in the USA on his superb purpose-built gallops at Tapeta in Maryland, he reflects upon how budding jump jockeys could better the starts to their careers. All those interested in National Hunt racing, he believes, should have a spell show-jumping: 'It's undoubtedly why Yogi Breisner, the well-known eventing instructor, has been such a help to numerous National Hunt jockeys and why they repeatedly go back to him for lessons.' Michael maintains that jumping a lot of fences within a tight area sharpens a rider's reactions, 'and there is always the emphasis on seeing strides and making quick decisions. Jumping show-jumps is the perfect foundation for riding over fences.'

When they practise over show-jumps, jockeys will find that they cannot ride too short, and when schooling over poles they learn to sit into their horses. It gives them the opportunity to appreciate the importance of not getting ahead of a horse's movement, and teaches them how to approach an obstacle in balance. Yet how many of today's aspiring jockeys could follow in Michael Dickinson's footsteps?

Keith Donoghue

Not many horses will jump five-bar iron gates or spring over huge walls and hedges onto busy roads and lanes from a standstill. But horses run for Keith Donoghue and jump for him, and this includes his wonder horse, The Governor, the brilliant 18hh grey hunter that he takes out with the Ward Union Hunt whenever he can, and for whom he has turned down a number of high offers.

Keith, known as Jacksie by his friends, has had an interrupted career in race-riding. Having at one time virtually hung up his boots due to weight problems, he has now bounced back into the limelight, mainly through partnering Tiger Roll to victory in the Glenfarclas Cross Country Chase at Cheltenham in 2018 and 2019.

Keith was brought up on a housing estate near Dunshaughlin in Co Meath, but he always wanted to ride, and his mother, who worked with the trainer Andrew Lynch as well as with Noel Meade, kept a pony for him at Lynch's yard. Some years ago, his brother Ian rode a winner as a National Hunt jockey for Gordon Elliott, hence Keith's later connection with Cullentra.

Jacksie was only eight when he became smitten by pony racing, and had his first ride at 11. He won the race. He then became extremely competitive and rode for five years in pony races until he was 16, racing against other children like Shane Foley, Bryan Cooper, Martin Harley, Oisin Murphy and Brendan Powell jnr. He ended up with 150 wins. He also took up show-jumping for a short while to get more practice over fences.

The keen young rider went hunting on his 13.2hh pony Muzzy, a rescue pony but a bold jumper. He also rode in hunter trials, and led up friends' horses at point-to-points. At 16, he went to Gordon Elliott's yard and took out his conditional licence, getting his first ride under rules in August 2009 in a handicap hurdle at Downpatrick. He did not win, but he gained his first success four rides later at the Listowel festival, on Gordon Elliott's Nino Cochise. In those days he could do 8st 12lb on the Flat, despite being 6ft tall, but he always knew that he would get heavier – 'my father is stocky and my mother is five foot eleven'.

Keith did really well in his early days as a jockey and acknowledges the help he received from Robbie Power. He also continued to go hunting with the Ward Union along with Paul Carberry, and says that he learned so much by copying Paul, whom he considers to be in a different league to any other jockey. Paul was always his god, and he still holds the rider in high esteem. Jacksie had an old rocking horse at home, and even put up mirrors around it so he could perfect his style along Carberry lines, and the colours he wore in pony races were those of Harchibald, one of the famous horses which Paul Carberry rode.

Yet after Keith Donoghue's good start to racing, he suffered a series of misfortunes. At 19, he broke his collarbone badly, and then the following year he had a severe leg break which kept him out of action for eight months. At 23, whilst out hunting, he hit the branch of a tree and almost lost an eye. To make matters worse, while he was on the sidelines, he put on a lot of weight, mostly due to depression, and at one time he reached 12st.

Fortunately, he gradually regained his confidence and returned to racing. Nowadays, he is an invaluable member of the Gordon Elliott team at Cullentra and rides many of the best horses at home. He will never be a lightweight jockey, but his horsemanship is universally recognised and Jacksie is extremely popular. Those victories on Tiger Roll at the Cheltenham Festival were exceptional, and he has plenty more years of race-riding ahead of him.

Frank Berry and Bobsline (nearside) jump the last en route to winning an epic duel with Noddy's Ryde in the 1984 Arkle

Rachael Blackmore, aboard her first Cheltenham Festival winner A Plus Tard, jumps the last before winning at Naas

Pony racing phenomenon James Bowen rides Push The Button to success at Ascot in July 2013

Nina Carberry jumps the bank at Cheltenham's cross-country course with Josies Orders in December 2015

The unique Paul Carberry takes the last fence on Pandorama to win the Lexus Chase at Leopardstown in December 2010

Harry Cobden cements his position at Ditcheat with King George VI Chase success aboard Clan Des Obeaux on Boxing Day 2018

Best friends and now part of the 1,000 winners club. Aidan Coleman (right) and Sam Twiston-Davies at Newbury in 2014

In another life champion Flat jockey Jim Crowley and Gentleman Jimmy (nearside) jump the last to beat Rapscallion at Wincanton in March 2006

Jim Culloty shows his delight after Best Mate landed an historic third Cheltenham Gold Cup for me in 2004

How Nico de Boinville made his name. Sprinter Sacre canters at Seven Barrows in Lambourn 2014

Michael Dickinson, riding Dorlesa, between Jeff King (nearside) on Canasta Lad and Steve Holland on Ben More during the 1974 Arkle

Keith Donoghue and Tiger Roll jump the last in the 2019 Glenfarclas Cross Country Chase at Cheltenham

Richard Dunwoody and Desert Orchid win the Agfa Diamond Chase at Sandown in February 1991

Jodami (nearside) carries Mark Dwyer to victory from Rushing Wild in the 1993 Cheltenham Gold Cup

Noel Fehily putting on his silks at Newbury in November 2018

A muddied Sean Flanagan after he and Tout Est Permis won the 2018 Troytown Handicap Chase

John Francome and Midnight Court win the 1978 Cheltenham Gold Cup

Barry Geraghty celebrates as Moscow Flyer wins the 2005 Queen Mother Champion Chase

Eddie Harty riding Harlequin at the Rome 1960 Olympic Games

Waiting Patiently carries Brian Hughes to victory at Kempton in January 2018

Richard Dunwoody MBE

It was May 6, 1995, and I was driving up the M6 to Haydock Park races with Shirley Brasher, wife of Chris Brasher, the famous runner and founder of the London Marathon. Shirley herself had been a top tennis player, and in her youth had won the French Open, and then she was a distinguished racehorse owner. She enjoyed analysing the finer points of sportsmen, but was extremely critical of jockeys, always wanting a jockey of her own choice to partner her horses. Richard Dunwoody was at the top of her list. Fortunately her horse, Moving Out, won that day, and naturally she put the victory down to its handling by 'The Prince', who had just lifted the jockeys' championship for the third time and, in her eyes, could do no wrong.

Richard Dunwoody was arguably the best jockey National Hunt racing has ever seen. He was the complete article: strong and stylish, with an inborn determination to win. He seldom made mistakes in a race. His epic battle with Adrian Maguire for the 1994-95 jockeys' championship demonstrated his all-consuming quest to ride winners. It was a punishing duel, mentally and physically draining for both riders. No jockey likes to get beaten, but Richard was an especially bad loser. He loved race-riding and he loved winning. For ten consecutive seasons, he rode more than 100 winners each year. He was driven to be successful, and his pursuit of perfection shone through. Only the best was good enough. So hard was he on himself that at times it was difficult to comprehend his outlook on life. But the racing public loved him, and his fans worshipped him like a god.

Richard rode a point-to-point winner for me when he was 19, and I subsequently followed his career with great interest. It was tragic that due to some bad falls he lost the strength in his right arm, which eventually forced him into retirement at the age of 35. Had he ridden for another five years his career total of winners, 1,874, would have increased significantly.

Richard Dunwoody was born in 1964 near Comber in Co Down. His father had long been fascinated by horses and had made them his life. As well as being a successful amateur rider, with more than 100 winners, he turned to training at a small yard in Ballyclare, Co Antrim. According to Richard he was single-minded and stubborn, traits he passed on to his son. George married Gillian Thrale, whose father Dick trained in Epsom – Indigenous, the five-furlong record-holder for many years when partnered by Lester Piggott, was one of his stars. Gillian, always knowledgeable about horses and a good rider, undoubtedly had a big influence on Richard.

At the age of two and a half, he was led round on a small grey pony at a horse show in Newtownards, and won his first rosette.

❢ I'm not sure when I became addicted to the buzz of riding horses, but Dad reckoned it started with Seamus, the donkey. He was a young donkey and could go. One day I took a heavy fall, but when Dad got to me there were no tears and apparently all I said was, 'Daddy, daddy, I fell off like a jockey! ❢

When he was five Richard was given Tony, a great little 12.2hh grey pony who played a big part in his early riding life. He did everything with that pony, including following his father's string of racehorses, and built a show-jumping course for Tony on the lawn beside the house. He hunted him with the North Down Harriers as well, and once, when only six years old, he stayed out for two and a half hours following closely behind the master. 'When I had Tony, we went from the cantering stage and my fear of going too fast to the point where he could not be fast enough for me.' From an early age Richard liked the idea of speed, and was determined to be a jockey. He attended the local point-to-points and his father often took him to race meetings, where he allowed him to lead up his runners, even though he was underage and had to be dressed up in a suitable cap to make him look older.

Although Richard's early education was at Dunover Primary School on the Ards Peninsula, close to his father's second training yard at Kilbrighthouse near Carrowdore, his main education took place in England at Rendcomb College near Cirencester. George had given up his training and the family had moved to Tetbury for him to become the manager at Charlton Down Stud. Tony the pony had travelled too, and Richard continued with his hunting as well as doing plenty of jumping and becoming a member of the Beaufort Hunt Pony Club. 'I enjoyed the Pony Club camps, and I even passed my "D" test.'

When George Dunwoody moved to Newmarket in 1976 to assist trainer Paul Kelleway, Richard was in his element, and began to ride racehorses. When he was 12 he began riding Ben Hanbury's hack, but in a very short space of time he was upgraded to Paul's thoroughbreds. 'The more experience I had of riding out, the more time I spent amongst racing people and the more I wanted to be a jockey.' At school he read John Hislop's books on racing and says, 'I practised the suggested exercises designed to strengthen the muscles most useful to a jockey.'

Unfortunately this obsession for wanting to race-ride went hand in hand with his fear of becoming too heavy and, almost along the lines of Fred Archer, he dieted to such an extent that he made himself ill. At 17 he was down to barely 7st and had lost a lot of his strength. When he did eventually sort himself out he got a job with Paul Kelleway as pupil assistant and began to learn the ropes through the eyes of a stable lad, before working himself up the ladder and doing plenty of riding on Newmarket Heath. Richard had been a bright pupil at school and had obtained ten O-levels, but after good mock A-level results he was never going to stay on for another year. Being a jockey was all that he cared about.

Although Richard enjoyed Flat racing and learned a considerable amount about race-riding from watching and talking to jockeys in Newmarket, his physique and weight meant he was always going to be a National Hunt jockey. In September 1981 he joined John Bosley's yard at Brize Norton in Oxfordshire and had his first taste of riding jumps-bred racehorses. During his time living with the Bosley family he was introduced to Captain Tim Forster, and during the bitter winter of 1982 moved to his big yard at Letcombe Bassett near Wantage, as a pupil assistant on £15 a week. There were plenty of hardships to be endured, especially in terms of the living conditions, but fortunately for Richard he was helped by Hywel Davies and Michael Furlong, both good jockeys and great teachers.

Although he had been riding from an early age, Richard still had plenty to learn about the jumping of racehorses. He was always self-critical and analysed his faults in great detail, in particular Hywel Davies encouraged him to let a horse get in close to a fence and teach it to fiddle. No racehorse can continually jump off a long stride and he explained to Richard that if a horse cannot shorten in front of a fence and is travelling at speed, sooner or later it will fall when meeting a fence wrong.

Richard did plenty of schooling at the Captain's, but by today's standards the sessions were somewhat unorthodox.

❝ The Captain would never use a lead horse for the youngsters, and on many occasions one of the babies would head for the wing of a hurdle or for the adjoining wire fence. There was always someone on the floor, and the guv'nor would just look at the skies and say, "My God, and you want to call yourselves fucking jockeys?"

The schooling over the fences was not much better, and there were numerous fallers. On one occasion Professor Plum took off with me having jumped the obstacles, and he made for the gate on to the Ridgeway. He cleared it perfectly, but I was deposited head first on the ground, while he galloped home to his stable. ❞

Tim Forster was a first-class trainer and produced three Grand National winners, but nobody would ever change his methods. He hated schooling mornings, and once a horse had been ticked off his list for having jumped the fences at home in a particular season, it would never jump again until the following year. One jumping session per horse, providing it cleared the obstacles, was the rule. He had no regard for style, or the shape the horse made over a fence. He just sighed with relief when the horses were safely back in their stables.

During Richard's first few months with Tim Forster he weighed about 8st 7lb, and was not strong enough to hold the horses who pulled hard. 'I rode too short, and although Hywel told me I looked stylish, I was too shy and lacked self-confidence.' It was not until he returned from a summer in Newmarket, riding out for Bruce Hobbs, that he progressed any further up the ladder, and got his first rides with his newly acquired amateur licence. He had his first ride in 1982, for Arthur Jones in a two-mile amateur Flat race on Mallard Song on the August Bank Holiday. In the spring of 1983, he had some welcome successes in point-to-points, primarily for the Old Berkshire Hunt Master Colin Nash, and on May 4, 1983, he had his first winner under rules when, for the Nash family, Game Trust won a hunter chase at Cheltenham.

Richard Dunwoody's rise up the ranks was rapid. After registering 24 wins as an amateur in the 1983-84 season he turned professional and, as well as riding horses for the Captain, he was taken on by Michael Oliver in the 1984-85 season. In 1986 he won the Grand National on West Tip for him. His close associations with David Nicholson in 1986 and 1987, and Martin Pipe in 1994 and 1995, supplied him with large numbers of winners. He was first jockey for both of them. Their horses definitely helped him take the jockeys' championship in 1992-93, 1993-94 and 1994-95. He won the Cheltenham Gold Cup in 1988 on Charter Party for 'The Duke', and his second Grand National in 1994 for Martin Pipe with Miinnehoma. As well as being an extremely positive rider, Richard was a great judge of pace and rode clever, tactical races. It is rare to see a jockey with a superb racing brain as well as an inborn gift for riding horses, but Richard was one of them.

When he started race-riding, Richard believes he overused his stick.

❜ I rode quite long in my races, because to begin with I rode too short and lost my balance. Indeed, I was twice unseated, and fell off twice in my first eight rides in point-to-points, but with my new style I couldn't use my stick very well, especially in my left hand. This annoyed me, and I got wound up and aggressive. Graham McCourt used to call me 'Mr Angry'. For the year 1983, I have an entry in my diary telling me to 'sit closer, grab hold of them and less stick'. ❜

Such was the future champion's determination to improve his riding style that he went to the British Racing School's chief instructor, Johnny Gilbert, and asked for help. 'Johnny thought the problem was rhythm, and he got me to practise on a bale of straw. In those days there were no designated jockey coaches.' Nowadays jockeys have far greater advantages: as well as having specialist tuition, they can practise on Equicizers, although at times too much emphasis can be placed on these machines and not enough on lessons on real horses.

Richard went to great lengths to study his style and analyse his weaknesses.

❜ The mistakes interested me more than the things I'd done well. In my rider's ledger I paid particular attention to the number of fallers I had, and especially to the number of times I was unseated. At the end of the 1985-86 season, 31 of the horses I rode had fallen, and a further ten had unseated me. That meant a fall for every 12 rides – close to the average for National Hunt racing, but too many. I knew where the fallers had come from – my demon-like desire to win. It did not matter if the horse was tired or not jumping well – whether he had a chance or no chance – I would throw him at the fence. I didn't wait for the fence to come to me. But I got better, and later in my career my average changed to one fall in 18 rides, which to me was acceptable. ❜

His last ever ride, Twin Falls at Perth in September 1999, was a winner, and during his final three days of riding, six of his nine rides were winners. 'Yes,' he wrote in *Obsessed*,

It was good to be champion jockey three times, and to ride more than 100 winners for ten consecutive seasons, but that wasn't what it was all about. I loved riding, I loved winning and I loved competing. I felt that I rode a racehorse as well as, if not better than, anyone else. I needed to believe that every time I walked into the weighing room. I liked being publicly recognised as a top jockey, and I always wanted to prove that the honour was deserved.

It's not surprising, given the extent to which Richard's quest to ride winners came to rule his life, that he found it hard to come to terms with his enforced early retirement at a time when he was still riding well and enjoying his life. Since his retirement, however, Richard has gone on to do some amazing work for different charities, including a 48-day trek to the South Pole, and a 2,000-mile trek across Japan. His mind remains active and he keeps himself supremely fit.

Now that he lives in Spain with his partner, Olivia, and young daughter Emilia, he seems far happier with his life and has plenty more adventures in the pipeline, but wherever he is in the world he will always be remembered as an exceptional jockey who rode some epic races.

Richard Dunwoody was known as 'The Prince' for a reason. He ruled jump racing, and the National Hunt game was his sovereignty. The four King George VI Chases he won, two on One Man and two on Desert Orchid, will be forever etched in the minds of his admirers, and he singles out the second grey as the most intelligent and competitive horse he ever rode. Both horse and rider inspired racegoers with their bravery, and neither of them liked being beaten. No wonder they were well suited. They were two of a kind.

Mark Dwyer

Mark Dwyer always wanted to be a jockey. Fortunately he had plenty of encouragement from his parents, who bought him a pony, even though they were not involved in the racing industry. His father Jimmy was a seed salesman, but he was also a regular racegoer, mostly around the Dublin area. Nowadays one of his sisters works for the horse sales company, Tattersalls, and breeds racehorses.

One of Mark's best friends, Eddie Woods, whose father Paddy had ridden Arkle during his jockey days, gave Mark plenty of advice, and at weekends the young boy would go to Galway and ride out for Kieran Egan, who had racing ponies as well as racehorses and helped Mark get good rides in pony races. He showed considerable promise on the 'flapping' circuit and had more than 40 wins. One of the best ponies he rode was Jonesborough, trained by Sean McGann at his yard close to Galway city. The mare was top of her grade during the years that Mark raced her.

In 1978, at the age of 15, Mark became apprenticed to Liam Browne on the Curragh and in July 1979 had his first winner on Cloneash Emperor at Limerick Junction racecourse (now called Tipperary). Liam had a strict work ethic and insisted that all the horses were ridden out with neck straps. He told his jockeys to keep their hands down and get their mounts to settle. Mark stayed with Liam until he was 19. He had 66 wins on the Flat and was champion apprentice in 1980.

Yet despite his Flat racing successes, Mark was steadily putting on weight, 8lb or 10lb a year, and in 1981 he had his first jumps winner when Bartlemy Hostess, trained by Denis Barry, was successful at Mallow (now called Cork) in a handicap hurdle. It was during his time at Liam Browne's that Mark had a call from Barney Curley, who had watched the young jockey ride winners over hurdles for Peter McCreery. He asked Mark whether he would be interested in moving over to England and riding for Jimmy FitzGerald.

The jockey duly moved to Yorkshire in 1982, but at that time had very little experience of schooling over fences and had only ridden in a handful of steeplechases. Consequently Ronnie O'Leary, who had applied for the job at the same time, rode the chasers and Mark rode the hurdlers, while retaining his Flat licence as well. In the 1983-84 National Hunt season he started riding some of Jimmy FitzGerald's chasers, but the jump schooling at home was very basic: the jockeys rode over a line of hurdles or a line of fences and were instructed to take the obstacles at speed.

It was obvious, however, that Mark was a complete natural, and he was quick to ride chase winners. His style was distinctive: he was a quiet rider who rode with a sensible length of leg and had exceptional hands. He maintains that it was his hunting with the Ward Union and jumping massive drains on his pony that had helped his balance and developed his technique. Tommy Carberry, recognised as one of the finest steeplechase jockeys ever, had begun with the same hunt, and later on Paul Carberry hunted as many days as he could with the Wards.

In 1985 Mark rode Forgive'n Forget to win the Cheltenham Gold Cup, and later that year won the Hennessy Gold Cup at Newbury on Galway Blaze – both horses were trained by Jimmy FitzGerald. In 1993 he won his second Cheltenham Gold Cup, this time on Jodami for Peter Beaumont, and to prove his versatility as a top-class jockey partnered the Richard Price-trained Flakey Dove to win the Champion Hurdle in 1994.

A broken elbow meant he had to retire from race-riding in 1996, and from then on he concentrated on buying and selling National Hunt horses from his 100-acre farm near Malton in Yorkshire. He has shown plenty of expertise when pinhooking foals and yearlings, many of whom have progressed to win decent races under rules.

In progressing from being champion apprentice on the Flat in Ireland to winning the blue riband of steeplechasing on two occasions at Cheltenham, Mark set an unusual precedent for young jump jockeys. Being runner-up in the National Hunt jockeys' championship on three separate occasions – once to Richard Dunwoody and twice to Peter Scudamore – was also an amazing achievement. His quiet style suited a variety of different horses, and he was a fine tactical rider.

Dominic Elsworth

When he was a child Dominic Elsworth had taken his pony Lord Marengo to a show-jumping class at the Bramham Horse Trials, and had found himself parked next to Harvey Smith's massive show-jumping lorry. 'Harvey was shouting a lot and giving orders to his staff. I was shit scared!' Little did he realise that later Harvey would be his boss.

Dominic was fascinated by racing from the age of ten. He would watch the Bob Champion film and *National Velvet* over and over again. When everything was quiet at the equestrian centre near Otley in Yorkshire where his mother was a riding instructor, he would pull up his stirrups when he rode his pony and pretend to be a jockey. His younger sister Natalie loved riding too and became National Junior Side-Saddle champion. Dominic took part in many show-jumping classes at local shows and was also interested in eventing, but he dreamed of being a huntsman. His parents told him he would be too big to be a jockey.

Dom left school at 16 and, despite having been intimidated by Harvey Smith when he was younger, he was advised to go to Harvey and Sue's yard for some experience of the racing world. Their stables and the farm were less than 15 minutes away from his home. Sue is an excellent trainer who has been responsible for many winners at Grade 1 tracks and she saddled Auroras Encore to win the 2013 Grand National.

Dominic arrived on his moped at the Smiths' establishment in Bingley in West Yorkshire thinking he knew everything about riding, but he soon realised the regime was tough going. On his first morning, wearing a wax jacket and a velvet hunting cap, he was run away with when riding a racehorse on the gallops. Yet the experience sharpened him up, and he ended up staying with the Smiths for ten years.

When there were schooling mornings at the yard, Harvey took charge, and he gave Dominic invaluable lessons. There is no better teacher. As well as racehorses, the aspiring jockey would ride plenty of young horses, and he helped with the breakers – the ones who came to the yard to be broken in. A number of top jockeys, including Jim Crowley, have learned their trade under Harvey's watchful eye, and for Dominic it was the best possible experience.

'Harvey is very good at giving a jockey confidence. He always stresses the importance of having horses travelling in a rhythm on forward-going strides. I learned such a lot with him.' In 1997, Dominic was granted a conditional jockeys' licence, but still did not quite understand what it meant to be a 7lb claimer. On his first ever ride, in a hurdle race at Market Rasen, he fell off. Harvey laughed afterwards and said to him, 'It's not as easy as what you think, lad.'

Despite this inauspicious start, the Smiths were patient with their young protégé and gave him plenty more rides over hurdles. In February 1999 he rode his first winner on Moonshine Dancer in a conditional jockeys' hurdle at Catterick. Dom went on to ride good winners for Sue Smith, including Mister McGoldrick in the Racing Post Plate at the Cheltenham Festival in 2008.

Yet in 2006, on the advice of AP McCoy, Dominic moved away from Yorkshire to join Oliver Sherwood's yard in Lambourn as first jockey. It was a huge bonus for him to get further experience in racing in the south of England, and as well as riding out in Berkshire he visited Paul Webber in Warwickshire, Lucy Wadham near Newmarket and me at West Lockinge. He was always a big asset on schooling mornings, and outstanding on young horses. Following his move from Yorkshire, he had plenty of rides and some good winners. Everything looked rosy.

However, in August 2009 Dominic had a horrendous fall at Ffos Las, and it took the medical teams 20 minutes to revive him. On the Glasgow Coma Scale, where 5 signifies 'Alive' and 0 means 'Dead', he was classified as '1'. Dominic was in a seriously bad way and, after his time in hospital and care from a top neurological team, he returned to his home near Hungerford in Berkshire to be cared for by his wonderful wife, Louise. He could not tolerate any light on his eyes, found balance difficult, and had to spend many months in darkened rooms. He could not even walk upstairs. He had nil energy and the best he could do was potter around in sunglasses.

Somewhat harshly, Dominic blames himself for the fall.

It was high summer and, with fewer rides at that time of year, it makes it harder for jockeys to keep their weight under control. I am five feet ten inches tall, and I had gone to extreme lengths in order to weigh out at ten stone for that fateful three-mile chase. I had spent a week wasting and I had been drinking very little water. I had taken a lot of fluid out of my body – too much in hindsight. When I went head first into the ground, the fluid that protects the brain was insufficient due to my dehydration. Harvey Smith always told me that hot baths, sweating and saunas were a bad idea.

Yet how many jockeys, in their struggles to do 'light', have punished their bodies? In the 1960s and 1970s the champion jockey Terry Biddlecombe would regularly shed 10lb in 24 hours by sweating in Turkish baths. Long term, he paid the penalty by losing his life at 72 when his body packed up. Excessive dieting is dangerous and undermines a person's health.

It was a long haul back for Dominic, but there was a massive cheer, when on his comeback ride in October 2010, he won on Edgbriar for Paul Webber at Cheltenham. Further successes followed, including wins on Somersby in the Grade 1 Victor Chandler Chase at Ascot in 2012 and the Haldon Gold Cup at Exeter in 2013. He was also victorious on Calgary Bay at Doncaster in 2012 in the Sky Bet Chase. These wins demonstrated that he had retained his riding skills, and that he still enjoyed racing.

Gradually, however, with fewer opportunities and rides, he realised that he needed to pursue another career, and in April 2014, with 450 winners to his name, he announced that he would not be renewing his riding licence.

Nowadays, Dominic Elsworth is a Level 3 jockey coach, which means that he helps young jockeys with their race-riding styles and techniques. He is greatly respected as a teacher and has had several promising riders on his list, in particular Jonjo O'Neill jnr, who has impressed the racing world with his cool riding and natural talent. He has the makings of a champion. Dominic is also helping Charlie Todd, who has graduated from the pony-racing ranks and is now based with Ian Williams. He too appears to be reaping the benefits of Dominic's tuition.

Dominic has an excellent way with horses and his balance and deep seat, coupled with good hands, were hallmarks of his riding. In particular, he did not rush horses into their fences. He remains a valued friend, and was a jockey whom I was always happy to let ride my horses. Above all, he had Terry's approval, and that was good enough for me.

Noel Fehily

Noel Fehily retired from race-riding in March 2019 with 1,352 wins over jumps. During his career, despite suffering numerous injuries, he enjoyed major successes including the King George VI Chase twice (Silviniaco Conti in 2013 and 2014), the Champion Hurdle twice (Rock On Ruby in 2012 and Buveur D'Air in 2017) and the Queen Mother Champion Chase in 2017 on Special Tiara. He was one of the most respected and likeable National Hunt jockeys in the business: 'The nicest guy you could ever wish to meet and a cool tactician in the saddle,' says Dan Skelton. He let his riding do the talking and became the undisputed role model for any aspiring young jockey.

When Noel was six his father, who drove milk lorries but also farmed on a small scale, took him and his sister to a local riding school near their home in Dunmanway, Co Cork. Noel took to his riding lessons like a duck to water. He would spend as much time as he could in his school holidays riding ponies, and was usually given the difficult ones to sort out for other children. 'I remember one pony that was particularly naughty, and it regularly dropped me. One day I was on the floor twelve times, but I always got back up for more. It was a challenge I enjoyed.'

Noel began riding out horses – mostly point-to-pointers – for his neighbour Ned Barrett, whose son, a few years older than Noel, took part in pony races. Noel soon got rides in them as well, and his ability was quickly noticed. He was offered plenty of rides from Co Cork handlers, and his father bought several ponies. In 1988 and 1989 he was the champion pony-race jockey in Ireland. 'Looking back on it,' he reflects, 'some of the tracks were horrendous and unbelievably tight, but I learned a lot.' The young boy rode out for Ned Barrett even when he was at school – 'I regularly missed the school bus, but the headmaster never really minded.' Noel stayed at school until he was 18 and completed his Leaving Certificate: his parents wanted him to finish his education and he never minded lessons.

Noel did not have much jumping experience in his teenage years apart from attending the occasional gymkhana, but Ned gave him a selection of rides in point-to-points and he rode his first winner for him in 1992 when he was only 16, on Squirrels Daughter at the Corrin point-to-point near Waterfall.

After he left school he clocked up 80 point-to-point winners, as well as a number of hunter chase wins, which gave him the taste for riding on the bigger tracks. For a while he worked in Robert Hawkins' yard in Innishannon, but he rode for a variety of point-to-point trainers including David Wachman, who at that time was not involved in the Flat racing world but trained close to Clonmel in Co Waterford.

In September 1998, on the advice of Richard Forristal, now the *Racing Post*'s Ireland editor but who at the time was working for Kim Bailey in Lambourn, and Ed Vaughan, who was then Charlie Mann's assistant, Noel decided to chance his luck riding as an amateur in Britain. He moved over to Charlie Mann's, but made up his mind to go back to Ireland by Christmas unless he had ridden five winners. He rode six. His first winner over hurdles was Ivy Boy at Plumpton in November, quickly followed by Siren Song at Lingfield.

In March 1999 Terry and I travelled to Ireland to the Lismore point-to-point, also in Co Waterford. It was there that we spotted Best Mate, who pulled up in the four-year-old maiden race, which Noel won on Bruthuinne, another horse who subsequently came to be trained at West Lockinge Farm. Terry was impressed by Noel's riding skills at the point-to-points.

Noel ended up staying in Lambourn for many more seasons, and whilst still an amateur he was fourth in the Pardubice in Czechoslovakia on Charlie Mann's Falcon Du Coteau. When he joined the professional ranks he became champion conditional jockey at the end of the 2000-01 National Hunt season with 42 wins. From 2008 until 2018, he continued to figure prominently in the overall jockeys' championship table, and was placed fourth on four separate occasions.

'The best thing I can say about Noel,' declared AP McCoy when Noel Fehily hung up his boots, 'is, thank God he wasn't properly discovered earlier, because it would have meant fewer winners for me.' Perhaps it is surprising that Noel was not noticed sooner, because he was always a good rider who made very few mistakes, but he never pushed himself into the public eye, and maybe trainers did not immediately spot his talents.

Technically and tactically, Noel was brilliant. He was a strong jockey with a quiet manner in the saddle, and many horses perform at their best when they stay relaxed and have confidence in their riders. Asked to elaborate on Noel's success, his agent, Chris Broad, responsible over the years for masterminding the careers of many top jockeys, put it down to 'the way he rides, the way he conducts himself, the way he looks after himself – everything. His attitude to life is great, because he is relaxed and chilled.' In retirement, at his home in Wiltshire where he currently breeds and produces top National Hunt horses, these admirable characteristics continue to shine through.

Mick Fitzgerald

Michael Anthony Fitzgerald has an unorthodox background for racing. His father was a mechanic and 'my mother was just a cleaning lady'. When he was nine, however, the family moved from Killarney to Wexford, a renowned horse county, and it was there that his involvement with horses began.

The Fitzgeralds lived at Camolin near Gorey and owned an acre of land around their bungalow. Several of Mick's school friends rode and his father was persuaded to buy him a pony, which was kept in the back garden. This first pony was stuffy and stubborn and did not last long, but then came Bracken, who was able to show-jump and thoroughly proved his worth. Mick's father drove him to a local show every Sunday in their converted lorry. Mick says he did not have any proper riding lessons, but was able to watch other children and develop his own style.

When Mick was 13, a family friend, Sean Doyle, had his car fixed by Mick's dad. Sean worked for the trainer Richard Lister, who later trained Anita's Prince to be placed in the King's Stand Stakes at Royal Ascot. He introduced Mick to the trainer, and subsequently Mick rode out at the yard every Saturday morning and in his school holidays. It was the start all would-be jockeys dream about. Mick obtained a jockeys' licence and had over 20 rides for the yard, but there were no winners, although he fondly remembers riding Panoe, owned by Major Victor McCalmont.

Mick Fitz had a great childhood, except for the time when he was bullied by a boy at school. But confidence is of the utmost importance for a jockey, and much of Mick's confidence came from the day that he stood up to the bully and took him on. It proved to him that he could win a battle.

When he was 16, the young Fitzgerald moved to the Curragh to be apprenticed to John Hayden, but even at that age he had weight problems and had to spend much of his time in saunas. With no racecourse successes in Ireland, yet still determined to be a jockey, he bumped into Stan Moore in Newbridge, who advised him to go to England. When he was 18 he decided to make the move.

To begin with, Mick went to Richard Tucker in Devon and then moved to Ray Callow, after which he joined Jackie Retter's yard, but there was no sudden rise to stardom, and at one point he almost emigrated to New Zealand. However, that elusive first winner eventually came in December 1988, courtesy of Lover's Secret at Ludlow, and in the ensuing season he had a number of high-profile wins on Duncan Idaho. Whilst at Jackie Retter's establishment he was champion conditional jockey but he needed to broaden his horizons, and started to look further afield. Thus he moved to Nicky Henderson's, and he remained there until his retirement.

At the time of his move to Berkshire, Richard Dunwoody was riding for Martin Pipe, and Jamie Osborne was with Oliver Sherwood, but despite formidable opposition among his fellow jockeys, Mick won a series of high-profile races from Seven Barrows, including the Triumph Hurdle on Katarino, the Ryanair Chase on Fondmort and the Arkle Chase on Tiutchev.

His enthusiasm and determination meant that he was in demand by trainers from other yards as well, and it was for Paul Nicholls that he partnered See More Business to win the Cheltenham Gold Cup and the King George VI Chase in 1999 and also Call Equiname in the 1999 Queen Mother Champion Chase. In 1996 he had been successful in the Grand National on Rough Quest for Terry Casey.

In 2008 the fall from L'Ami in the Grand National forced Mick into retirement, but being told to stop race-riding hit him hard. He was on the crest of a wave and had ridden more than 1,300 winners. He had been a great asset to Nicky Henderson's yard. Selflessly, however, Mick Fitzgerald did not allow his own misfortunes to stop him contributing to the racing industry, and over the years he has put a great deal back into the sport. In particular, he has a strong interest in helping young jockeys and he enjoys teaching them.

Mick believes that the only way to learn is 'through making mistakes and getting things wrong', and he prefers his pupils to be riding horses rather than practising their styles on Equicizers. 'Too much use is made of these machines. It is the horses that teach a person how to ride.' He also says that too many trainers 'can't read a race, can't teach their jockeys and don't offer them enough help or encouragement'.

Mick Fitzgerald, Fitzy, is still obsessed with racing and he is an eloquent broadcaster on television. Viewers respect and admire his knowledge, positive attitude and common-sense approach. He is a great ambassador for the sport.

Sean Flanagan

When in 2016 Sean Flanagan was appointed stable jockey at Noel Meade's powerful Tu Va stables in Co Meath it was a great honour because he was stepping into the shoes of the peerless Paul Carberry. Subsequently, Sean has shown he is well up to the task.

By good fortune, when Sean was at primary school in Co Wexford, the children were encouraged to miss a few hours of school each week and go to the local riding school at Boro Hill in Clonroche for lessons on the ponies. Right from the beginning Sean enjoyed these outings, and when he was ten years old his parents were loaned a pony to keep on the acre of land at the back of their house. Jenny was a bay mare, 12 hands high, and was good to ride but had an awkward temperament and was vicious in the stable. Fortunately this did not deter Sean from looking after her and he learned a lot more about riding when she occupied the field. When Jenny was returned to her owners, Sean's father bought him a pony of his own. This was Flash, a 14hh strawberry roan Appaloosa cross-bred who turned out to be a great pony and Sean grew up with him. He joined the Wexford Pony Club and enjoyed his days out hunting as well as attending the pony club camps and competing in show-jumping classes at the local shows.

Sean Flanagan's secondary school, Good Counsel College in New Ross, had strong horseracing connections: Aidan O'Brien, Enda Bolger, Shane Foley, Tom O'Brien and Tom Doyle had all been former pupils. One of the teachers used to take his class to race meetings, and on a certain occasion organised a school trip to Aintree. This definitely intensified Sean's interest in horseracing. Throughout his teenage years whilst riding ponies, all he wanted to do was to become a jockey. He did manage to get 15 rides in pony races, but although he discovered the adrenalin flow he never rode a winner.

After leaving school, Sean began working a few hours each day of the week on a local farm but his ambition to be a jockey took him, every weekend, to trainer Liz Doyle's yard in Crossabeg close to Wexford town, where he started riding racehorses. In 2005 he began a ten-month course at the Racing Academy and Centre of Education, RACE, in Kildare. It was the perfect introduction to the racing industry and he spent a number of weeks at Martin Brassil's yard near the Curragh. Martin is a good trainer and was responsible for the 2006 Grand National winner Numbersixvalverde.

Back at Liz Doyle's yard with an amateur licence, Sean got his first ride on the track with On Your Way. The horse was unplaced, but when he was 17 Liz did provide him with his first ever point-to-point winner – Red Royalty scored at Tinahely. Although he was grateful for all the support that Liz gave him, Sean moved later in the year to work for Eamonn 'Dusty' Sheehy at Graiguenamanagh in Co Kilkenny. He stayed as an amateur and had plenty of rides being second in line to Kevin Power. His first winner on the track was in 2006, on Keevas Boy in a handicap chase at Down Royal, where he beat the top rider Conor O'Dwyer. He continued to get more experience in point-to-points and had more than 50 rides and two more winners.

Sean turned professional at the beginning of 2007, and before the end of that National Hunt season he had ridden 14 winners, finishing in third place in the conditional jockeys' championship. During the next two seasons he rode a further 50 winners, and was second in the table.

Yet just as his career as a jockey was on the up, disaster struck. A series of bone breaks – shoulder and arm – caused him to be sidelined and when he returned to race-riding he found it harder to get winners because he had lost his claim. In 2011, he decided to spend some time in Britain, and went to Evan Williams' yard in Wales. But his fortunes worsened, and during his eight months across the Irish Sea he did not have a single winning ride.

In 2012 Sean was at a low ebb but Dave Niven, who works in Dusty Sheehy's yard, put him in touch with the leading American jumps trainer Jack Fisher. The man is a serious horseman who was also a champion jumps jockey in the US, best known for his unmatched successes in timber races on Saluter in the 1990s and his win on Revelstroke in the 1994 Maryland Hunt Cup. The move to the States provided Sean with a much-needed turn of fortunes. He had 14 winners there and greatly enjoyed his time in Maryland, learning plenty more about jumping racehorses, and especially how they are schooled.

He went back to Ireland and started afresh. He rode 16 winners for the Co Tipperary trainer Harry Kelly, as well as for a number of other trainers including Liz Doyle and David O'Brien, giving him 30 wins during the 2014-15 season.

However, in the summer of 2015, Sean's decision to ride out for Noel Meade marked the turning point of his career. Davy Condon, one of Noel's regular jockeys, was no longer able to race-ride following a bad fall at Aintree, and in September Paul Carberry broke his left femur for the third time, ultimately putting an end to his race-riding career, and opening the door for the lesser-known jockey.

To have successfully climbed back from rock bottom in 2012 to riding winners for Noel Meade in 2015 was a remarkable achievement, and demonstrates the importance of perseverance in sport. Nowadays Sean is riding with supreme confidence and has had wins at the top level, including in significant Grade 1 races. He is in a great frame of mind and looking forward to the future and to further successful riding days. Having recently obtained his pilot's licence, he can now look down on the world and thank his lucky stars for his enviable position in a top National Hunt yard.

John Francome MBE

John Francome left school in 1969 at 16 with virtually nothing to show for twelve years of education. 'There were only two pieces of pink paper as proof of my ever having been to school at all. One stated that I had obtained a low pass in metalwork, and the other showed I'd gained an even lower one in geography.' Such certificates were useless to a boy whose parents had envisaged their son becoming a vet.

However, exam results can be extremely misleading and John had always been a bright, quick-witted child. He still exhibits that amazingly sharp brain, and has put it to good use over the years, but in those days 'lessons came a poor third behind ponies and football'. Yet John was always a forward thinker and highly focused, and in particular he has always been clever with his finances.

❛ We weren't the most academic bunch but we certainly knew what two and two added up to and how to get it. For most of my mates making money was a necessity, but for me it was just a game. I loved doing it then and I love doing it now, not because I am greedy but because I enjoy the challenge of a deal. Anything that made money was fair game, whether it was legal or not. My business interests at school ranged from running the tuck shop to printing counterfeit lunch vouchers, which I sold to a number of pupils at half price. ❜

Although John had been riding since he was six, he had never been interested in racing, and certainly never considered a career as a jockey. His riding talent had given him numerous successes in the show-jumping world, but he knew there was a vast difference between competing at shows for a hobby and jumping horses for a living.

Therefore, that John ended up going to Fred Winter, the champion National Hunt trainer in 1969, and staying with him for 16 years until he retired from race-riding in 1985, is an amazing story, and it transpires that John's whole career in racing was solely based on the advice of a carpenter, 'who probably didn't even know which end of the horse to feed but, as it turned out, was a good judge of character'.

John had never heard of Fred Winter, but this friend of his father had once done some work for the boss at his Lambourn yard. John's interview at those famous stables was the biggest turning point in his life, presenting him with a ticket to stardom that would yield 1,138 winners and earn him seven National Hunt jockeys' championships. He had always been competitive and greedy for success when riding his ponies in horse shows, but his eyes were opened far wider when he was put on the staff rota at Uplands. There were no shortcuts and he was made to work hard, but through his mistakes and the bollockings he got from the brilliant head lad, Brian Delaney, he quickly understood why discipline and high standards are so important in top National Hunt yards.

John Francome had been born in Swindon in 1952, starting off in life in a council house with his parents and twin sisters, but by the time he was presented with his first pony, at the age of 16, the family had moved to a house of their own on the edge of town and closer to the countryside. Neither of John's parents had any connection with horses: the only link was a distant relative 'who went to prison for selling a blind horse to a lady as a hunter'. His father was a fireman on the Great Western Railway, who 'used to cut people's hair and sweep chimneys in his spare time to earn extra money'. According to John, absolutely nothing ever bothered him, which was obviously the part of his genetic make-up that he passed on to his son. 'No matter how many things went wrong in the day, Dad was never miserable, and one of his favourite sayings was to "make work a pleasure".' John's mother Lillian was a great worker too, and kept chickens in the garden to help pay the rent. It's clear both parents always encouraged and supported their children in whatever they wanted to do, giving them the perfect platform from which to create their future lives, and the confidence to embark on anything.

John had his first taste of riding on a trip to the seaside at Barry Island. He only sat on a donkey on the sands, but back home he began helping the local milkman at weekends in return for a ride on his horse after the milk rounds. His first pony, Black Beauty, had belonged to the milkman's daughter and cost £50. She was kept in an old red railway wagon in the family allotment and fenced in with barbed wire. For a whole year she only had a bridle – there was no saddle because the Francomes couldn't afford one. So the future champion did all his riding bareback.

When Norman left the railways, his fortunes changed. He started up a building business of his own that proved highly successful. As a result, two more ponies could be bought, and their accommodation was upgraded with a railed paddock and a stable. By now John had become smitten by the riding bug, and in the winter would go hunting on Saturdays with the VWH Hunt. His best friend was Peter Wightman, whose father had a big farm near Fairford in Gloucestershire. He would take the children's ponies to the meets in his trailer pulled by a Land Rover. This was a big step up from the days when Black Beauty travelled around the countryside in a transit van with three scaffolding planks serving as a ramp.

Horse shows and gymkhanas took up a large part of the Francome summers, but John also spent time with Peter on the family farm, where they got up to all kinds of tricks. Sometimes they would help round up the bullocks into an old air-raid shelter. 'We would tie ropes around them and ride them like the cowboys in the rodeos.' This may not have been much fun for the bullocks, but it was a great way for the children to improve their balance. John's riding would later be characterised by his apparently inborn ability to ride his horses in a balanced way. 'My first year of riding with no saddle was the best thing that ever happened to me,' he says now, 'as it taught me to grip properly with my legs, which in turn helped me to balance myself without needing to lean on the horse's mouth.'

Apart from attending the Pony Club camp and having a few lessons with Mrs 'Molly' Sivewright at the Talland School of Equitation near Cirencester, coupled with some show-jumping tuition from the renowned Dick Stillwell near Holyport in Berkshire, John was self-taught. 'I learned through experience and from watching the best people doing whatever I was interested in, whether it was show-jumping or racing or anything else connected with horses.'

Imitation is certainly the best way for any beginner to learn. In nature, animals learn from watching their parents. Yet nowadays so few would-be jockeys get the opportunity to study the styles of those at the top at close quarters and copy them, because, contends Francome, so much emphasis is put upon 'getting your position on an Equicizer and sitting correctly'. Consequently riders don't develop their own styles through practice, and few acquire a natural balance. Riding bareback or without stirrups is seldom done, because these days it goes against health and safety rules. The young jockeys are taught artificially without having a real horse or pony to practise upon.

John Francome loved his childhood, and it proved invaluable to his future race career. The family support that he had when progressing from ponies to horses and upgrading to top-class show-jumping was tremendous. His father, bitten by the show-jumping bug, answered an advertisement in the *Horse and Hound* for a Grade A show-jumper in Cheshire and bought it. This horse, named Red Paul, was the catalyst of John's jumping career, and the teenager revelled in the challenge of being able to ride over the open tracks at places like Hickstead or on the County showgrounds. Harvey Smith and David Broome were his idols, and John used to watch them ride as often as he could to copy their techniques and improve his own style. The Francome trailer was swapped for a horsebox with living accommodation and there was plenty of travelling around the country. It was with Red Paul that John represented Great Britain abroad and won the Young Riders' European Championships at Hickstead in 1970.

More often than not, it was John himself at the wheel of the horsebox on the road to the shows, even though he was only 16 and had no licence. He usually took his mother with him as his father was too busy at work, but on one occasion Norman Francome was laid up following a bad car accident and his wife had to stay at home to look after him, so rather than miss the shows John drove the horses all on his own. There were no motorways in those days and usually he drove through the night, his father reasoning that he would be less likely to be stopped by the police when it was dark and in the early hours. The driving was a challenge, but even then John exuded the confidence that was to become his trademark.

There is no doubt that John Francome's show-jumping was an enormous help to him when it came to riding as a National Hunt jockey. Fred Winter was quick to spot his talents and gave him plenty of opportunities to school and educate the horses he was later to ride in races. Over the years John rode some fantastic horses on the track, and his name will always be linked with Midnight Court (Cheltenham Gold Cup) and Sea Pigeon (Champion Hurdle) as well as with Lanzarote, Sonny Somers, Wayward Lad, Observe, Bula, and his favourite horse, Osbaldeston, on whom he won 17 races.

John loved the schooling sessions on the training grounds at Lambourn. He took enormous pride in teaching horses to jump correctly, and spent many hours educating them to adjust their strides in front of the fences and making them go deep, rather than standing off too far. 'Any horse can stand off. It's teaching it to put in that extra stride when it meets a fence wrong.' His instructions to other jockeys were always, 'Concentrate on what your horse is doing and keep your head in the right position.' A jockey's head is the heaviest part of his body, and if it goes too far forward or else the rider sits too far back then the horse is easily taken off balance.

I took real pleasure in teaching the young horses to jump properly. With a horse who doesn't want to jump it is important to know straight away whether it is nervous and needs encouragement, or whether it is taking the mickey and wants a good crack round the backside. If you make the wrong decision with a nervous horse you can spoil it for a long time. The main point is always to remember that if a horse doesn't enjoy himself, he will never be very good at his job. 〝

As well as being a top National Hunt jockey John Francome has an excellent philosophy on life. His enviable if inimitable style, coupled with his courage and happy-go-lucky approach, set him apart from his contemporaries, and indeed from most present-day jockeys as well. Horses jumped well for him, and he seemed to inspire them with confidence. 'In life one must always think forwards,' says John, 'and so must the horses we ride. Positive thoughts are all-important. Negative thoughts are to be avoided, and if they are the only ones one has it is probably better not to think at all, since indecision is dangerous.'

The Francome family bond, so evident when John was developing his riding skills, is there for everybody to see. It is great when someone can look back and say that their childhood days were some of the happiest in their life. Success is often achieved through having the right attitude, and in the champion jockey's career this was clearly the case, although John also stresses the role of luck, and he believes he was fortunate to have met the right people at the right time. With his wicked sense of humour, he is a great ambassador for the sport he loves. When he retired he was greatly missed by his fans, but his style is there for all to copy.

Dean Gallagher

Even when Dean Gallagher was growing up around the Curragh in Co Kildare he was saving up his pocket money to buy *Pacemaker* magazine every month. From the age of 11 he was also riding in pony races and was already convinced he would be a jockey. He chose to ride in the famous Robert Sangster colours of emerald green and royal blue.

Dean loved those weekends on the pony racing circuit. He and his father Tom Gallagher, who in the early 1960s had worked for the trainer PJ 'Darkie' Prendergast, with Meadow Court and Noblesse the stable stars, would drive all over Ireland with the little trailer behind the car. Mark Dwyer had just stopped riding on the circuit, but with Charlie Swan and John Egan two of his rivals, Dean was extremely competitive and a tough nut to crack. As his skills became recognised he was offered numerous outside rides on top ponies – sometimes four or five in a day.

By the time Dean left school his father, having had a short spell of training privately in Co Donegal, had moved to the renowned Jim Bolger's at Coolcullen as travelling head lad. Therefore Dean went too, and began his apprenticeship for the Flat – it never entered his head that he would end up as a National Hunt jockey.

Many top figures in racing have started off at the Bolger establishment, in particular multiple champion jockey AP McCoy and the champion Flat trainer Aidan O'Brien, and Jim was a great man to work for. Dean says he was hard but fair, and built up a young lad's confidence. Dean had 16 winners on the Flat, and his first winner was for his boss on Keynes at Roscommon in 1984. Extraordinarily, it was on the very same horse that he lost his claim when, many years later, he rode him to win a hurdle race at Southwell for John Jenkins.

Unfortunately, a rapid rise in his weight meant Dean did not finish his three-year apprenticeship with Jim Bolger. In 1986 he weighed 8½st, and this was considered too heavy for a Flat jockey, so he completed his apprenticeship with Dessie Hughes on the Curragh, managing, during his six months there, to incorporate plenty of jumping as well – mostly schooling over hurdles – and this gave him a good taste for the National Hunt game.

At 18, he was approached by the *Daily Telegraph* correspondent Tony Stafford, who had noted the young rider's successes in Ireland, and Dean moved to England to be employed by Rod Simpson in Lambourn. He spent three years with the colourful Simpson, and watched many good jockeys schooling horses on the Lambourn Downs. He rode plenty of winners, mostly over hurdles. However, when his trainer lost the patronage of Terry Ramsden as his principal owner, Dean moved on to Jenny Pitman's yard, where David Wachman and Ian Williams were also working.

Jenny was a fantastic teacher, says Dean, and she helped him massively with his riding. He rode a number of good horses for her, and Royal Athlete winning the Long Walk Hurdle at Ascot in 1989 gave him a great thrill. Dean was then retained as first jockey by the Jersey-based owner Paul Green, and he also rode as second jockey for Charlie Brooks behind Graham Bradley, and for Paul Webber who trained near Banbury. In 1995, he won the Hennessy Gold Cup at Newbury for Charlie on Couldn't Be Better, and in 2001 was victorious for Paul in the Scottish Champion Hurdle when partnering Ulundi. Dean also had a great liaison with the fine racemare Dubacilla, who was bred and owned by Henry Cole, trained by David Nicholson and won a number of good chases, finishing second in the 1995 Cheltenham Gold Cup behind Master Oats and fourth in the Grand National that same year.

Dean is a deep thinker, and his judgement in a race and ability to work out tactics were always superb. His assessment of Cheltenham, the Mecca of steeplechasing, is of particular interest.

It's a quirky track. It is very hard to come from behind in a race, but at the same time it's hard to win from the front: you have to be able to judge pace. Sometimes they go very fast, and if you use your horse too much early on you won't get home, but if you drop off too far you can get caught when they kick going on down the hill. It's hard to ride on the inside, as you are turning quite a bit and you get a lot of traffic there. A horse has to be there or thereabouts when going down from the top of the hill into the third-last. You need one with plenty of pace, but it has to be able to stay as well. Speed and stamina are all-important, but the jumping is vital. If a horse does not jump well, it cannot win at Cheltenham. **'**

A series of unfortunate brushes with the racing authorities began in 1998 when, alongside several fellow jockeys, Dean was wrongly accused of race-fixing. He continued riding whilst on bail, but the distress and financial worry of having to pay solicitor's bills as well as a mortgage played deeply on his mind, and to escape the pressures he turned to cocaine. Having been cleared of all race-fixing charges, he eventually paid the penalty for drug-taking by receiving an 18-month suspension.

On his return, Francois Doumen offered him a lifeline as first jockey to his establishment in France, and Dean rode for Francois for two years, successfully partnering the Paul Green-owned Hors La Loi III and keeping the ride when the horse was sent to England to James Fanshawe, from whose yard he won the 2002 Champion Hurdle.

The French trainers are experts when it comes to schooling their horses, teaching them to jump from an early age, and Dean was fortunate to have many successful years in France. After spending time with Doumen he moved as first jockey to Francois Cottin, who trained more than 100 horses in Chantilly. Altogether his time in that country yielded 126 winners. He won the Prix du President de la Republique (the French Grand National) in 2005 and 2006.

However, later in 2006, at Cagnes-sur-Mer, Dean had a bad fall and fractured several vertebrae in his neck. Although he returned to race-riding, he was already thinking about calling it a day and when his favourite horse, Musica Bella, suffered a fatal fall in the Grand Steeple he decided to relinquish his licence and look for an alternative opening with racehorses. 'Enough is enough,' he said when I spoke to him, telling me how upset he had been by the loss of the mare, 'and I was not getting any younger,' but during his years as a National Hunt jockey Dean rode more than 600 winners.

In February 2010, Deano, as he is known to his friends, began riding out for Aidan O'Brien at Ballydoyle. He now has an important position at this powerful yard, and does plenty of work-riding on the superb horses that are trained there. He says he feels fitter than he has ever been and, with his partner Radka, daughter Chloe and young son Dylan Thomas, he has rediscovered his enthusiasm for life. He is once again a happy man and an invaluable member of the champion trainer's team.

Barry Geraghty

In January 2019 Barry Geraghty rode winner number 1,876, and became the fourth most successful jockey in jump racing history.

Co Meath is a good part of Ireland in which to grow up as far as racing and bloodstock are concerned. Fairyhouse racecourse was only just down the road from the Geraghty home in Drumree, and from the start Barry benefited from the family's racing connections. His grandfather bred the peerless Golden Miller, who when owned by Dorothy Paget won five Cheltenham Gold Cups and in 1934 both the Gold Cup and the Grand National in the same season. Barry's father always farmed cattle as well as having a few horses, and he enjoyed hunting and point-to-points. Barry's brother Ross race-rides in America.

It is little wonder that Barry Geraghty always wanted to ride, and he set his heart on being a jockey. When he was 11, his parents opened a riding school next to their home, and this provided a great opportunity for the child to ride different ponies. He was soon helping to improve the riding school ponies, many of whom were naughty at the beginning. As a member of the Meath Pony Club Barry received valuable lessons from the late 'Chich' Fowler, and went to the local shows, but he preferred hunter trials to show-jumping. He loved hunting with the Meath Foxhounds and the Ward Union Hunt.

When he was 14 Barry Geraghty rode in a number of pony races, against top riders like Jamie Spencer and Jason Maguire. 'We learned how not to clip heels – if we did this we had falls. It was a great lesson.' Meanwhile, he was riding a wooden Equicizer at home and, contrary to the opinions of many of his fellow jockeys, he firmly believes that this improved his balance and his style.

Barry left school at 17 and based himself with Noel Meade at the famous Tu Va stables near Navan. He found Noel to be a good teacher and very explicit when it came to tactics in a race. The jockey soon obtained an apprentice licence to ride on the Flat, but he never rode the winner of a Flat race. Nevertheless, it was for Noel Meade's yard that Barry rode his first ever winner, Stagalier, in January 1997, in a maiden hurdle at Down Royal.

After three years with Noel, Barry moved to Jessica Harrington's establishment in Co Kildare. 'Jessie has such a positive approach to riding and nothing ever fazes her.' She is an accomplished horsewoman in her own right and she gave the young jockey plenty of valuable tips on style before later entrusting him to ride the brilliant Moscow Flyer. 'She gives a rider confidence,' says Barry.

Barry Geraghty became famously associated with Moscow Flyer – on whom he won two Champion Chases – and then with Kicking King and Bobs Worth, both of whom won the Cheltenham Gold Cup. He also rode Buveur D'Air, Jezki and Punjabi to win Champion Hurdles as well as partnering the brilliant Sprinter Sacre in a number of top races, including the Champion Chase, an event he has won five times. In 2003, Barry won the Grand National on Monty's Pass for Jimmy Mangan. He has an enviable racing CV and is a deep thinker who takes the game extremely seriously. He is up to date with the breeding and form of all the horses he rides. Indeed, he is an encyclopaedia of racing and has strong views, but he usually keeps his opinions to himself, unless specifically asked to divulge them.

Although still riding in races and having had a double at the 2019 Cheltenham Festival for his boss JP McManus, for whom over the years he has ridden countless winners, Barry, who was born in September 1979, is possibly nearing the end of his career as a National Hunt jockey, largely due to the number of serious injuries that have befallen him. A broken leg at the 2019 Grand National meeting was slow to mend. However, at his magnificent home near Ratoath in Co Meath, he has some fine stables and paddocks for rearing young horses, and when he does retire he is sure to continue with a close involvement in the sport.

His contribution to National Hunt racing is legendary and Barry's knowledge of the game is unparalleled. His successful career demonstrates the advantages of the lessons learned in the Pony Club and on the pony racing circuit. He sets a fine example to aspiring jockeys of today and is a role model for their chosen careers.

Eddie Harty

Eddie Harty has led a remarkable life, all of it connected to horses. He never remembers a time when he was not surrounded by them. 'I was born to be a horseman,' he says. 'Nothing else.'

Eddie's illustrious father, Captain Cyril Harty, an officer in the Free State Army, was the founder of the Irish show-jumping team and the anchor rider in numerous competitions, in the days when his team members rode former army remount horses. Captain Harty once had the distinction of winning the Heavyweight Hunter Championship at the RDS horse show, and then, in the same week, being a member of the first Aga Khan Show Jumping Team, before winning the High Jump class. He had a trio of successes in the space of five days. As a jockey he won the 1922 Military Cup at Punchestown on Santos, before training Knight's Crest, ridden by Martin Molony, to win the Irish Grand National at Fairyhouse. The Captain was Eddie's idol and he exerted a big influence during his son's riding career.

Eddie was always a natural rider, and at the age of 11 won the 13.2hh children's open show-jumping championship at the RDS on the brilliant little mare, Rossa. In those days the class was held in the main arena, presenting a big test of nerves for any child to ride over show-jumps in front of a vast, cheering crowd. Eddie, however, was fearless: nothing fazed him, as demonstrated later on in his life when he rode as a steeplechase jockey.

Eddie's grandfather was a public trainer in Co Limerick – the first to have a stable of racehorses 'beyond the pale': it was considered to too adventurous to train so far away from the Curragh. When the Harty children travelled to Co Limerick for hunting, the ponies were hired from Paddy Punch, who had a varied assortment in his yard. Eddie first went out hunting when he was six, and riding with the hounds became the highlight of his childhood. On one occasion, his father took him to the hireling man but there were no ponies left. The child was almost in tears but then, by chance, another pony came back into the yard 'after pulling its cart and milk churns on its rounds from the creamery'. It was immediately snatched from the shafts, washed off and saddled up so that Eddie could join the hunt.

Eddie Harty had his first ride in a hurdle race at 14 – not something that could happen today, as amateur jockeys are not granted licences until they are 16. He was unplaced that day, but then finished second in his next race. Those who knew the horse maintained it should have won but it had not been given its usual drink of stout and poteen before the off. In the point-to-points in the 1950s and 1960s it was generally accepted that horses were given alcohol before they ran, but occasionally too much was administered and the horses behaved like drunkards.

Despite his inauspicious start to race-riding, Eddie did have his first winner in Ireland when he was 17, Loyala, trained by his father, won a hurdle race for three-year-olds at Navan but his first winner under rules had been a year earlier when he had partnered Flaming Dome for Earl Jones in a three-mile chase at Exeter. He remembers one of his early rides under rules, in a hunter chase at Market Rasen as a 16-year-old, where he was watched by the well-known jockey Dick Francis. 'If you want to live longer, don't ride so short, and don't sit so far up the horse's neck.' At that time Eddie believed all jockeys should ride with their knees above the saddle.

When Eddie began riding in point-to-points many of the races were run over banks, and if horses missed their footings on the tops they would flip over and could break their backs. He remembers a race at Templemore in which the mare he was riding fell and landed on top of him. He was buried beneath her. In those days first aid at point-to-points was minimal, and it was a while before he was freed from beneath his motionless mount. He suffered considerable pain and had to hold his head in his hands, but his father insisted that his son was well enough to ride his fancied runner in the last, and the doctor duly passed him as fit to ride. The horse won in a canter and many of his father's friends benefited from a massive gamble. Some years later, Eddie Harty met that very same doctor, who remembered the occasion well. 'I had to pass you,' he explained, 'as I had been told to have my £10 bet on you in the last race.'

At the same time as riding more than 50 winners in point-to-points Eddie continued with his show-jumpers, and also became interested in eventing. In 1960 he represented Ireland in the Three-Day Event in the Olympic Games in Rome, on an ex-racehorse called Harlequin who had been trained by Ryan Price in England and Willie Rooney in the north of Ireland and, whilst not that speedy, had won races under rules. After a few seasons in training, Harlequin became Hack Champion at the RDS horse show, and was then sold to Iris Kellett as a show-jumper. To qualify for the Olympics, all that Eddie and the horse had to do was take part in a single one-day event as well as a two-day event before being allocated a place on the Irish team. When taken to Rome, Harlequin trotted unlevel in the dressage test but had clear rounds in both the show-jumping and cross-country phases. He finished up in ninth place overall – an amazing achievement for an inexperienced ex-racehorse. What would the RoR think of that today?

After all his exploits hunting, show-jumping, point-to-pointing and eventing, Eddie then spent time in England race-riding for leading trainers, in particular Toby Balding, Tim Molony, Fred Rimell and Fred Winter. In 1969 he won the Grand National on the Toby Balding-trained Highland Wedding, and during his time with Fred Winter he rode the brilliant but ill-fated Killiney. When riding for Fred Rimell, Eddie's best win came on Jupiter Boy in the Mackeson Gold Cup.

In 1971 Eddie Harty was forced to retire from race-riding after shattering his arm in a bad fall. He afterwards concentrated on training racehorses on the Curragh from his yard at Strawhall. He knew the game inside out, and he made and sold many top horses to Britain, notably Fifty Dollars More and Half Free to Fred Winter, as well as Katabatic to Andy Turnell and I'm Happy to Toby Balding.

Eddie and his devoted wife, Patricia, have derived great satisfaction from seeing their sons Eddie jnr and Eoin continuing to follow in the family's footsteps. The former currently trains on the Curragh, close to where Eddie was raised, and Eoin lives in the USA where, having spent time as an assistant to Bob Baffert, he now trains Flat horses for Godolphin.

Eddie Harty sets an unprecedented example to present-day jockeys by demonstrating that good horsemen can switch from one field of equestrianism to another and be successful in whichever discipline they choose, provided they have enthusiasm, determination and a good work ethic.

Adrian Heskin

When Adrian Heskin was at school he would ride early in the morning as well as when he got back at night – even if it was dark. He first sat on a pony when he was three. His ponies mostly did charity rides, but he always wanted to make them go faster, and often rode up Sean O'Brien's gallops pretending to be a jockey.

Growing up near Kilworth in Co Cork he did not go hunting nor to shows, but from the age of 12 he went to pony races as a spectator and later managed to pick up some rides. Thus his riding career took off and he was fortunate to have the support of a number of top trainers on the pony circuit. He only weighed 7st – ideal for pony racing – and he had plenty of winners. The races were highly competitive and nearly all run right-handed, which meant that the ponies tended to become one-sided in their mouths. Many were pure thoroughbreds and had come off the tracks, probably discarded by their trainers for not going into the stalls or refusing to settle. Adrian believes the child riders can learn a huge amount from riding these unpredictable animals at speed and around tight corners.

After leaving school Adrian went full-time to Michael Hourigan's training establishment in Co Limerick. He stayed there for five years. Andrew McNamara and Tom Doyle were resident jockeys at the same time and Adrian was given accommodation in Michael's house. Life was tough but he thoroughly enjoyed it.

Adrian was granted an amateur licence when he was 16, but only kept it for six months and only rode in two point-to-points. He soon took out a conditionals' licence and his first winner was in February 2009 when partnering Mystical Breeze to victory in a handicap hurdle at Naas. His first ride in the paid ranks had been less successful. He had ridden at Fairyhouse, and was run away with and unseated at the third hurdle. There were plenty of winners for the Hourigan team, and Adrian rode out his claim. He did a lot of schooling at the yard, as well as helping with the 'breakers'. After riding them initially for three days in the indoor school, they would be taken out to the gallops and cantered behind a lead horse – with no shoes, no neckstraps and no pads under their saddles. 'It was a question of "close contact",' reflects Adrian, 'and getting really close to the horse you rode.' Michael used to follow the young horses up the gallop in his jeep and bang on the door if they were not going forward.

During his last years at Michael Hourigan's Adrian rode out once a week at Enda Bolger's – the 'King of the Banks', and the best man to teach a horse to jump anywhere in Ireland. He considers he learned more with Enda than with anybody else he ever rode out for. If Enda believed in a jockey and saw he was enthusiastic then there was nothing he would not do to improve that rider's technique. Young jockeys can consider themselves extremely fortunate when they get help like this from the top professionals. Adrian had a number of rides for Enda in the top banks races at Punchestown and rode Love Rory to win a novice hurdle at the Listowel festival in 2013 when, at 33-1, he beat Barry Geraghty on a horse of Michael Hourigan's that he had been jocked off.

After Michael Hourigan's, Adrian went freelance for a year and rode for Liz Doyle, Jonjo Walsh, Mick Winters and Eddie Harty. He had a first-class agent too, Garry Cribbin, of whom he speaks very highly.

At 21, Adrian got a top job riding for Barry Connell, which meant living close to the trainer Alan Fleming at Tully East, near the Curragh. It was a retained position which he greatly enjoyed, but unfortunately injury led to a spell on the sidelines, after which he moved to England and rode as stable jockey for Tom George. Adrian is still in Britain, and currently retained by the McNeill family, who have first-class horses with a number of top trainers. His short riding career has to date yielded some notable winners, including the 2010 Cross Country Chase at Cheltenham with A New Story and the Whitbread Gold Cup (now the bet365 Gold Cup) at Sandown on Church Island in the same year. He has an interesting career ahead of him and is a fine horseman.

Brian Hughes

In January 2019 Brian Hughes registered his 1,000th winner in National Hunt racing, and his hold across the racecourses in the north of England is virtually untouchable.

Growing up near Newry in South Armagh, Brian rode ponies 'as soon as I could walk' – there were always horses and ponies in the family's fields, mostly half-breds and show-jumpers – but his parents were never riders: his mother worked in an old people's home and his father is a joiner by trade and a building control officer for the Northern Ireland government. Yet Brian had most of his riding lessons from his father. He loved jumping and regularly went out hunting, primarily with the Oriel Harriers or the Newry Harriers. He often rode his ponies at some of the local shows and gymkhanas.

The secondary school Brian attended, St Michael's and St Paul's, was the second largest school in Northern Ireland, with 1,600 pupils, but he hated it and was never happy there. 'I was a small child due to having been born a month prematurely. I'd also been ill for several months early in my childhood with meningitis. I could not wait to leave.' So at 15 Brian left to go to RACE, the Racing Academy and Centre of Education, in Kildare, which in many respects is the Irish equivalent to the British Racing School in Newmarket. He well remembers arriving there in 2001 because Galileo won the Irish Derby on the same day.

His heroes at that time were AP McCoy, Pat Smullen and Mick Kinane, but because of his weight – fully dressed he barely weighed 6st – he presumed that he would end up as a Flat jockey. However, when he went home at weekends he often rode out for trainer James Lambe, who lived 15 minutes away. 'When he came to me as a teenager,' says James, 'he once rode 22 horses in a single day. He never questioned the tasks ahead of him and he never said "No". His attitude was always positive, and I used to speak to him as though he was an adult, not a child.'

Brian vividly remembers the day when as a 16-year-old he accompanied James to Down Royal racecourse to ride one of the racehorses in a gallop – at least that was what he presumed – but the trainer had other ideas. James asked him to show the horse one of the chase fences, and in no time Brian, riding the four-year-old Winter Star, was following an older horse around the whole course. Neither horse nor jockey had ever jumped a proper steeplechase fence before. 'I was run away with, and I had no licence. I ended up leading, but the horse was a great jumper and it was a lot of fun.'

The trainer advised his young protégé to get an amateur licence – he already had his apprenticeship papers from the Racing School – and thus he ended up with both a jumps licence and a Flat one. James was true to his word and gave Brian his first rides on the tracks. On one occasion he rode a horse called Boleys Pride over hurdles. It was set to run with nearly 12st, but the fledgling jockey, even with his breeches, boots and colours, only weighed 7½st. He rode with 4½st in his weight cloth.

During his ten months at RACE, Brian was sent out every morning to Charlie O'Neill's yard, which was half an hour from Kildare town. It was a great experience. 'I learned how to muck out my horses, tie them up, groom them and ride them properly. There was a nice sand gallop as well as a cross-country course. Charlie's yard gave me a great start to my racing career.' In his second and third terms he was placed with Kevin Prendergast on the Curragh, which he considers was a great honour. The legendary trainer had been responsible for producing and winning with many famous horses, including Nebbiolo, Ardross and Oscar Schindler, and many well-known jockeys have learned their trade in the Prendergast yard. Kevin's stables are run on proper old-fashioned lines:

If a lad was cheeky and cocky, he would soon be brought down. I was always one of the lesser apprentices but I worked hard and learned to keep my mouth shut. On many occasions I most probably got to ride horses I shouldn't have done, but the trainer seemed to trust me, and in 2002 I rode my first ever winner on the track when partnering Perugino Lady at Downpatrick in an apprentice handicap. **,**

Brian rode for three seasons on the Flat in Ireland, but as his weight crept up he realised he would not be able to keep pace with many of his lighter and more experienced contemporaries. So, thanks to Bobby O'Ryan, who had sold numerous good jumpers to England, in particular Inglis Drever and Tidal Bay to Graham Wylie to be trained by Howard Johnson, Brian got a job in the Johnson yard and he moved over from Ireland.

Although he had ridden in a few hurdle races in his native land and schooled horses for jumping, he never dreamed that he would ride 11 winners in his first six months in County Durham. Graham Lee was the stable jockey at the time, and was extremely helpful to Brian. 'I used to ask him a million questions. I loved his style – he was such a quiet rider. Tony Dobbin and Alan Dempsey were other jockeys who came in regularly to school horses. They too were exceptional horsemen and role models for me to copy.'

Brian stayed at Howard Johnson's for two years. In the early months everything went well, but in his second season he had only three winners. Graham Lee left and Paddy Brennan arrived, and Brian became downhearted and contemplated giving up altogether. Fortunately he pushed on and had a number of rides for smaller trainers, in particular John Wade and Alan Swinbank. At the end of the 2007-08 season he was crowned champion conditional jockey, and won the prestigious Swinton Hurdle for Richard Fahey on Joe Jo Star. Brian has continued to ride freelance, and formed excellent links with a number of northern trainers, riding 140 winners for Malcolm Jefferson before he died in 2018. In that year, the Jefferson-trained Waiting Patiently gave Brian his first Grade 1 success in the Ascot Chase.

Brian considers he has been extremely fortunate as a National Hunt jockey, because he has been surrounded by the right people

at the right time. He may have been fortunate, but he has worked
his way into the top league, and he remains highly professional and
extremely ambitious. Like AP McCoy and John Francome, he has
never been a drinker nor a smoker. Apart from Lucy, his wife, and his
two lovely children, race-riding is his life.

No jockey takes his racing career more seriously than Brian
Hughes, and when riding in a race he is a pleasure to watch: he
knows his courses and walks all of them prior to racing. Every race he
contests is the subject of careful forethought. He is always ready to
discuss his tactics, and his feedback to owners and trainers is always
appreciated. He is definitely a jockey to have on one's side. If he were
to leave the north of England for the southern tracks, he could easily
become a champion.

Richard Hughes

Despite most people classifying Richard Hughes as purely a Flat jockey, he has jump racing in his blood. In the years that he rode over hurdles he did well. His 5ft 10in height would point to him being a National Hunt jockey rather than a Flat one, and numerous jump jockeys have begun riding winners on the Flat before a rise in weight has pushed them into National Hunt. However, with Richard Hughes it was the other way round, even though many of the jockeys start off with similar backgrounds. There is a fine dividing line and several top riders have surprisingly switched codes.

Richard's father Dessie was a leading jumps rider who partnered Monksfield to victory in the Champion Hurdle in 1979 when he beat Sea Pigeon. He also trained a number of top National Hunt horses, including Hardy Eustace who, under Conor O'Dwyer, won two consecutive Champion Hurdles in 2004 and 2005. Yet despite Dessie Hughes becoming synonymous with National Hunt racing in Ireland, he only switched to riding over hurdles and fences when his weight got the better of him and made it impossible for him to continue on the Flat. 'Like Dad,' says Richard, 'I too started my career on the Flat, but he made it abundantly clear that he wanted me to stay there. He did not want me to be a jump jockey, even though I did make occasional forays into the National Hunt game and enjoyed them.'

Like a large number of aspiring jockeys in Ireland, whether destined for the Flat or for National Hunt, Richard began his riding career in pony races. When he was only seven he was presented with a supposedly unrideable two-year-old 12.2hh thoroughbred pony by the father of one of his schoolfriends. Chestnut Lady became a superstar on the pony circuit. She was Richard's best friend, and his whole life revolved around her, from mucking her out before school to riding her in the afternoons and evenings. 'She was the most prolific winner of my entire riding career.'

It is hardly surprising that Richard's pony-racing days were such a success. As soon as he was ten he was accompanying his father's racehorses onto the gallops on the Curragh. Dessie was a first-class teacher, and taught his son to sit correctly and ride in balance. Richard used to wear a set of Monksfield's colours, and on racedays his sister Sandra would organise his rides. In Ireland the Turf Club has no jurisdiction over 'flapping' racing and as a licensed trainer Dessie was not allowed to get involved in the pony-racing circuit. Unsurprisingly Richard's winners were plentiful, and he was well rewarded financially by owners and trainers for whom he rode.

Pony racing was not like the Pony Club Mounted Games. You did not get a rosette for winning: instead you got money. From the age of ten I never needed to ask my parents for pocket money. Usually the riders got £5 given to them by the trainer for every pony they rode, and £20 if it won. When I was paid at the races I would slip the notes down the sides of my riding boots. On the way home in the car, I would take off my boots and shake out the money.

The pony races in Ireland are extremely popular, and those taking part become streetwise and clever. For the successful children, pony racing is a lucrative way of life, and it is not uncommon for a child to have seven or eight rides at a single meeting. Yet the Irish approach tends to be frowned upon in Britain, where the children never race for money.

Richard Hughes' first winner over hurdles was in 1993 at Punchestown on Amari Queen, trained by his father, for Michael Ward-Thomas, who had won the Queen Mother Champion Chase at Cheltenham with Martha's Son.

Richard's second winner was at a lesser track in March 1994, when he partnered Conclave to win a maiden hurdle at Tralee. He had a number of rides over hurdles, but never any in a steeplechase. He used to think that he was not tough enough to enjoy riding over fences, but later in life regretted that he never gave it a try. He was partly put off jump racing whilst spending time in Lambourn with the top National Hunt jockey Norman Williamson. On many occasions he witnessed the pain Norman endured after falls on the tracks.

Richard's CV for National Hunt racing reads well. In 1997 he won the Irish Champion Hurdle on the Noel Meade-trained Cockney Lad and those early years of race-riding showed that the future champion Flat jockey could easily have been just as successful in another sphere.

Indeed, Richard had the perfect style for jump racing: he had superb balance and sat well into his horses. He never rushed them into the obstacles. During the winters of 1996 and 1997, when he rode jumpers for his father as well as for Noel Meade, he was even able to give Paul Carberry a few lessons. In those days, according to Richard, Paul was sloppy and untidy, but later he copied the finer points of Richard's Flat-racing style. The jockeys were good friends, and often rode against each other over hurdles. Their positions in the saddle were similar.

In many ways, it was a shame Richard Hughes did not take his National Hunt career any further, but financially he had far better rewards by staying on the level. He won the Flat jockeys' championship on three occasions, in 2012, 2013 and 2014, and in the middle season rode 208 winners. From the hours spent on the rocking horse that he was given during his childhood to his brilliant career in the saddle as a Flat jockey, which yielded 2,180 winners worldwide, Richard's riding was always superb and his style was universally admired.

Tim Hyde

A fine picture of Prince Regent adorns one of the walls in Camas Park in Co Tipperary. In 1946 Tim Hyde snr won the 1946 Cheltenham Gold Cup on this famous horse, having already won the Irish Grand National in 1942. Prince Regent was a real old-fashioned type, a magnificent individual with near-perfect conformation, plenty of bone and a lovely shoulder setting off his superb front.

Tim Hyde's father had bought Camas Park in 1940, the year before Tim jnr was born. A great sportsman who rode in many point-to-points over natural hunting country, as well as producing and showing top-class hunters, he also show-jumped to a high level and became a top professional jockey in the 1930s, riding mostly for Tom Dreaper. He partnered Workman to win the 1939 Grand National, having finished second the previous year to the Reg Hobbs-trained Battleship. In 1950, however, Tim Hyde snr suffered a career-ending accident when he had a fall over a bank in a show-jumping competition in Co Cork. The fall left him paralysed from the waist downwards but it did not stop him training horses or buying top ponies for his children, and Tim Hyde jnr, today's Master of Camas Park, began riding when he was only four.

The Hyde family is laced with generations of famous connections, with present-day members spread the length and breadth of Ireland and recognised in most corners of the equestrian world where classy thoroughbreds are to the fore.

When Timmy Hyde was growing up there were always ponies around the house, yet when he was six he had a fall from one of them and his foot got lodged in a stirrup iron. He was dragged for almost three-quarters of a mile around a field and ended up unconscious for ten days. When he recovered, he remembered very little of the incident, and fortunately his nerve was unaffected. He always loved going hunting, and would go out regularly with the Golden Vale Hunt, which his father founded, or with the Tipperary Foxhounds.

Tim Hyde snr had been responsible for show champions at the RDS (Royal Dublin Society horse show) on numerous occasions, and he bought show ponies for the young Tim, who won many championships on his 12.2hh pony from the age of nine, even though he preferred jumping. He won the 14.2hh show-jumping championship at the RDS when he was only 15. There was no pony racing in the 1950s, and Timmy never rode in point-to-points because he was too light – he weighed a mere 6½st.

However, he was always fascinated by racing, and although his parents wanted him to be a vet, he had other ideas and set his sights on being a jockey. Every summer, after riding in the RDS horse show at Ballsbridge in early August, he would spend a couple of weeks riding out for Toss Taaffe, who trained close to the Curragh. When ending his schooldays in Cashel, at 15 he became apprenticed to Harry Wragg at Abington Place in Newmarket. 'He was a wonderful man whose stable management was superb. He was very meticulous.'

It must have been quite a shock for a young boy to leave home and venture from his native Ireland to start his career in England, but even though he was homesick, he quickly adapted to his new way of life and stayed with the master trainer for three years. 'We rode up and down the streets in the town. Even the biggest strings only had forty horses. Training in those days was a lot more peaceful, and of course there was hardly any traffic.' Tim Hyde rode his first winner at Newmarket during his apprentice days, but as he grew up his weight increased, and he left racing's headquarters when he was 18.

His father was training a few horses at Camas Park, and his great friend Major Tim Vigors, who owned Coolmore, was also training from that now famous establishment in Co Tipperary. In December 1959 Timmy Hyde applied for his jump jockeys' licence and, claiming 7lb, rode his first winner later that month for the Vigors family on Libertina in a handicap hurdle race at Limerick City, a racecourse close to the town that sadly no longer exists.

In the 1960s and 1970s Tim Hyde rode for a number of different trainers as a National Hunt jockey, but his name will forever be linked with the Duchess of Westminster's fine chaser Kinloch Brae, on whom he won the Cathcart Chase at the Cheltenham Festival in 1969. He was an accomplished and fearless rider and an excellent horseman with good hands and a good eye for a fence. He combined race-riding with show-jumping, and even though he raced in the winter months he still enjoyed competing at the big horse shows during the summer – in the 1960s and 1970s there was no summer jump racing. He spent his time educating young horses and sold many of them abroad. Several Olympic horses passed through his hands.

In 1973 Timmy retired from race-riding having amassed more than 200 winners. Residing at the magnificent family home, Camas Park, he became increasingly more involved in the buying and selling of thoroughbreds. He has always had an eye for a good horse, and although he specialised in show-jumpers during his race-riding days, he quickly established his name in the Flat and National Hunt worlds for trading at the top level. Some class Flat performers have been through Timmy Hyde's hands, notably Alexandrova, Al Bahathri, Soviet Star and Indian Skimmer. When his breeding operation subsequently took off as well, the likes of Capri, Toast Of New York and Ten Sovereigns further advertised the Camas Park name. Timmy also bred the 2016 Kentucky Derby winner Nyquist. He enjoys pinhooking and has bought a number of his best horses in America.

The Hyde family will always be synonymous with horseracing, and Timmy's son, another Tim, who is a qualified vet, himself rode 45 winners under National Hunt rules. He now supports his own son – yet another Tim – in his growing passion for race-riding. Camas Park is a special place and its current master has done a massive amount for racing. His sense of humour and way with people have put him at the top of his profession, and he is universally popular – both at home and abroad.

Richard Johnson OBE

In 2019 Richard Johnson was awarded an OBE for services to horseracing. One of the most enthusiastic National Hunt jockeys in the sport, he puts in an unbelievable amount of time and energy, yet still gets a huge kick out of winning races. He is prepared to travel the length and breadth of the country to achieve his goals. From 1995 until 2015 Richard was 16-times runner-up in the jockeys' championship to AP McCoy, but when the champ finally retired he captured the coveted jockeys' award himself in the 2015-16 and 2017-18 seasons. Nor, at 42 years of age, does he look like stopping, even though many of his contemporaries have hung up their boots. He lives for winners.

Dicky Johnson was born in Herefordshire. His father Keith was an amateur jockey who enjoyed point-to-points, and together with Dicky's brother Nick is an avid farmer, with the pair sharing two farms at Madley, mostly grassland. There are plenty of cattle as well as horses. Richard's mother trained racehorses, initially with a permit and then with a full licence, and indeed in 1993 provided Dicky with his first win under rules when she trained Rusty Bridge to win a hunter chase at Hereford. Her son was only 16.

As a child, Richard began with a quiet grey pony that he could 'kick around the farm', but he progressed on to his liver chestnut 13hh pony, Tasty. She looked like a miniature racehorse and would do everything that her rider wanted. She was the only pony that the Johnsons never sold. As a member of the Radnor West Pony Club, Dicky used to take Tasty out hunting as well as to local gymkhanas, cross-country events and tetrathlons. She gave him a lot of fun, and he thoroughly enjoyed his summers at the Pony Club camps, becoming well known in Herefordshire horse circles.

Like Peter Scudamore, Richard Johnson went to Belmont Abbey school near Hereford, enjoying the emphasis on sport. He left before his A-levels, his mind already set on racing: indeed, he would rather read the *Sporting Life* than textbooks. Thus at 16 he was sent to David Nicholson's training establishment to work as a lad. 'The Duke' was a great teacher and brilliant with young jockeys. He had a strict work ethic but knew all the finer points of jockeyship and was a huge influence in Dicky's life.

The young jockey was quickly noticed with his winners on the tracks, and as a fledgling professional he progressed to win the conditional jockeys' championship at the end of the 1995-96 National Hunt season when he was still only 18.

Over the years, Richard Johnson has ridden for a number of top trainers, but he has always had a particularly close association with Philip Hobbs, for whom he won the 2003 Champion Hurdle on Rooster Booster, as well as the Triumph Hurdle in 2017 on Defi Du Seuil. He also partnered Menorah to win the Supreme Novices' Hurdle in 2010, and rode the same horse to win a number of top chases. In 2018, Dicky won the Cheltenham Gold Cup on Native River, trained by Colin Tizzard, having previously won the race in 2000 on Looks Like Trouble for Noel Chance, whose daughter Fiona is now his wife. Other big-race wins on the Johnson CV include the Queen Mother Champion Chase with Flagship Uberalles in 2002 and the Stayers' Hurdle of 1999 with Anzum, the latter trained by his early mentor David Nicholson.

Richard Johnson's enthusiasm for race-riding sets a fine example to the many younger jockeys of today, and his philosophy on life is enviable. 'I've never understood why you have to be an unpleasant person to be a big winner. I have always felt one should treat people in the way one expects to be treated oneself.' Dicky is a top professional with an outgoing personality and an engaging smile. His popularity is widespread. The champion jockey's appetite for winners is insatiable: 'I still get an enormous thrill from going first past the post wherever the race may be.' With no suggestion of retirement, his tireless agent Dave Roberts presses on with booking his rides. 'I would like to get to 4,000 winners, but it would be hard to beat AP's record [4,359].'

As the reigning champion over jumps, Richard Johnson has a full life, but enjoys his chosen career and is happy to spend many hours on the road travelling to racecourses. When there are days without racing he stays at home to watch over his National Hunt broodmares and his youngstock. Menorah is prospering in his retirement in the Johnsons' Herefordshire fields, and Fiona loves riding him with the children, Willow, Casper and Percy. He is a fine-looking horse, and I feel proud to have bought his mother, Maid For Adventure, as an unbroken three-year-old. She won three races for me on the track and was easy to train.

Lizzie Kelly

By winning some high-class races Lizzie Kelly has done a great service to the cause of lady jockeys. She has helped put them in the public eye. Lizzie spent her childhood in Devon at Culverhill Farm in South Molton. It is the home of her mother, Jane, and stepfather Nick Williams, both of whom are successful racehorse trainers, and her half-brother Chester is proving to be another capable jockey under rules. Lizzie remains close to her father, Shaun, a social worker who works with people with learning disabilities. He fully supports Lizzie's riding career.

She was a natural in the saddle from the age of five, and by the time she was eight she was riding thoroughbreds. As an active member of the Dulverton West Pony Club, Lizzie thoroughly enjoyed going hunting on her ponies. Later, she experienced a number of fun days when she took the racehorses out with the hounds. This either freshened them up or qualified them for point-to-points. Lizzie took part in two pony races, but she found them boring because they are run over the sprint distance of five furlongs: 'They were over too quickly, and there was not enough excitement.'

From an early age Lizzie was ahead of her game. She would watch races on television and study jockeys' styles. She was determined to be among them when she grew up.

I was riding breakers for Nick at the age of twelve. I had my fair share of falls but they didn't bother me. I always got back on the horses afterwards – I assumed falls were just part and parcel of the game. However, I did not enjoy the stable management as much as the riding, and when I went to the Pony Club camps and rallies I was marked down on this. The assessors gave me low marks.

Two days after her 16th birthday, Lizzie Kelly had her first rides in point-to-points. 'I finished third and fourth and it was great.' Altogether she won 25 races, mostly on homebred horses that she knew well and had educated from the start of their careers. 'I enjoyed riding the maidens. I had taught them at home and I trusted them. Some of them were sold on, but others we kept and they went into training.' Lizzie's first winner under rules was when, at the age of 17, she rode Blackstaff at Exeter in a hunter chase; she went on to ride him in the Foxhunter Chase at Cheltenham as well as at Aintree.

Lizzie also did well at school, studying diligently and getting her A-levels before going to Winchester University to read Event Management. She passed out with a 2:2 degree at 21, but knew that a career as a jockey was her goal. During her years at college she spent the summers in Ireland. She had two spells at Willie Mullins' Closutton yard and two summers with Joseph O'Brien. 'I went to Ireland to learn more about racing and see how the horses were trained over there,' says Lizzie. 'I didn't have any rides on the racecourses in Ireland, and I did not expect them, but it was great experience to work over there.'

Lizzie Kelly's career as a National Hunt jockey has been meteoric, and she has picked up her rides without the help of an agent. She believes that jockeys' agents have become too powerful and can hold back good jockeys through unsuitable bookings or no bookings at all.

❛ If an agent believes in a certain rider he will give him the cream of the rides available, but if he is near the bottom of the list then he may not get the help he deserves. While making champions, many agents have destroyed the careers of lesser jockeys who would, on many occasions, have done better if they had ploughed their own furrows and gone forward with confidence and belief in themselves. ❜

In March 2019, Lizzie won the Brown Advisory & Merriebelle Stable Plate Handicap Chase at the Cheltenham Festival on Siruh Du Lac, trained by Nick Williams. She rode an excellent, well-judged race and thoroughly deserved the victory. It was the week when three female riders took centre stage – Bryony Frost and Rachael Blackmore were also winners – but Lizzie was the more experienced having already won there in 2018 when Coo Star Sivola had taken the Ultima Handicap Chase.

It is not just in chases that Lizzie excels, even though she won her first Grade 1 race on Tea For Two in the Kauto Star Novices' Chase at Kempton on Boxing Day in 2015 before going on to take the Betway Bowl on him at Aintree in 2017. On Agrapart she won the valuable Betfair Hurdle at Newbury in 2016, whilst Tea For Two was also successful in the Lanzarote Hurdle at Kempton in 2015.

Lizzie Kelly is an extremely versatile rider who has a cool head when the pressure is on. She is also tough, as I can testify when, at 15, she came to West Lockinge Farm for work experience. She badly cut the base of her thumb by inadvertently wrapping it around a lead chain, yet despite the pain she refused to go to the local surgery and covered the wound in plasters. She never stopped working.

Lizzie fully deserves further successes in her race-riding career, and demonstrates the advantages that jockeys are afforded by riding young horses in their teenage days. There is no substitute for being in a horse environment from an early age and Lizzie has taken full advantage of the opportunities that have been offered to her.

Jack Kennedy

Jack Kennedy was the star of the Irish pony-racing circuit and his progress as a National Hunt jockey has been meteoric. He ended up with 221 pony-race winners – a record. His talents were spotted early, and he rode in his first race when only nine years old. His main rides came from Jerry Daly in Co Kerry and the Finnerty brothers who lived near Roscommon. Dawn Dancer, owned and trained by a family friend, Tom Baker from Dingle, was his first ever winner.

After the initial excitement of seeing his son win a race, Jack's father, a welder, purchased his own racing pony and transported it in his trailer to the races for his son to ride. In no time at all, there were nine ponies at the Kennedy home. Jack's career snowballed, and at the same time Oisin Murphy and Connor King were having plenty of successes on the pony racing circuit. Jack rode ponies all over the country: 'I went everywhere. One day at Newmarket in Co Cork I had fifteen rides and five winners. The race meeting put on twenty-two pony races that day due to all the divides.'

Jack, who was born in April 1999, is the youngest of four sons. His brother Michael trains and brings on young horses at Innishannon in Co Cork and his eldest brother Paddy, who also rode in pony races, is another proficient National Hunt jockey. He finished second in the 2019 Grand National on Magic Of Light. Paddy owns a 60-acre farm in Kildangan, close to Monasterevin in Co Kildare, and gives his younger brother plenty of support. Jack was always keen to ride, and had a pony of his own when he was only four years old. Buddy was 12 hands high and became his teacher. The child attended school under sufferance. He did little or no homework and instead rode ponies on as many evenings as he was able.

Jack's tremendous run in pony races came to an end when he was 15 and it was then he went to Flat-race trainer Tommy Stack. He stayed for six months and was granted a professional licence. He greatly enjoyed riding work on the well-bred Flat horses, but his weight increased and he soon yearned to ride jumpers. Jack had learned about jumping when his brothers had driven him down to Eugene O'Sullivan's yard near Lombardstown in Co Cork. He had also spent some time during his school holidays with Gordon Elliott, and in 2015 he moved to Gordon's stable at Cullentra for a full-time job.

Since working in Co Meath, Jack has not looked back, despite having spent a few months on the sidelines with two leg fractures. Gordon has proudly watched the young superstar rise up the ranks and has given him a number of enviable opportunities in top races. 'He seems to be one of those riders who come along once in a long time,' observed Enda Bolger. Despite being 5ft 9in in height he is very light for a jump jockey, and it is testament to his ability and quiet riding style that from the age of 17 he was given the rides on class horses – Apple's Jade and Samcro being two of his favourites.

However, it is endearing that the child prodigy remains modest despite his successes. Jack speaks well in his interviews and is sharp on form, but never forgets his roots and constantly thanks his parents for having driven him to so many pony-race meetings in his childhood. He undoubtedly showed natural talent from an early age, but like many jockeys is fortunate to have had the backing of his family. It is unusual for a jockey to have had such a single-minded determination to race-ride, right from the days when he started riding ponies. Jack has already had winners at all the major National Hunt festivals, in England and Ireland, and he is championship material for future years. His style is easy to pick out in a race. Above all, after all his experience on the pony-race circuit, he is a tactical rider and an exceptional judge of pace.

Graham Lee

Graham Lee is a leading Flat jockey, and in 2014 was third in the championship table. In 2015 he won the prestigious Ascot Gold Cup on Trip To Paris, and in 2018 was successful in the Nunthorpe Stakes at York on Alpha Delphini, but he started his race-riding career as a National Hunt jockey.

Graham is the eldest of four boys, all of whom were cared for and brought up close to Galway City in Ireland by his 'superstar' mother Mary, a hard-working woman who as well as dealing with her children was employed in the offices of two major companies. Neither of Graham's parents had any interest in horses, and out of the four boys he was the only one who wanted to ride, even though his younger brother, Malcolm, worked in racing later in life. It was football they followed, not horseracing. His grandfather had played for Kilmarnock and been capped for his national team.

Graham grew up close to Galway racecourse and was always fascinated to hear the thundering hooves and the shouting from the track, especially during the August festival. He would climb up onto the hill that looked over the last two fences, and from there he could see most of the racing. He soon discovered that Michael McDonagh, who had trained I'm Confident to win the Galway Hurdle in 1989, owned some riding stables nearby, and he went there on Sunday mornings to have riding lessons. This was when he first sat on a pony, and from the very beginning he wanted to be a jockey.

When he was 15 he went to the racing stables of PJ Finn on the Curragh – it is a good yard and Seamie Heffernan was there at that time – but he was hopelessly homesick and returned to Galway a week later. After this inauspicious start into racing his fortunes looked up, and for the next two years he spent his school holidays with Mouse Morris at Everardsgrange near Fethard in Co Tipperary. Set in the most scenic part of Ireland, it is a yard with a good feeling to it, and Graham was happy there. He rode the racehorses on a daily basis.

Graham's first proper job was with Noel Meade at Castletown, and he stayed there for a couple of years, having his first ride in January 1992 in a novice hurdle at Naas. It was one of five rides that he had for his boss.

❛ I was a rubbish rider, and it is surprising that I was given any opportunities. The only schooling that I did was with Noel but I had barely jumped anything when I first ventured onto a racecourse. I had no idea how to be a jockey or how to race-ride, even though I had ridden in a few pony races and won a couple of them. ❜

From Noel Meade the jockey moved to Dessie McDonogh's, also in Co Meath, the trainer who had famously produced Monksfield to win two Champion Hurdles. In November 1992 Graham won his first race, on Blushing Pearl at Navan in a handicap hurdle.

❛ I rode two winners for Dessie and stayed with him until the end of 1992, but I knew basically that people thought I was useless, so when Ger Lyons got me a job with Mary Reveley in England, I remember telling the trainer that I was off to try my luck across the water. ❜

The young jockey's fortunes changed dramatically when he went to Yorkshire, and he spent nearly six years working for the Reveley family. It was an efficiently run yard, and the trainer was a true horse person with amazing knowledge. Her stable management was superb. Graham was given plenty of rides and he rode many winners – he even rode the stable star Cab On Target to win a hurdle race at Sandown. After Mary Reveley's, he moved to Malcolm Jefferson and was stable jockey there for several years.

When Graham started getting winners in the north of England he was noticed by the top trainers and offered a selection of outside rides. He hit the heights in the first ten years of the century and, although mostly riding freelance, was approached in 2002 by Howard Johnson to be his stable jockey and ride for Graham Wylie. He stayed at White Lea Farm in County Durham for a couple of years, during which time he rode class horses, notably Inglis Drever, on whom he took the World Hurdle at Cheltenham in 2005, as well as No Refuge, Arcalis and Grey Abbey. On the latter he was successful in the 2004 Scottish National, having a few weeks earlier won the Grand National for Ginger McCain on Amberleigh House.

Graham rode his 1,000th career winner on January 7, 2012, but he was starting to find that the opportunities in National Hunt racing for riding top horses were on the decline. Over the years, as well as registering some major successes – including many for popular trainer Ferdy Murphy on the likes of Kalahari King, L'Antartique and Divers – he had also experienced a number of bad falls and broken many bones. He was finding the months of convalescing increasingly more frustrating. Worried about the loss of income during the weeks on the sidelines, he often thought about going back to riding on the Flat, especially since he was a light weight and finally, in April 2012, whilst lying in Nottingham hospital with a dislocated hip, he announced to his agent Richard Hale: 'I'm going to be a Flat jockey,' and from that day he turned his attentions to a different code. For years AP McCoy had been telling him, 'If I was your size I'd be a Flat jockey.'

However, despite being successful in his switch to the Flat, Graham found the weighing-room atmosphere extremely different to the one he had been accustomed to on the National Hunt circuit.

When I first became a jump jockey I was sharing the weighing room with the likes of AP McCoy, Jamie Osborne, Richard Dunwoody, Adrian Maguire and Norman Williamson – they were my heroes and I was living the dream. There was plenty of craic and I loved it, but when I went over to the Flat I realised that Flat racing is a business. The horses are not expected to last like they are in National Hunt racing. Flat racing is commercial and closely linked to breeding. The horses have shorter racing careers and are either retired to stud or sold. The summer is one mad rush – racing, racing and racing. Day meetings and night meetings – we are always on the road, and there is little time for close camaraderie in the weighing room. It is a job, and it can take a while for Flat jockeys to understand and accept fellow riders from a different code. **'**

Graham has always been a highly sensitive person and a deep thinker – even as a child he spent many hours weighing up his path to a career in racing. His life is never stress-free, although this does not come across to those who do not know him. In 2016, while still doing well as a Flat jockey, he started taking the associated downs too much to heart. Perhaps he did not have race-riding in the correct perspective and, despite having the perfect home life with his wife, Becky, and two children, he gave his career priority over everything else in his life. He got himself into such a state that he could not see beyond the racecourse, and when everything got on top of him his anxiety became unbearable.

That summer the jockey was diagnosed to be suffering from depression, something his beloved mother considered to have been dormant in him for many years. In 2016, it was triggered and produced a recognisable illness. Fortunately, Graham agreed to counselling and talked to the right people. With depression it is essential not to keep anxieties bottled up – sufferers must open up and discuss their problems. Nor can depression be put right unless the sufferer recognises the gravity of the illness and the importance of communication. A strong shoulder to lean upon is invaluable.

At the top level in sport there is always pressure, and those taking part are constantly driving themselves to achieve goals. Life can be tough and lonely. The highs go hand in hand with contrasting lows, and sometimes it is difficult for individuals to come to terms with the bad days.

After months on the sidelines, Graham came through his depression and resumed his career as a jockey, but with a different outlook on life. He is now enjoying his job and riding well: 'I am now giving it a hundred and ten per cent.' At last he is relaxed and happy again, but his mind is just as sharp.

When Graham rode horses from my yard I always enjoyed talking to him, and we had many pleasing results, including winning the Warwick Classic Chase and the Peterborough Chase. He was both consistent and reliable, and I never had to give him any instructions – good jockeys don't need to be told how to ride. We had a mutual understanding in the paddock and his words were always the same: 'Let's keep it simple.' He is an exceptional man and an inspiration to young riders. May he have many more successful years in the saddle.

Carl Llewellyn

In the public phone box in Lambourn Carl Llewellyn was inserting numerous two-pence pieces into the coin box. He was trying to ring the Wiltshire trainer, Jim Old, about going to work for him having been advised to do so by Hywel Davies, a fellow Welshman who was regularly riding National Hunt winners at the time. There were no mobile phones in the 1980s but Carl persevered with the red phone box and he got the job. He then remembers travelling down the M4 on his moped to meet his new employer. Yet he was soon pulled over and stopped by the police, who promptly told him never again to ride it on a motorway. He thus took a different route to Jim Old's, via the back roads and lanes.

Carl Llewellyn is the prototype of a jockey rising to fame from ordinary beginnings without being spoilt by his parents. As a child he was never afraid of hard graft and he later stamped himself as a rider of true worth. He was always a trier and made his own life, pushing himself to the limit in order to reach his goals, firstly as a National Hunt jockey and then as a licensed trainer. Nowadays he is a valued assistant to Nigel Twiston-Davies.

Carl's father is a farmer in Pembrokeshire, and there were always horses and ponies around the farm. Riding came naturally to the young lad, even though he did not sit on a pony until he was nearly ten. He quickly got the taste for the excitements of hunting, which he regularly did on Saturdays with the South Pembrokeshire Hunt, and in the summer months he competed at the local pony shows. He particularly enjoyed show-jumping. His only regret being that he did not ride his ponies bareback, even though his father often rode his own horses without saddles. Nowadays, Carl would advise all children to ride without stirrups. It is a great way of developing natural balance and grip. Nobody taught Carl to ride when he was a child: he taught himself, and he learned by his mistakes – when he did things the wrong way he fell off. He had plenty of competition because his elder brother, who later trained point-to-point horses, also rode ponies, and his younger sister was a highly proficient winner in the show ring.

Carl did not enjoy school and was always longing to leave, which he did as soon as he was 15. 'I left on the Wednesday and did not wait to be picked up – I thumbed my way home, and by the Sunday I was in Lambourn at Stan Mellor's yard.' For some years he had set his sights on being a jockey and, not being someone to sit back and leave it to others, he knew from that day he left school that if he wanted to succeed it would be important to go to the best trainers. Thus, he wrote letters to the top men – to Stan Mellor as well as four others: Josh Gifford, Fred Rimell, Fulke Walwyn and Fred Winter. However, they had no vacancies, yet Stan was happy to take him straight away.

Carl learned plenty during his spell in Berkshire, and found his chosen trainer an excellent teacher, but he did not start riding under rules until the 1980s, despite successfully partnering some point-to-point winners in Wales trained by his father and by Peter Bowen. In only his second year of point-to-pointing he was novice point-to-point champion with five winners. However, the competition has since become far stronger since Carl's days, and to become a champion today the riders need many more wins – when James Bowen was novice champion in 2017 he had 30 winners to his name.

Carl only managed to ride seven point-to-point winners during his years between the flags but his landmark first victory under rules was in 1986, when at 21 he rode Stargetic to win a novice handicap chase at Wolverhampton for Roy Robins.

After spending 15 months with Stan Mellor, which coincided with the days of those good horses Royal Mail and Pollardstown, Carl made his famous switch to Jim Old's yard due to Stan concentrating more on Flat horses. Carl spent five years with Jim, but still only managed to get 80 rides.

Carl's next move was to join Captain Tim Forster in Letcombe Bassett near Wantage. This was again on the prompting of Hywel Davies. He started off as a stable lad, but then rode winners for the Captain and at the end of the 1987-88 season he was the leading conditional jockey. Unfortunately, when he was promoted to first jockey, he had a bad fall and broke his elbow and his leg, both of which took a long time to mend. These injuries lost him his job, and when he was mended he needed to look further afield for another vacancy.

As luck would have it, Nigel Twiston-Davies, whom Carl had met at a barbecue and for whom Peter Scudamore was riding as number-one jockey, invited the champion conditional to ride out at his yard at Grange Hill Farm near Naunton. He was quickly given the job as second jockey to Scu but when the latter began riding more and more for Martin Pipe, the younger rider's career took off because Peter then accepted the offer to be Pipe's number one. The Welshman got instant promotion and became Nigel's first jockey.

The two men had a fine innings together and Carl stayed with that trainer for 19 years, during which time he partnered many famous horses to victory in prestigious races. He had seven wins at the Cheltenham Festival and two in the Grand National, one for Nigel – Earth Summit in 1998 – as well as Party Politics for Nick Gaselee in 1992. He rates Tipping Tim as the best horse he ever rode, and he won the Mackeson Gold Cup on him in 1992. In total, Carl Llewellyn rode 995 winners under National Hunt rules.

Although Carl maintains that he rarely had any proper lessons with his riding, he remembers, as a child, watching the ITV 7 racing programme every Saturday and studying the ways in which jockeys rode. He worked hard to improve himself and always walked the courses before he rode in his races, something that jockeys rarely do these days but which Terry Biddlecombe considered an important part of a jockey's itinerary.

If riders walk the course they can assess the ground and decide upon the best place to jump a fence. Sometimes too, if the underfoot conditions are poached and rough, it is advantageous for jockeys to look for better ground on bends – but unless a course is walked an accurate assessment cannot be made. Nowadays, they rely too much on watching races on the television.

Carl Llewellyn considers that today jockeys have become lazier and less dedicated. They are too reliant on modern technology and they are spoilt by mobile phones, agents and the internet. Too many riders in the 21st century call themselves jockeys but the actual riding of horses is secondary to them: 'They are not prepared to put in the work to fully understand the horsemanship side of being a jockey. They thrive on personal appearances and some would be happy to get beaten as long as their style looks good to viewers.' Maybe that's why there are fewer good young jockeys coming through the ranks compared with 20 years ago.

An excellent mixer, sharp and with a good sense of humour, Carl is extremely knowledgeable about racing and he is a much-respected registered jockey coach having helped a number of young riders. When he takes somebody under his wing he asks them a simple question: 'Do you want to ride horses, or are you only interested in being a jockey?'

Blessed with a light frame, which meant he never had to diet, and inborn natural ability, Carl always looked stylish on a horse. He had sympathetic hands and appeared to have a good eye for a fence. He communicated well with the horses he rode, and they responded to his drive. These attributes, coupled with his steel nerve and his ability to read a race, served him well during his years as a jockey. If he had not been plagued by injuries he would undoubtedly have ridden many more winners and easily surpassed the 1,000 mark.

Adrian Maguire

Adrian Maguire deserved to win a National Hunt jockeys' championship. In the 1993-94 season he rode 194 winners, but lost by a margin of three to Richard Dunwoody. Altogether he won 1,024 races in Britain, and had he not been forced to retire from race-riding in October 2002 at the age of 31 following a fall at Warwick, in which he broke his neck and was fortunate to escape paralysis, he would surely have won many more. In the opinion of Yogi Breisner, the renowned Swedish riding coach, Adrian possessed the best eye for a fence of anybody he has ever taught. His judgement for a stride was exceptional.

Adrian always wanted to ride, but had no real horse connections: his father was a greenkeeper on the Royal Tara golf course in Co Meath, and his mother was a nurse in Trim. Yet he remembers watching racing on television with his youngest brother, Finny, when he was barely six. His elder brother Michael, Jason Maguire's father, also became a jockey, but was 13 years older than Adrian. When he retired from race-riding he began to give his younger brother riding lessons on his ponies. Adrian's best memory is being put onto an unbroken 13.2hh Connemara pony with which he formed a special bond. The child always rode without a saddle – it was the best way to learn.

Michael Maguire bought and sold a number of ponies, and had a good understanding with the famous Irish horse dealer Ned Cash. Adrian would regularly ride these ponies in local gymkhanas in Co Meath, and remembers hacking to shows through towns, since at that time his family had no horse transport. He loved educating the ponies, which were then sold on, and he did plenty of show-jumping. Hunting with the Tara Harriers, the Ward Union Hunt and the Meath Hunt taught him a huge amount about balance and the importance of not interfering with horses' mouths when jumping obstacles. Adrian always had superb hands as a jockey, and always sat naturally on the horses he rode.

At the age of nine, the budding jockey began pony racing. He was extremely light and at times needed special weighted saddles. Peter Fahey from Galway had a famous racing pony called Salmon Leap – the same pony that Mark Dwyer was also fortunate to ride – and Adrian loved riding it. The pony races made his adrenalin flow, his results were good and it was then that the vision of one day being a licensed jockey really crystallised. His brothers Michael and Seamus would take him all over the country to ride in races, and soon, due to being a small, neat and astute rider with plenty of victories to his name, he was in great demand as a jockey for the top ponies. The courses varied enormously and so did the ponies he rode. Yet over and over again Irish pony racing has proved to be one of the best springboards for aspiring jockeys. Many top names have come through the pony racing ranks.

The Irish pony races differ a great deal from those seen in Britain. They are much rougher and are run on widely varying terrains. The Irish children become amazingly streetwise and sharp. Their reactions are quick in adverse situations. They practise on many different animals and learn to negotiate a lot of different gradients. Some of the tracks are unkempt, with sharp bends and difficult cambers. At any one meeting a good pony-race rider could have six or seven rides in a day. More often than not he or she would never even have sat on any of the ponies beforehand. No mollycoddling of the children: the races are highly competitive, with fierce betting. As Adrian says, 'One quickly learns how to get a position in a race, and provided one is sharp-witted and wide awake one can see what is going to happen before it does.' In any sport, thinking ahead is of vital importance. The children riding in pony races learn how to get good starts and keep an eye on those around them when assembling behind the starting tapes. Adrian did seven years of pony racing in Ireland and won more than 200 races. He remembers riding his 12.2hh ponies at weights under 6st. He had a special little red saddle, which he still treasures today.

As Adrian progressed from pony racing he began riding

racehorses at weekends for Joanna Morgan, and it was through her that he went to work for the shrewd trainer Michael Hourigan in Co Limerick. The living conditions associated with the establishment were far removed from what Adrian had been used to at home, but his years with Michael were good ones. His first winner was Gladtogetit at Sligo in 1990, and he had plenty more successes as an amateur, including riding Omerta to win the Kim Muir at the 1991 Cheltenham Festival, on his first ride in England, followed by the Irish Grand National on the same horse less than three weeks later. Adrian also spent three seasons in point-to-points and rode 38 winners. He was overall champion in his third year.

Adrian was a natural as a jockey and after his time as an amateur he turned professional in the 1991-92 season. He moved to England as a conditional jockey in Toby Balding's yard. It was from there that he won the 1992 Cheltenham Gold Cup on Cool Ground. Afterwards he was had up by the stewards for excessive use of the whip, but Toby Balding was a brilliant trainer who fully understood the sport. He accompanied him to the hearing and far from berating his star jockey, he praised him and told the stewards that 'if he'd missed the horse once with the whip he wouldn't have won'. Adrian was not known as a 'whip' jockey, but in a race like the Gold Cup to win at all costs has to be in a jockey's mind. Champion jockey Richard Johnson won on Native River in 2018, and afterwards he too was harshly treated by the stewards for excessive use of his whip. Sometimes, one wonders how much the offiicials really understand about race-riding.

Adrian could never have been so successful without his chief mentors, Hourigan and Balding. They believed in him and gave him great opportunities, as did David Nicholson when he moved to Jackdaws Castle in the Cotswolds. In his days with 'The Duke' he won two Scottish Grand Nationals, on Baronet (1998) and Paris Pike (2000), the Queen Mother Champion Chase in 1994 on Viking Flagship, and the King George VI Chase on Barton Bank for David Nicholson and then again on Florida Pearl for Willie

Mullins. In 1998 he won the Whitbread Gold Cup at Sandown on Call It A Day.

Having to retire from race-riding in 2002 came as a severe blow to Adrian Maguire, but for a while he successfully took up training from his home in Co Cork. On relinquishing that licence in 2017 he was taken on by Aidan O'Brien at Ballydoyle as a work-rider, which demonstrates the high opinion the champion Flat trainer has of him as a horseman. It is great to see the ex-jockey continuing to contribute to racing, and once again demonstrate his fine riding skills on top horses, whilst his son, Finian, is riding plenty of winners on the track as an amateur and keeping the Maguire name in the headlines.

Sir Anthony McCoy OBE

Anthony Peter (AP) McCoy's contribution to National Hunt racing cannot be over-emphasised. He has done an unbelievable amount for the sport that has taken over the major part of his life, and all from a predominantly non-horse background. His formative years were punctuated by a series of important landmarks, all of which put him in the right place at the right time, and his career was a succession of phenomenal achievements. To have been champion jockey for 20 consecutive years from 1995, and to have won virtually every big race in the jump racing calendar, from the Grand National to the Cheltenham Gold Cup, is an unprecedented record, and one unlikely ever to be equalled. Even before he retired in 2015, AP had been awarded an MBE, and in 2010 he was voted BBC Sports Personality of the Year. In 2016 he was knighted in the New Year's Honours List for his services to horseracing, and all this from the shy child who disliked interacting with people.

The pathway to becoming the confident, well-spoken man of the world who exhibited an amazing career was an unusual one, but fortunately the jockey's natural ability was channelled in the right direction. AP was born in Co Antrim, Northern Ireland on May 4, 1974, and he grew up in the little village of Moneyglass, where his father Peadar, who has been a significant help to his son all the way along the line, was a carpenter but 'could turn his hand to almost anything'. He always liked horses and followed racing. The champ's mother, Claire, who died in December 2017, was a special lady with a wonderful sense of humour and always one to speak her mind.

Claire had six children, yet managed her day-to-day life with efficiency and cheerfulness. She even ran a small shop close to the bungalow that Peadar had built as their family home. However, she endured many days of anger and frustration when her eldest son continually refused to attend school in Randalstown, and her dealings with the attendance officers became regular occurrences –

'Wee Anthony did everything that he could to avoid sitting at his desk in the classroom.' He didn't find his lessons difficult and was, from all accounts, a quiet unassuming pupil, but he could not see the point of books and a blackboard when there were better attractions outdoors. He was undoubtedly stubborn and single-minded from an early age.

Co Antrim is not a renowned horse county, but in 1970 Peadar McCoy, with his passion for horses, had bought a mare named Fire Forest. She was related to the Grand National winner Kilmore, who, ridden by Fred Winter, had been successful in the race in 1962. Fire Forest was in foal to Steeple Aston, and when trainer Billy Rock heard about the purchase he arranged to meet Peadar and they struck up an immediate friendship, which was to last until Billy died in 2003. This chance liaison was the springboard for AP's involvement in racing.

If Dad wanted me to take an interest in horses he never told me so, and he never pushed me, but I was in contact with them from an early age. Indeed, there is a photograph of me sitting on Misclaire, the daughter of Fire Forest, when I was barely three years old. I was perched on her bare back and I was holding on to her mane with little spindly legs dangling down her sides.

Every Easter, when AP was small, his father would take him to the annual horsefair in Toomebridge, where the gypsy folk would buy and sell their horses and ponies. Horse fairs in Ireland, both in the north and the south, were renowned trading days, and Peadar's little boy loved the atmosphere and seeing all the different animals. At eight, 'Wee Anthony' was taken to the local riding school run by Mrs Kyle for lessons, and he soon realised how much he enjoyed his connection to ponies. He began asking for a pony of his own and, when he was nine, Peadar bought him one.

She was a horrible pony with a high proportion of thoroughbred blood in her. She was attractive but wild, and had never been ridden. Once she was broken in and I started to ride her, all she wanted to do was bury me into the ground. Dad thought she would get better and calmer with work, but she got worse. I had endless falls, but surprisingly was not put off. We called her Seven Up, because that was about the number of times she would drop me every day that I rode her. **9**

Fortunately, this unrideable pony got sold, and was replaced by Chippy, a 13.2hh strawberry roan who was amenable, fast and a great jumper. The pony did plenty to help AP with his early riding. Such was the child's determination to make a go of his new-found passion that he found some poles, painted them black and white, and built a show-jumping course on a grassy patch of ground between two busy roads in front of his house. He spent many evenings after school – on the days he attended – going round his course and trying to beat the times he had clocked up the day before.

This marks the beginning of his love for jumping fences at speed. He went to a number of local pony shows and won many classes, but decided, after a while, that a show-jumping career was not for him: there was too much hanging around and waiting your turn to jump. AP was impatient even then. He always wanted more excitement and the adrenalin rush. He was not prepared to waste time when he could be doing better things – the same applied to his infrequent days in school.

It was during the years when AP was jumping Chippy in shows that Peadar used to visit Billy Rock's yard on Saturday mornings. He began taking his son with him, and once the future champion started watching the racehorses it was as if a fire had been lit, his mind set alight by the thought of riding them himself. He would watch racing on television whenever he could, monopolising two of the four TV channels every Saturday. He persuaded his mother to buy him the *Pacemaker* magazine every week – in those days £2 was a lot of money – but at least it gave him something to read. The young Anthony McCoy also enjoyed football and was an Arsenal supporter right from the start. His interest in snooker sprang largely from Belfast-born Alex Higgins winning the World Snooker Championship in 1982, and the 'Hurricane' became one of AP's heroes. But as he grew up it was horseracing that truly got into his veins, and took over from all other sports.

Billy Rock, who had spent time with Mick O'Toole on the Curragh and ridden in point-to-points, became like a second father to AP. He took the racing-mad child under his wing, and the young lad experienced all his early riding on racehorses on the Billy Rock gallops. His mentor believed implicitly in the child's natural ability, and the likelihood of him one day becoming a top jockey. One of the first horses AP rode, when he was 12 years old, was Wood Louse. At the beginning he was allowed to trot him round one of the sheds, but later he would canter him on the gallops. By coincidence, he led up the very same horse when it won a race at Down Royal under Conor O'Dwyer in 1989. Now that racehorses had come into Anthony's life, his ponies were instantly forgotten and Chippy was found a new home.

Billy Rock's racing stables in Cullybackey were about 11 miles from Moneyglass, but the distance did not deter the young McCoy. He would get a lift with a local butcher who had to pass by his door every morning, but when this convenient mode of transport ceased he persuaded Peadar to buy him an old racing bike and he cycled to work.

❝ Even if the yard had been a hundred and eleven miles away I would still have got there on my bike. They were great days. I was paid £100 per week, which was huge money for a fourteen-year-old, but I did not have anything to spend it on as I did not go to discos or pubs. I saved up my wages and I was well off, even though there were times when I had to lend money to my elder sisters, who were mad about going out and were always broke. But I made sure they always knew they were loans, not gifts, and I used to keep track of all that they owed me in a special ledger. For once the maths that I had practised at school proved useful. ❞

AP rode a number of different horses at Billy Rock's, and often the difficult ones. Billy was a sound trainer and had winners on the big tracks with horses such as Eddie Wee and Helynsar, but he did not give his young jockeys an easy time.

❝ I had a million falls. The lads used to laugh their heads off at me trying to stay on some of the mad fresh animals that Billy told me to ride. He would just chuck me up onto some yak to see how I'd get on. I would get buried regularly, but I used to dread telling him about some of the horses because, however bad they were to ride, it was a challenge, and staying on them made me even more determined. If Billy told me to get up on one then I rode it. I was often run away with as well, even though the gallop was circular and on deep sand. The main problem was my weight. I was too light and less than six stone. I tried to make myself heavier on the horses' backs by riding out in big old-fashioned breeches like the ones I'd seen pictures of Richard Dunwoody and John Francome wearing at home. I wore proper jodhpur boots. I just became addicted to the gallops and the speed. ❞

Some years later, in 1995, shortly after AP had won his first National Hunt jockeys' championship in Britain, he remembers being with Conor O'Dwyer and the late Anthony Powell in a Chinese restaurant in Naas, during the Punchestown festival. Conor told the story of how, in the past, he and Anthony, both top jockeys, had ridden horses for Billy Rock in races, yet many of them had been wayward and had no steering. Joey Kelly and Dr Jekyll were two unrideable examples. They were crazy and had no mouths. On one occasion the former had virtually run off the track. The jockeys told Billy his horses were dangerous and that they no longer wanted to ride them, but all he said in reply was, 'Well, Wee Anthony rides them every day, and Wee Anthony never complains.' Little did they know, back then, that he was referring to the star young rider, Anthony McCoy. 'Billy obviously saw something in me, a talent for riding, from an early stage. He was convinced I was going to make it as a jockey. He never doubted me.'

In August 1989, AP left school – even though it was two weeks into the new term. Billy had told him he'd be far better off riding horses. Claire was not happy about her eldest son shelving his studies for a career in racing, but Billy was an astute man, and his other occupation was working for the Department of Agriculture importing semen for cattle from the Netherlands and Canada for the artificial insemination of cows. If her son's planned career as a jockey failed, he told Claire that he had taught the boy how to do the AI and in the future he could easily make a living 'bulling cows'. . . In the young lad's mind, however, there was never any doubt that he would make his name by riding in races.

After these formative years with Billy Rock, AP's mentor advised him to move down to Co Kilkenny to join Jim Bolger – he had already been there on a two-week trial. 'He would strike the fear of God into many of his lads, and they would scarper if they saw him coming down to the yard,' he remembers.

Thus in April 1990, 'I left Punchestown races and went down to Coolcullen in the horsebox with Tom Gallagher – Dean's father – who was the travelling head lad. I was desperately homesick and used to cry myself to sleep at nights, but on principle I did not dare return home even though I missed my parents.' Billy had decided to send his protégé to Bolger, whose quiet yard is hidden amid lanes and hills, rather than to the Curragh, because he reasoned that it was in the middle of nowhere and the young boy would be unlikely to get into trouble.

Jim is famously responsible for having made numerous top jockeys – Christy Roche, Willie Supple, Aidan O'Brien, Seamie Heffernan, Ted Durcan and Paul Carberry all had attachments to the yard in the years AP was there. David Wachman was also part of the team and as the new boy arrived Kevin Manning was just leaving. 'Anthony was tall and very slight,' Aidan remembers, 'but an unbelievable rider for his age. It was the way he sat and the balance that he had. He was very quiet and mannerly. For a young fellow, he was unbelievably dedicated, committed and very focused. He had a lot of wisdom for his years.' Seamie Heffernan recalls that 'McCoy impressed everyone at the yard, because he was always stylish and very determined. He was a natural rider.'

During his four years at Coolcullen, AP rode his first ever winner in March 1992, when Legal Steps won a maiden race at Thurles. The horse carried 8st 1lb. He had nine winners as an apprentice, but after badly breaking his leg on the gallops in January 1991 he gained weight whilst convalescing, and it was obvious that it would always be a struggle for him to be light enough for top Flat honours. He would have to turn his attentions to National Hunt, even though Jim Bolger had declared, having seen him crying in pain after his fall on the gallops, that he would never be tough enough to make a jump jockey. The truth was that Jim did not want to lose him because he had been riding many of the top horses, including Jet Ski Lady, the 1991 Oaks winner, and St Jovite, who won the 1992 Irish Derby and the King George VI and Queen Elizabeth Stakes at Ascot.

In 1994 the future champion was getting some rides and winners over hurdles, and in the July of that year the English trainer Toby Balding, who had already put Adrian Maguire on the map, saw the young Northern Irish jockey in a hurdle race at Wexford. He finished second that day on Havin' A Ball, but Toby was happy with what he saw and invited him over to England. This marked the turning point in the jockey's career, and shortly afterwards he moved from Ireland to spend two years at the Balding establishment at Fyfield near Andover. With Dave Roberts as his new-found agent the winners flowed, and at the end of the 1994-95 National Hunt season he was crowned champion conditional. From the 1995-96 season onwards he was the champion jockey for 20 consecutive years. In 1997 AP moved to Martin Pipe's, and the pair dominated the sport for the next six years, before Anthony was signed up in 2004 by the leading owner JP McManus to ride in the famous green and gold colours. He based himself with Jonjo O'Neill at Jackdaws Castle in the Cotswolds.

AP maintains that he mostly taught himself as a rider by watching and copying others.

> At Billy's, I would go round on a horse on a sunny day and look at my reflection in a car or shop window. I would check to make sure I was looking good. I don't know why but I always believed, even as a child, that I could ride and fortunately Billy was of the same opinion. He used to call me the next John Francome. When I was at Jim Bolger's my Flat-race hero was Mick Kinane – the most perfect jockey I have ever seen – and I also admired Steve Cauthen.

When he was at Jim Bolger's yard AP remembers the boss saying, 'You might not be able to ride in a race like a jockey, but at least you should try to look like one at home.' Over the jumps, AP was a huge fan of Richard Dunwoody, and he also loved watching Conor O'Dwyer.

> I thought Conor was a brilliant rider. He always gave his horse a ride, but if it wasn't the horse's day he did not subject it to a hard race. He did not beat a horse up to finish fifth or sixth when he could give it an easy time and finish seventh or eighth – just to keep him for another day.

How many stewards would allow this under current rules? Sadly, too many are uneducated with regard to the training of horses, and do not understand that horses can have off days. In the present climate it is all about finishing in the best possible position, which leads to jockeys unnecessarily pressurising their mounts, which is completely wrong, and at times can ruin a horse for life, especially when jockeys resort to their whips on a tired animal.

AP McCoy's years as a jump jockey, finishing with a total of 4,359 winners, are justly famous. With the backing of Dave Roberts, he reached heights that were hitherto unheard of, and what he achieved was phenomenal. Yet his style was unique, and no present-day jockey should try to copy it. His determination and obsession with riding winners set him apart from all of his contemporaries. At times he experienced excruciating mental anguish in pursuit of his ambitions, but he never let it get the better of him. He was hard on himself and suffered numerous injuries, but would still travel to any racecourse, however remote, if there was the likelihood of a winner. AP had complete tunnel vision. Every part of his body was pushed to the limit, and he consistently gave the horses he partnered powerful rides, never taking no for an answer if there was a race to be won; as well, he could accurately assess their ability. His feedback to owners and trainers was spot-on.

In retirement AP still spends a large part of his time working in the racing industry. He constantly watches the riding styles of today's jockeys and questions how they have come up through the ranks to ride in National Hunt races. He rues the limited backgrounds that many of them have: indeed, a number of them have had minimal jumping practice before taking to the racecourse. He believes insufficient riding experience as children is why standards have fallen among the younger generation of jockeys. Admittedly AP himself did not do a great deal of schooling over hurdles or fences before joining Toby Balding – indeed, on his first ride in a chase at Galway for Paddy Graffin in 1994 he had never previously jumped a steeplechase fence – but his childhood show-jumping days were invaluable.

Nowadays, says AP, many National Hunt jockeys ride too short and lack natural balance. At Jim Bolger's all the lads had to ride with a proper length of leg before they went onto the gallops, and the boss insisted that the horses were walked and trotted on the bridle with their heads held in the right place. Many of today's riders have no idea how to get a horse to carry itself correctly in its slow paces.

I have huge respect for Jim Bolger. The time I spent at Coolcullen was the making of me. I learned so much, not just about horses and about riding but about people and about life. I didn't fully realise it back then, but as time has gone on, the more I have come to appreciate the years that I spent with that trainer.

AP has also been backed throughout his life by his family, and during his riding days by his loyal wife Chanelle. Their two children Eve and Archie appear to have inherited many of AP's competitive genes, and show unlimited energy in their own sporting activities. Eve already enjoys show-jumping and fearlessly rides her ponies at speed, just as her father rode Chippy, while Archie is incredibly athletic and has the perfect build for a jockey. AP was tough and ruthless when riding, but beneath that hard exterior he is an extremely sensitive man who adores his family. There will be no lack of support when his children set out on their own careers. Loyalty is everything in life, and where would AP have been without it? It is something he learned to appreciate from an early age, and has carried it with him throughout his career.

With his dry sense of humour and razor-sharp brain, 'Wee Anthony' deserves all the accolades he has received. He has taken National Hunt racing to a new level, and there will never again be a jump jockey of his calibre.

Jody McGarvey

At 16 Jody McGarvey had never ridden a racehorse but he still remembers the excitement of buying his breeches, boots and skull cap – the compulsory racing kit – when he set off to the south of Ireland for the Racing Academy and Centre of Education, RACE, in Kildare. He embarked upon a career in his favourite sport.

Jody is a fine example of a National Hunt jockey who comes from a family without any equine connections. His father drives lorries, but he was always interested in racing, and as a child it was always racing that Jody loved watching on television. The local riding stables were conveniently close to his birth town of Coleraine, Co Derry, and after a series of lessons Jody used to compete in shows on their 13.2hh and 14.2hh ponies. He also spent days out hunting with the Route hunt. The nearby yard had a number of good jumping ponies and show-jumping was its trademark. Jody was always a small, light child. He was ideal for the ponies and received plenty of help and praise.

Jody had a great time at the racing school before being allocated a place in Christy Roche's yard on the Curragh. He was fortunate to have been sent to such a renowned trainer, and one who had been a distinguished jockey as well. He obtained his conditional jockeys' licence and was given more than 100 rides. His first winner, Code Of The West, was for JP McManus in 2009 in a handicap chase at Down Royal. It was a significant win and led to a number of rides for the leading owner. When riding in the green and gold colours, Jody received support and help from Frank Berry, who is in charge of JP's jumping string.

By the time that Jody was 19, Christy was winding down his training operation, and it was suggested that a move to England would give him more race-riding opportunities. Thus, he spent a year with Evan Williams, but he did not settle away from Ireland and pined to return to his native land. His time in Wales was then cut short when he broke his leg in a car crash.

Nowadays Jody is freelance and based back at the Curragh. He rides out for many of the top trainers, including Joseph O'Brien, and has ridden some good winners for a number of different yards. He is a neat rider and has a good eye for a fence having spent his early years on show-jumping ponies. He remains at a good weight and can ride at 10st 5lb. With JP McManus giving him plenty of rides, he has a bright future and is a fine example to aspiring young jockeys having started out with no expectations yet worked his way up the ladder.

Jeremiah McGrath

'It was the best grounding I ever had,' says Jeremiah – Jerry – McGrath. He's speaking about a summer he spent at Dermot Weld's yard on the Curragh. Dermot Weld, himself a former top National Hunt jockey, as well as a qualified veterinary surgeon, is one of Ireland's most respected and successful racehorse trainers, and Jerry could not have gone to a more professional man nor a better yard. Not only has Dermot Weld trained British and Irish Derby winners as well as taking two Melbourne Cups, but he has also, as a trainer, won the Irish Grand National and both the Triumph Hurdle and the Irish Champion Hurdle, which shows that his successes have not been confined to Flat racing. It was at Rosewell House that Jerry developed his style in the saddle as well as learning how to relax horses on the gallops. Riding on the Curragh is a great experience for any young racing enthusiast, and Jerry thrived on the months he spent there.

There is no racing background in the McGrath family, but Jerry's father always had show-jumpers and enjoyed hunting, and his son had a pony from the age of four. As a member of the local pony club in Cork he enjoyed hunting with the South Union and Killeady Hounds with his brother Tom. He also took part in all the local pony activities but racing was never the topic of conversation in the McGrath household, even though from the age of 12 Jerry would watch it on television. He never rode in pony races or point-to-points, but when he left his school in Cork he was sent to RACE in Kildare, after which he went to work with Dermot Weld.

After his spell on the Curragh, Jerry returned home to study for his school Leaving Certificate, as agreed with his parents, but he had already become hooked on racing and was allowed to spend his 2007 summer holidays in England. He went to Brendan Powell's yard and was given his first ride on the track when he took part in an amateur riders' handicap at Newbury. The horse was unplaced, but Jerry stayed on in Lambourn for another week and rode Bathwick Quest to win a bumper at Newton Abbot for the same trainer.

Having completed his studies in the summer of 2008, Jerry returned to England. 'I did my last exam on a Wednesday, but was back in the UK by Friday.' He spent the next 12 months at Brendan Powell's yard and rode a few more horses for him in amateur races. 'Brendan is a very good teacher. I was told off a lot and he was strict, but he was extremely helpful, and it was through Brendan that I was introduced to the jockeys' agent Dave Roberts.' Despite a degree of uncertainty as to whether or not he was making the right move – he had filled in forms for university – on Brendan's advice Jerry rode out for Nicky Henderson, who was looking for more young jockeys. His trial days were successful and he then moved to Seven Barrows. He has been there ever since.

Jerry McGrath is undoubtedly one of the backbone riders at Nicky Henderson's powerful yard, and his fine horsemanship has always been highly prized. Not only does he spend a considerable amount of time helping to educate the young horses, but he is also a competent National Hunt jockey who has already won two races at the Cheltenham Festival. In 2012 Une Artiste was successful in the Fred Winter Juvenile Handicap Hurdle, and in 2019 Beware The Bear won the Ultima Handicap Chase, both supremely popular winners.

As a sideline, National Hunt breeding is one of Jerry's prime interests and, with his good knowledge of pedigrees, he should go far in the bloodstock world when his racing days are over. He has an interesting background and a good brain. He has learned his trade from highly respected professionals and has a wide circle of friends.

Paul Moloney

Paul Moloney was born in 1978 at Lagganstown in Co Tipperary. His father was a farmer and did not come from a horse background, yet Ursula Ryan, a near neighbour, had numerous horses and ponies, the majority of which were hunters.

Paul would go down to her yard whenever he could and constantly watched her horses cantering around the fields. He saved up his pocket money and at the age of ten bought his own pony. Any extra pennies would go towards riding lessons, in particular from Gareth Dooley, who ran the riding school at Rockwell College near Cashel. Paul always knew from those childhood days that he wanted to ride in races, and he became obsessed by the idea of being a jockey.

In his early teens Paul used to go to Jim Bolger's famous training yard in Co Carlow and learn to ride the racehorses. At 14 he spent his school holidays at Michael Hourigan's in Co Limerick, and from there got the chance to ride in a handful of pony races – Timmy Murphy, David Casey, Shane Broderick and Kevin O'Brien were all at the Hourigan establishment at the same time. David Wachman was Michael's head lad, and it was a great environment for young jockeys and future trainers. Paul loved every minute of it. Whilst still at school but with an amateur licence, he rode in several bumpers and in 1997 had his first winner, on Vain Princess, at Clonmel racecourse.

At the end of 1997, in order to go a step further up the ladder, it was suggested that Paul contact Christy Roche, who trained on the Curragh and whose career as a jockey had been outstanding. In March 1998 Christy offered Paul a job, but in the meantime David Wachman had moved into his own yard near Clonmel, and Paul went to him to ride in point-to-points, and he also rode horses for Liam Burke. After two seasons he had amassed 20 winners between the flags and was crowned champion novice rider. When he later moved up to the Curragh the winners continued to flow, and he shared the amateur riders' title with Philip Fenton, even though the latter was ten years his senior and had a great deal more experience.

Unfortunately, early in his career with Christy Roche, Paul broke his leg and was prevented from race-riding for a year, but after his recovery he bounced back and kept on as an amateur until the Galway festival, where he won a bumper. It was after this that he turned professional and he stayed at his Curragh base for five and a half years. In one season he rode 48 winners and ended up fourth in the jockeys' championship.

Despite his successes, it was nevertheless difficult for Paul to keep the rides on the top horses when established jockeys with bigger profiles were also attached to Christy's yard. On the advice of Barney Curley and Jamie Spencer, the jockey moved to England and had spells with Ian Williams, Tom George and Ferdy Murphy. He was well regarded in Britain, and many top trainers asked him to ride for them. In 2005 he joined up with Evan Williams and rode a number of the Ruckers' horses including State Of Play, who was victorious in the 2006 Hennessy Gold Cup at Newbury. Paul also had a fine record in the Grand National at Aintree and finished in the first four on seven occasions.

In 2017, Paul had another bad fall and severely damaged the nerves in one of his shoulders. He was 36, and in a 20-year riding career as a National Hunt jockey he had ridden 843 winners. It was then that he decided to call time on race-riding and handed in his licence. He returned to his native Ireland after telling the *Racing Post* that, although he would miss the buzz of riding in races, especially on steeplechasers as well as the thrill of winning, that 'all good things come to an end'. Paul has always had a great way with horses, and despite no longer being a jockey he is still closely connected to the racing world. Like Adrian Maguire, he rides out daily for Aidan O'Brien at Ballydoyle, and has a house with land barely a couple of miles from where he was born. His wife, Louise, works in the hospital in Clonmel and his three children greatly enjoy their daily life back in Ireland.

Paul Moloney was an excellent jockey and was particularly good on young chasers. At West Lockinge Farm, he did much of the early work on Somersby and rode him to win his first chase at Warwick in 2009. He was a quiet rider with good hands and balance. He sat deeply into his horses and encouraged them to jump well. He was also a good judge of pace, and seldom positioned himself in the wrong place in a race. Paul has a strong eye for a horse, and his current breeding operation, which he runs from his home, is sure to be successful: he has the right people behind him and is a fountain of knowledge. Every move that Paul has taken in life has been carefully thought out, and he is unlikely to make any rash decisions with his bloodstock ventures.

Arthur Moore

When I used to visit Ireland in the 1970s to inspect young store horses as prospective purchases for the late Captain Tim Forster, it was Arthur Moore who drove me around the countryside. The days were highly educational and enjoyable, but I was always a nervous passenger, since my guide was somewhat erratic at the wheel. There were times when I felt more like a co-driver in the Monte Carlo rally. However, Arthur has a vast range of experience with racehorses – hurdlers and steeplechasers in particular – and not only does he have a great eye for a horse, but he is also extremely knowledgeable when it comes to assessing pedigrees.

Arthur is the son of the legendary Irish trainer Dan Moore, who had also been an accomplished jockey, and twice won the Irish National on Golden Jack in 1943 and Revelry in 1947. As well as training L'Escargot to win the Cheltenham Gold Cup in 1970 and 1971, Dan produced him to win the Grand National in 1975. Arthur never remembers a time when he was not surrounded by horses and ponies. Originally, his father trained at Fairyhouse, in the fields behind the present-day Tattersalls sales complex, and Arthur, his sister Pamela, who later married the brilliant jockey Tommy Carberry, and brother Jonathan always rode as children.

There is a lovely photograph of Arthur on the wall in his house showing him, mounted on his 11hh pony alongside his parents in front of their house at Fairyhouse. Nobody taught him to ride, he says: he just picked it up from what he saw. He went out hunting, which helped his balance, and rode out on racehorses from an early age at his father's yard. 'I was self-taught: I copied the lads and the jockeys on the gallops.'

After a public-school education at Downside in Britain, Arthur returned to Ireland and from an early age, dreamed of being a jockey. Indeed, in 1965, when only 16, he had his first ride in public in a bumper for his father. Arthur has meticulously kept albums of photographs, newspaper cuttings and race write-ups of all his rides, something few other jockeys have done, and those scrapbooks, which include cuttings from his trainer years, are fascinating. They are an education in themselves as to how racing has progressed over the past 50 years, and would take days to study in depth. Arthur's interest in history is further reflected in the bookshelves in his kitchen and adjacent rooms.

Once he had begun race-riding, the young jockey struck up an excellent relationship with Georgie Wells, who trained King's Sprite, a horse close to Arthur's heart since it gave him his second winner under rules and his first hurdle win against professionals. In 1969 Arthur Moore was the joint champion amateur rider in Ireland, tying with Dermot Weld. In 1971, when he had turned professional, he again partnered King's Sprite, this time to win the Irish Grand National. Other notable wins included the Ulster National for Willie Rooney on Copper Kiln VI, and both the Troytown and Thyestes Chases on the Vulgan-sired Veuve. He rode in four English Grand Nationals, and on the fourth occasion completed on The Vintner for Fulke Walwyn. Arthur's experiences in the saddle benefited him enormously when it came to taking out a training licence in 1975, but he continued to ride for a while even while training, and won his last race in 1977. His tally of more than 50 winners may not have been in the same league as the champions of today, but his riding was workmanlike, he had a good eye for a stride and could read a race. He never knew the meaning of fear.

Arthur is tall for a jockey – just short of 6ft – but he did not have to diet vigorously like his modern-day counterparts. He once rode at 8st in a maiden race on the Flat at Dundalk, and remembers that when he had to ride at 9st 11lb for the Irish National, he went out for a meal the night before and ate a good steak and salad, plus two glasses of red wine 'to flush me out', as it was conveniently thought to do in those days.

It's always interesting to see how breeding comes into the making of jockeys as well as good racehorses, and obviously the Moore genes are powerful in the racing world. Arthur was born to carry on the family tradition of race riding and training – horses were in his blood from the beginning. It was something he always expected to do, and he has executed it superbly well.

Arthur Moore's patience and understanding are the hallmarks of his trade. He has the right temperament for his involvement in the bloodstock world, and his assessment of pedigrees is outstanding. His opinions at all the major National Hunt bloodstock sales are greatly valued, as is his ability to source future winners from numerous points of the compass in Ireland, Britain and France. I learned a vast amount from him on our travels around the countryside. Quite simply, he was the catalyst in my passion for jump racing.

David Mould

Generally regarded as one of the most stylish National Hunt jockeys of his day, David Mould will forever be associated with the many horses he rode for 16 years for Queen Elizabeth, the Queen Mother, in particular Makaldar and Inch Arran.

'Makaldar was a big, lazy horse with extra big, almost loppy, ears but he was so genuine and unlucky not to win the Champion Hurdle in Saucy Kit's year. He was carried across the course by the wayward Aurelius.' In 1973, David won the Topham Trophy over the Grand National fences at Aintree on Inch Arran, an eyecatching grey horse who captured the imagination of the racing public.

As well as riding for Her Majesty, David also rode for the famous actor Gregory Peck, who owned the talented racehorse Different Class. 'He was the best stamp of a horse you could ever see. He was a gent and he was beautiful. He twice won for me at the Cheltenham Festival and was third in the 1968 Grand National.' Yet another owner for whom David rode was Sir Winston Churchill, whose funeral he attended even though he had his leg in plaster, the result of one of the many accidents that befell him on a racecourse.

David Mould's father was a military man who fought in the First World War and afterwards became a horse dealer. 'My mother, Edith Lilien, had been a society lady in her youth and her father had been Lord Mayor of Windlesham.' David considers he had a great childhood, because he grew up surrounded by horses and ponies.

I was a tiny little thing as a child. I was a war baby and there was food rationing. When I was 14 years old I barely weighed 4½st, but because I was so light I could ride all my father's ponies – even the little ones. I rode a lot of them without a saddle, and I enjoyed riding bareback. It teaches one balance.

David took part in all the Pony Club activities including the local shows and gymkhanas, and spent days out hunting, usually with the Garth Hunt. 'All I ever wanted to do was to ride, and Dad used to lend me out to ride ponies for other dealers as well. I got so much experience from riding all those different animals.' David was always a natural rider and had lovely hands. He was well taught, and on several occasions was given lessons by the legendary show-jumping and eventing coach Dick Stillwell, who had been shortlisted for the Olympics in the 1940s. He was a tough instructor but a brilliant teacher, and helped many top riders, including Richard Meade, Jennie Loriston-Clarke and Lucinda Green.

In his teenage years, David attended Kenyngton Manor School in Sunbury where, having been brought up by two well-educated parents, he was – unlike many would-be jockeys – a well-behaved, intelligent pupil. He never minded being in a classroom because he had plenty else to occupy him when he was out of it. He rode his ponies at weekends, as well as on summer evenings and in the holidays.

At 14, however, he left school and his father sent him to Staff Ingham's racing yard in Epsom. He became an apprentice and earned half a crown each week. It was a spartan existence and Major Ingham, who had been an RAF squadron leader and was a friend of David's father, was a hard taskmaster. The idea had been for the young boy to become a Flat jockey, but 'I shot up a foot and put on two stone'. His Epsom mentor, who believed in his ability, got him a job with Major Peter Cazalet, a top jumps trainer at Fairlawne in Shipbourne, Kent, close to Sevenoaks. Previously a jockey and a good cricketer, Major Cazalet was champion National Hunt trainer three times in the 1960s.

David remembers his Fairlawne days with great affection and, having joined Peter Cazalet in 1957, remained with him until he died in May 1973. In November 1958, he rode his first winner, Straight Hill, in a novice hurdle at Plumpton. 'She was a tiny rabbit of a thing, and I only got the ride because Arthur Freeman, who had ridden Mr

What to win the Grand National earlier that year, did not want to partner her.'

Peter Cazalet's training establishment would have been an eye-opener for trainers of today. The gallops were uphill and on grass – there were no all-weather surfaces in those years – and they were barely two furlongs long.

People say that Martin Pipe started interval training, but I can tell you we did it at Fairlawne in the 1960s. We would go up those gallops numerous times and walk or trot back down the sides of the park in between. If the boss wanted to do a bit more with his horses he would box them up and take them to Knole Park ten miles away, where a mile grass gallop had been specifically made.

Fortunately, unlike the big strings of today, there were only 35 horses trained at Fairlawne each season, and they were always extremely fit when they went to the racecourses. Peter Cazalet was a genius of a trainer. It must have been a magnificent estate – all the houses in the village were owned by the Cazalet family – and the schooling ground for the racehorses was painstakingly laid out within the park. 'There were three sets of fences – all in lines, small, medium and large plus three rows of hurdles. A lot of attention was given to schooling and the horses were always known to be good jumpers on the racecourses.' The Queen Mother, for whom David rode a total of 106 winners, had her own suite in the main house, and regularly travelled to Fairlawne as she loved to watch her horses working. It was a cruel day for her when Devon Loch had his mishap on the run to the finishing line in the 1956 Grand National but, although trained by Peter Cazalet, it was before David Mould's riding days and Dick Francis had been the jockey.

The 1960s were great days for National Hunt jockeys and produced many top riders, but their ways of dieting and keeping fit were vastly different to today.

❝ I could not do weights under 10st 5lb, and in my riding years we had no saunas nor physiotherapists on the racecourses. I spent a lot of my time in Turkish baths all over the country, and in particular I remember spending many hours in the baths in Gloucester with Terry Biddlecombe, who would always take a bottle of champagne with him, since he maintained that nobody could sweat properly without drinking. ❞

A number of jockeys in the last century would have failed current breathalyser tests, but they rode great races.

David Mould's early life paints an interesting picture for young jockeys of today. The strict discipline he endured in Epsom and at Fairlawne undoubtedly contributed towards the image he subsequently presented to the racing public. He was always a dapper jockey and immaculately turned out. David was a fine horseman as well, and looked very tidy in a race. 'I thoroughly enjoyed my riding days despite the injuries I received – I earned a living having fun, and I rode for some wonderful owners.' For him it was 'the Sport of Kings' in every sense.

Nowadays, happily married to former ace show-jumper Marion Coakes, renowned especially for riding the diminutive Stroller, he can look back on his racing days and compare the styles of the jockeys in the 1960s and 1970s with those of the younger jockeys currently riding. David deplores the modern trend for excessively short stirrups and the bumping about on the horses' backs – he was always taught to sit quietly on the racehorses he rode and his results were outstanding.

As the jockey who won on Tingle Creek on his first appearance in Britain, and then created more records with his supremely popular wins in the famous Queen Mother colours, David was never a champion, largely due to his many injuries, but he still rode 606 winners before retiring at the end of the 1974-75 season. 'My father and mother were war people, and as far as I was concerned Sir Winston Churchill and the Royal Family won the war for us.

Peter Cazalet was the Queen Mother's trainer and I was his jockey.
I was just fortunate to have been in the right place at the right time.'

Danny Mullins

Yet another member of the powerful Mullins dynasty, Danny – who was born in April 1992 – is the son of Tony, who was twice champion Irish National Hunt jockey and renowned for riding the wonderful mare Dawn Run to many of her successes. Danny's mother, Mags, was champion lady rider on two occasions and an accomplished horse person as well. Both Tony and Mags currently train racehorses in Co Kilkenny, although they have gone separate ways with their lives.

As a child, Danny was small and light. He loved riding ponies and had the right physique to show-jump and race them. Mags took him all over the country to compete, and he won the 12.2hh pony show-jumping championship at the RDS horse show twice, but although he continued with his 13.2hh ponies it was pony racing that especially captured his imagination, and he had some great times on the 'flapping' circuit. The jet-black 12.2hh pony, Mania, was famous and, despite her bad attitude in the stable, she won numerous races for him. Everybody knew her.

Danny rode more than 150 winners on the pony racing circuit, and was the rider all his fellow jockeys feared. Sharp, talented and deadly, he seldom lost a race, and it was then that he knew he wanted to be a jockey. He reckons the 'flapping' races focus a rider's mind, but also that many bad habits were picked up too, especially with overuse of the whip. It is well known that child riders in the Irish pony races are well remunerated, and such were the 'perks' Danny received – money stuffed down his boots by satisfied punters and trainers – that he was able to buy his first car from the profits of his pony racing days.

In 2008 Danny could not wait to leave school, and went to Aidan O'Brien's yard at Ballydoyle for two weeks' work experience having already spent two weeks in 2007 at Jim Bolger's establishment. He planned to ride out for several more Flat trainers, including Dermot Weld and Ger Lyons, but that initial visit to Jim Bolger had been so successful that he decided upon further months at the master trainer's yard, and he ended up being at Coolcullen for three and a half years. At 16 he had taken out his apprentice licence and he had a number of rides on the Flat. His first winner, in a seven-furlong handicap at Leopardstown on My Girl Sophie, was in May 2008. On his first seven rides, he had five winners.

Although in total Danny's Flat-racing days provided him with more than 70 winners, his weight began to rise and he soon struggled to do anything below 9st 2lb. He thus turned his attentions to jump racing, and in 2010 Malande was his first ride over hurdles – this same horse had also been his first ride on the Flat. His first season jump racing was not a huge success, and he found the change from the Flat a big step: 'I did not have a daily jumping mentor to correct me, and I was not surrounded by jumping people.' Jim Bolger did not appreciate him riding over jumps during the summer months and, having broken his thumb and collarbone in one of the hurdle races, he finished his apprenticeship six months early and turned his attentions to riding out for his uncle Willie Mullins, spending some time along the way with Enda Bolger, whom he praises greatly for the help he gave him with his jumping. There is no better teacher.

As a jump jockey Danny has had his fair share of winners, and is extremely adaptable. On his 21st birthday he had his first Grade 1 winner when Mount Benbulben won at Punchestown for owner Barry Connell. He has also more than once ridden a winner for both his mother and his father on the same card.

Danny is an enthusiastic jockey whose background of show-jumping and pony racing has given him a solid grounding. To date, he has had no winners at the Cheltenham Festival, but has ridden a number of second-placed horses and continues to have time on his side. He enjoys life and is a popular rider on the National Hunt circuit.

David Mullins

Another grandson of the late Paddy Mullins, whose name will forever be linked to the wondermare Dawn Run, David Mullins is an established National Hunt jockey who regularly rides for the champion trainer Willie Mullins. His father Tom, Willie's brother, also trains, and over the years has himself saddled an array of Grade 1 winners, but these days he has a smaller string to manage and concentrates more on his bloodstock interests. In 2016 David won the Grand National at his first attempt when he partnered the Mouse Morris-trained Rule The World. He had not even reached his 20th birthday, making him one of the youngest jockeys ever to have been successful in the race.

David's mother has a show-jumping background and her sister Marion Hughes jumped for Ireland. Thus, throughout his childhood he was well supported by his parents in his equestrian interests. David had a number of good ponies, enjoyed hunting and hunter trials as well as show-jumping, and jumped on several occasions at the RDS horse show.

He particularly enjoyed it when young ponies were bought and he could educate them before they were sold on. He has an inborn dealer streak in him, and is a shrewd man when it comes to buying and selling horses. Schooling ponies is an undoubted art, and David was always a natural rider who stood no nonsense with the young ponies, but he always disliked stable work and admits there were many times when he was lazy in the yard.

When I was fourteen I used to hate getting out of bed in the mornings, and my father almost despaired of me and my approach to life, but he got me to pull myself together. I was ordered to the yard and made to muck out the stables. Dad also told me I would never make a good jockey because I was too tall.

Gradually, and at times under sufferance, David became more interested in racing. He enjoyed attending the sales, and particularly remembers watching his father buy a Definite Article three-year-old at Goffs: this horse, Some Article, went on to win the Land Rover Bumper at Punchestown. It ignited David's interest in the bloodstock markets.

At 15, still at St Kieran's College in Kilkenny, David began riding out racehorses, and after taking his Junior Certificate he left full-time education to begin riding in bumper races. His first winner was Rathvawn Belle, who was victorious at Punchestown in February 2013. As a 17-year-old, he began riding out for Willie as well as for his father, and also spent two weeks with Gordon Elliott. The winners flowed, and at the end of that year he turned professional. Fosters Cross, trained by Tom, provided him with his initial win in the paid ranks when winning at Thurles in December 2014, but it was not long before the jockey rode out his claim and notched up more than 60 winners.

Despite his height of 5ft 11in, David Mullins is a sound jockey who has ridden a number of tactical races for top trainers, in particular when partnering Nichols Canyon for Willie Mullins to take the Grade 1 Morgiana Hurdle at Punchestown in 2015, defeating the then unbeaten Faugheen. David rides with a sensible length of leg and sits into his horses, having been given valuable lessons by Ruby Walsh. His riding career looks certain to produce more successes, but long term it is the buying and selling of bloodstock that is sure to feature highest on his list of priorities. Despite David's way with horses, he is a businessman at heart.

Patrick Mullins

Patrick Mullins holds a remarkable record for a National Hunt amateur jockey. He has already been Irish champion on 11 occasions, and when he reached the 546-winner mark he surpassed Ted Walsh's long-standing figure. In 2012 Patrick's 74 winners were more than had ever been achieved by an amateur in a single season, although in 1915 Billy Parkinson had recorded 72 wins. In Ireland it is accepted that top amateur riders are on a par with the best professionals – in many cases they are better. However, many remain in the amateur category due to issues with their weight and the enjoyment they get when contesting the top amateur races at the festivals.

The Mullins family has deep roots in National Hunt racing. Paddy, father of Willie, was a brilliant trainer and most of his sons rode in races – Tony, in particular, had wins on Dawn Run and Willie was champion amateur on six occasions, winning the Aintree Fox Hunters' Chase on Atha Cliath in 1983 and the Champion Bumper at Cheltenham in 1996 with Wither Or Which.

Patrick, Willie's only son, was born in Dublin, but brought up in the country at his father's training establishment, Closutton in Co Carlow. His mother, Jackie, hunted and evented in England, and later became an accomplished amateur rider in Ireland. Patrick had his first pony, Breeze, when he was five. His cousin Emmet, George Mullins' son, was a similar age and rode his pony Missy, and the two young lads would race their ponies around Willie's gallop and have one-lap races, but Breeze usually got the better of Missy because the latter was too fat. Both children hunted with the Carlow Farmers hunt and went to Pony Club activities at Warrington near Kilkenny. Emmet and Danny, Tony's son, were good at show-jumping, but Patrick's next pony, a JA, tended to hot up too much, especially when he took him to the gallops. Patrick only rode in one pony race because he was tall and too heavy – 'on a 13-hand piebald mare who had come from gypsies. Emmet won the race on a sharp half-bred pony. I had not appreciated that we had to go round twice: I only got going on the second circuit and I finished fourth.'

Always a bright child, Patrick was well educated at Clongowes, Ireland's premier boarding school, at Clane in Co Kildare. The high fees paid off as nowadays Patrick is not only a talented jockey but also helps on the administrative side of Willie's powerful training operation, and writes newspaper articles. He speaks exceptionally well and handles the press and media in an highly professional manner.

Patrick did ride in a few point-to-points and had one winner for his Aunt Mags, but at 16 he had his first ride as an amateur in a bumper race at Thurles on Screaming Witness, owned by his parents. It failed to win, but it gave him the taste for race-riding. His first success was in June 2006 in a Flat race at Limerick on Diego Garcia. The horse was the stable's second string, but unfortunately Jackie and Willie were on holiday and not present to see their son's triumph. Patrick then rode three more winners in the space of a week. It was a brilliant start for a child who was still at school.

Although he started his career on the Flat, Patrick had plenty of jumping tuition. Willie does not school his horses much at home, but at 16 Patrick was sent to Enda Bolger's in Co Limerick for some intensive cross-country jumping, and he later had a ride for Enda over fences. At that time, he was able to do 9st 13lb. Jumping banks at Rathcannon is every jockey's idea of heaven, and Patrick thoroughly enjoyed his stay.

On one occasion, during his summer holidays, Patrick went to Guillaume Macaire's yard at Royan la Palmyre in France. The 14-time French champion jumps trainer has sold many good racehorses to Britain and Ireland, including to Willie Mullins. French jumpers are schooled intensively – far more than in Britain and Ireland – and the Macaire system was an eye-opener for Patrick, for whom riding on the schooling grounds was an especially valuable experience. He also spent time with Francois Cottin, another top jumps trainer who is based at the famous Maisons-Laffitte training centre close to Paris. There are jumps to be seen everywhere.

After finishing at his school, Patrick spent three years furthering his education at college in Maynooth and, despite his upbringing and sound grounding for race-riding, he did not ride full-time on the track until he was 21. He is now 30, but to have won the amateur championship on 11 occasions is a massive achievement.

At 6ft 1in, Willie's son is a dedicated jockey with extensive racing knowledge. Not only does he have successes in bumper races, but he excels over hurdles and fences. His cool approach to race-riding and his unflappable nature help him enormously. He is a tactical rider and balances his horses particularly well, never rushing them around bends nor pushing them out of their strides on the approaches to the obstacles.

In 2015 Patrick rode his first Grade 1 chase winner when partnering Douvan in the Racing Post Novice Chase at Leopardstown. Just over a year later, he won his first Grade 1 hurdle when Bacardys took the Deloitte Novice Hurdle on the same track. To date, he has ridden four Cheltenham Festival winners, namely two Champion Bumpers, with Cousin Vinny (2008) and Champagne Fever (2012), and two winners of the controversial National Hunt Chase on Back In Focus (2013) and Rathvinden in 2018. In 2018 he also won the prestigious Galway Hurdle on Sharjah. Patrick looks certain to carry on the family training tradition in years to come, and his attention to detail has already been shown. He pays serious attention to his personal fitness and never ceases to turn heads when, bedecked in his running gear, he is seen running around the racecourses during the majority of the meetings he attends. He leaves no stone unturned.

Timmy Murphy

Nobody would dispute that Timothy James Murphy had a varied and tempestuous start to his career. He has always been a complex individual and, in his own words, 'never a really happy person, though probably the happiest when I was a child at home and riding my pony'. On his good days, Timmy was one of the most admired jockeys in his profession, yet his career was punctuated by a number of unfortunate incidents, some of which can probably be traced back to his childhood. At times he was brilliant but on other occasions erratic, depending on how the mood took him.

Fortunately, riding saw Timmy's inborn ability mostly to the fore. He is an artist in the saddle and he usually rode with the confidence of a horseman who knew he was better than most of those around him. He always liked to be in command. He was firm with his mounts and at times harsh on them, but he was always positive, and kept them going forwards in balance and rhythm. Riding with no apparent urgency, he made up their minds in no uncertain terms. His distinctive 'switch off' style meant that he never hurried the horses, but when he said 'go' they had to obey.

It might seem that Timmy started out in life with everything handed to him on a plate. His parents, both of whom came from Co Cork, were from horse backgrounds; his father, Jimmy, was well known on the point-to-point circuit and rode numerous winners. His grandfather on his mother's side was a greatly respected blacksmith. 'It was always Dad's intention that I would ride, and I don't really remember any time in my life when I couldn't. Dad bought me a rocking horse when I was ten months old, and I was given a pony when I was three.' There were always horses around, and when Timmy's father became the manager of Newberry Stud in Co Kildare close to the Curragh, mares, foals and youngstock were everywhere. From the day he helped his father to break in a tiny thoroughbred filly – the first racehorse he ever sat on – he knew it was racehorses he wanted to ride.

Horses were my father's life, and if I hadn't been into horses, I probably wouldn't have spent so much time with him. He made it easy for me to ride, but it was never a case of having to do it. We used to go riding out: me and Dad and my pony Bluebell. He was a great little pony: he was 13.2hh and grey. He was a huge part of my life. I went to gymkhanas with him and I went hunting and pony racing on him. He was stronger than me. When we were out hunting I couldn't hold him at all – we were always up in front. Once the hounds started to run he'd be off and he would jump anything. He used to frighten the life out of me, but it got the adrenalin going and he taught me so much. Dad taught me an awful lot about riding too, although we used to have terrible rows – 'hands down, stirrups down' – but I wanted to be a jockey straight away and I always wanted to perch up like a jockey.

Yet Timmy's childhood was not straightforward. Although he had countless opportunities, there were many days when he was unhappy and frustrated with his lot. He admits that he had a temper from day one. If his father tightened him up when they galloped together around the corners of their fields, Timmy would fly off the handle and, on returning home, would throw his helmet on the kitchen floor. Jimmy was strict with his son and wanted him to ride as well as possible, but he seldom gave him any praise.

I never remember Dad telling me that he loved me, and he often laughed at me when I had falls, but he toughened me up. But I became obsessed with getting things right. He had an old book in the house on riding styles, which I used to read a lot, and I'd check out which was the right way to fall. I'd practise curling up and rolling and making myself as small as possible. I used to strap my saddle to the chair in my bedroom and ride on it. I wanted more than anything to be a good rider. I used to practise using my whip while on the chair and switch it from hand to hand. I'd say I rode a million finishes and changed over my whip two million times! I always just managed to get up on the line. **'**

In his dreams, he won 32 Gold Cups and 48 Grand Nationals. As a child, Timmy loved watching the racing on television.

'Yet even then I watched the races through the jockeys. I had my favourite horses, but the jockey was the most important thing to me. Frank Berry was my jockey in Ireland, and Jonjo O'Neill my role model in England. They were my heroes. I used to have pictures on my wall of horses and jockeys where other kids would have pictures of football players or pop stars. As long as they were good horses and the jockeys looked stylish they had a good chance of making it into my bedroom. **'**

Jumping rated high on Timmy's list of what he enjoyed doing most, and all the practice he had in his formative years certainly paid dividends. He and his brother Brian built jumps on the hill beside their house and, because they rated the Grand National as the most exciting race of the year, they built fences to emulate those seen at Aintree. 'We'd collect old Christmas trees and chop down furze bushes from around the Curragh. We'd make our own Becher's Brook, and we'd make our fences as high as we could with steep drops on the landing sides.'

As well, Timmy and Brian would spend summers with their grandfather and Uncle Mick in Co Cork.

'We visited many different yards where they'd been called out to do some shoeing, and they had a donkey on the farm at home that we used to ride, and we'd have bets with each other to see who could stay on it for the longest. It's not easy to stay on a donkey's back when it does not want you there. We also used to ride the cows when they came down from the hill to be milked. **'**

Timmy's Uncle Mick used to tell his nephew he'd make a great jockey and that he'd get him going in pony races. His encouragement undoubtedly had a huge impact on his nephew, giving him the confidence that is so important when riding in a race. Timmy rode in a number of pony races for some highly respected people, in particular Jonjo Harding and Con Horgan, but never won any, despite being placed. 'I loved the pony racing. I loved the buzz. I loved the smell of the grass and smell of the horses and the chip vans. You felt like a real jockey, getting into your boots and colours and feeling the tension beforehand.'

It was clear that school was not the place for him, the vice-principal at Two Mile House actually telling Timmy's mother: 'His heart isn't here – it's on the Curragh.' He left school in the summer of 1990 when he had just turned 16 and never looked back.

❧ I didn't really have any interest in the lessons side of school. I struggled with most subjects – you have to have an interest in something if you want to be good at it. I wasn't stupid: if Dad had been a solicitor or a doctor then I would probably have taken my education more seriously, but he was a horseman and that's what I was interested in. I was quite a restless child, and I had very little patience, yet in my spare time I used to sew a jockey's colours – white spots on maroon polo necks – in the belief that I would ride for Lady Clague, the owner of Newberry Stud. I also made tassels for hats and whips from scraps of leather, and I used to sell them to lads on the Curragh. ❞

Timmy Murphy's rise as a jockey was not straightforward. His lack of patience, his hot temper and his association with alcohol led to some stormy times when he ventured into the racing world. Even as a teenager he was sacked by both Dermot Weld and Declan Gillespie for his drinking and poor timekeeping, with the former also criticising him for being hard on his horses. 'If a horse wouldn't do what I wanted it to do,' he writes in *Riding the Storm*,

I was a bit quick with the whip. Even though I loved horses, I lacked patience. I wouldn't give them a chance. If they weren't co-operating with me my first recourse was to the stick, not the carrot. *You will do what I want you to do and you will do it now.* That continued to the racecourse when I got older. Horses who weren't trying for me, I'd just beat them. It was something that was just in me and it took a long time for it to register.

Fortunately for Timmy, after his bad experiences on the Curragh he found his saviour, Mick Halford, who allowed him to start with a clean slate.

Mick always was, and still is, a great man to give a young fellow a chance. Fortunately he thought I got on well with horses, but this was a long way from the message that came from Weld's about me not liking horses. I'm not sure how those different perceptions of me came about. Maybe when I was young I did not really like myself, with the result that I probably took it out on whatever I could, mainly on the people closest to me and the horses with which I was working. But it was different at Mick Halford's. I felt at ease with him, and I would listen to whatever advice he gave me, be it on riding, on working or about life.

Timmy Murphy's first race-ride was for his father in a point-to-point in 1991 on Snuggledown. 'I had never jumped a proper steeplechase fence before I jumped the first on that day. I had done lots of schooling at home over poles and artificially made-up fences together with a big log in a field with bushes thrown over the middle of it.' That first ride was unsuccessful, as were his next six, but in 1993 he rode his first point-to-point winner when Gayloire won at Kilmuckridge in Co Wexford, trained by George Halford – Mick's uncle.

Most of the schooling of racehorses that Timmy did was with

Michael Hourigan, whose establishment he joined in 1993 on Mick Halford's advice. The trainer taught him an enormous amount. Between 1994 and 1996 he rode over 50 point-to-point winners, and 38 winners under rules. It was the start of an illustrious career in jump racing, and his winners in Britain, where for many years his name was linked with David Johnson, included the 2008 Grand National on Comply Or Die as well as a number of high-profile Cheltenham Festival wins.

His riding lessons continued in Britain, and Timmy still has high praise for Yogi Breisner.

He was great for riders. Yogi would say that it makes no difference how big or small a fence is: all you have to do is to keep the horse balanced. You can't make him do it, you just have to help him. Keep your hands still and you will feel the horse lengthening or shortening underneath you. I used to think, if a horse is running away with me going into a fence I can't just sit still and I always used to try to shorten a horse into a fence, especially the last fence, since I thought it was the best way and the safest, but Yogi changed the whole way I rode over an obstacle. I kept my style, but I was quieter. It was all about balance – not sitting too far forward or too far back, and always keeping the horse in a rhythm and letting him do the jumping rather than you.

Horses jump fine when they are loose – as can be seen when they are jumping in loose schools – but so often it is the jockeys who confuse them and cause them to make mistakes.

Though there were marked highs in the TJ Murphy story, these went hand in hand with mental and physical lows. His career is laced with dramatic incidents, none more so than his unacceptable behaviour on an aeroplane when he was returning from riding in Japan under the influence of alcohol. He served time in prison afterwards. Throughout his life, it would appear Timmy has lived on a knife edge. He has often found it hard to conceal his inner feelings, and these were undoubtedly linked to insecurity. He has always been hard on himself – the best jockeys are – and clearly there have been many days of anxiety and pent-up emotion that have caused him more mental anguish than he ever deserved.

Timmy Murphy is gifted as a horseman and was an outstanding jockey, who when he retired from National Hunt racing further demonstrated his inborn skills by successfully riding winners on the Flat. Yet the demons in his head have undoubtedly accounted for the many stormy days that he has encountered across the board.

During his race-riding days, Timmy received many cautions for excessive use of the whip, which strangely contrast with his basic love of horses. However, as a jockey he was labelled as one of the most sympathetic and patient of riders because he would wait for his horses to find their strides and never rush them, always maintaining that there is a maximum speed at which a human or a horse can go for a given period of time. In long-distance races, in particular, he argues: 'If the horse is made to go faster than the pace at which it is comfortable there will be nothing left at the end. The trick is to find the horse's natural cruising speed and let him go at that speed to conserve energy.' Timmy's winning ride on Comply Or Die in the Grand National was copybook. At his best, his rides were pure poetry, but much depended upon his frame of mind on a particular day. He was fiercely competitive but unfortunately there were times when his quest for winners outweighed his common sense and he paid the penalty.

Tomás O'Brien

Tomás, Tom, O'Brien has horseracing in his veins: his father, Jim, is Aidan O'Brien's brother, and his aunt, Liz Slevin, is the champion Flat trainer's sister. Jim originally had his own haulage business, but is now deeply involved in racing as right-hand man to his nephew Joseph O'Brien at his successful yard on Carriganog Hill in Owning, Co Kilkenny. His mother, Stella, has always worked for Credit Union in New Ross. Tom's grandparents were farmers, and as a child he was more interested in lorries and tractors. However, when he was 12 he went to the Slevins' busy yard, close to his home and he was given his first riding lessons. His cousin Mark Slevin – jockey JJ's brother – is just six months younger than Tom and they are great friends. They both learned a vast amount from Shay Slevin's tuition.

I much enjoyed hunting the ponies. We went out with the Wexford Hunt or the Bree Hunt, and jumping those narrow-topped, crumbling banks taught me such a lot with regard to balance. However, I did not become a Pony Club member, because there was seldom an opportunity to attend any of the rallies or shows, as the Slevin ponies were mostly youngsters and they specialised in buying and selling.

Tom was born in November 1986 and when he was 13 his uncle Aidan invited him to visit Ballydoyle, the world-famous racing establishment at Rosegreen in Co Tipperary. Once he began to ride the racehorses he was smitten and was determined to become a jockey. He would get taken there whenever it was possible, and went to the yard every weekend as well as in the holidays. School soon became a chore, but he completed his exams and did not finish his education until after his Leaving Certificate at the age of 17. Aidan was a huge help to his nephew and always gives valuable advice to young jockeys. Whilst earning a decent wage, the teenager lived for his weekends, and was even able to afford a car. On occasions he was allowed to accompany the O'Brien runners to England, especially when they travelled across the Irish Sea in special planes. He was spellbound by the efficiency of the yard staff and he much enjoyed his visits to British racecourses. On the gallops at Ballydoyle he cantered many of the well-known Flat horses, including High Chaparral and Rock Of Gibraltar.

As Tom's weight rose, he realised that National Hunt racing was going to be his game. He loved watching the British races that were televised in Ireland, and when it came round to the Cheltenham Festival he longed to be closer to his jump-race heroes and get involved in the action. Timmy Murphy and AP McCoy were the two jockeys he admired the most. At 16, he had done an amateur rider's course at RACE, and Shay Slevin had given him two point-to-point rides as well as rides in two bumper races.

In September 2004 Tom went to England for a weekend to Philip Hobbs' training establishment in Somerset. At the end of his days away he enquired about the likelihood of being able to join the yard. 'I can offer you a job,' he was told by Philip, 'but I can't promise you any rides, however I will let you school some of the horses.' Fired with enthusiasm, he returned to Ireland to pack his bags before going back to Hobbs' headquarters at Sandhill Racing Stables for a longer spell.

At the end of November he had his first ride, finishing second in an amateur riders' hurdle at Taunton and receiving praise from Richard Pitman on At The Races. Dave Roberts approached him to say he would like to be his agent. In December Tom rode his first winner, The Names Bond for Andy Turnell at Warwick, in another amateur riders' hurdle race.

During his early years with Philip Hobbs, Tom rode a number of point-to-point winners in the West Country. As well as winning a good maiden race at Larkhill, he won several hunter chases including the prestigious John Corbett Cup at Stratford in May 2006. He ended the 2005-06 season by winning the amateur riders' championship from Tom Greenall, and when he turned conditional in the autumn of 2006 he rode plenty more winners, which helped him to win the conditional jockeys' championship in the 2006-07 season.

Tom O'Brien has a particularly fine record at Aintree, having twice won the Topham Chase for Peter Bowen on Always Waining, as well as being successful in the Becher Chase for Philip Hobbs on Chance Du Roy. In 2007, he was second in the Grand National on McKelvey. He has also won two Welsh Nationals, plus three Grade 1 novice hurdles including two Tolworth Hurdles. That he chose from the outset to move away from Ireland and concentrate on racing in Britain is unusual for a jump jockey, but that decision has paid dividends.

Tom, like many other members of the O'Brien family, has an astute racing brain and a genuine interest in the horses he rides. His career demonstrates that his childhood days spent with ponies, plus priceless visits to Ballydoyle, have provided him with the perfect stepping stones towards National Hunt racing.

Derek O'Connor

Being a top amateur jockey in Ireland has always been a full-time occupation, and Derek O'Connor's record in point-to-points is phenomenal. In February 2015, when partnering the Gigginstown-owned Death Duty – trained by the astute Pat Doyle – at the Cragmore fixture in Co Limerick, he became the first jockey to ride 1,000 point-to-point winners, but since then that figure has steadily risen and now stands closer to 1,250. His cool approach hides his brilliance and depth of knowledge. He is a clever man and seldom misses a trick. Derek has also won a number of races on the track, and his four Cheltenham Festival victories, together with the amateur riders' championship in Ireland in the 2003-04 National Hunt season, further demonstrate his skills.

Born at Beagh in Co Galway in 1982, Derek now lives near Tubber on the Galway/Clare borders, which is only a short distance from where he was brought up. His father was a cattle dealer and his mother had a number of point-to-point wins to her name and, according to those who knew her, was a fearless rider with a profound knowledge of horses. Having spent a number of years in the legendary Tom Costello yard near Newmarket-on-Fergus, her stable management was also of the highest class.

Together with Davy Russell, with whom Derek gets on well, he worked as a teenager in trainer Eugene O'Sullivan's yard. Apparently when the boys were there, there was constant banter and they got up to numerous tricks. They both remember fighting over the one and only stable broom. 'It was lucky the broom had a short handle or else Derek might have killed me,' says Davy.

Through riding horses with Eugene, the two jockeys developed similar styles and they both positioned themselves in the centre of balance, with their horses jumping in a lovely rhythm. Eugene is an outstanding teacher who spends considerable time jumping his horses. Even when he was the pony-racing champion in the second decade of the 21st century, top National Hunt jockey Jack Kennedy used to be driven down from Co Kerry to Eugene's yard to get jumping tuition.

When he left that educational Co Cork yard, Derek was close to his present-day height of 5ft 11in. He moved back to Galway before being given a job by the brothers Pat and John Lynch in Co Clare, at their stables close to Dromoland Castle. The Lynch family reared cattle and had a number of point-to-pointers as well as a few runners under rules. Their facilities were basic but sound and there were some nice horses to ride. 'I learned a lot. It was a great experience and I rode my first point-to-point winner, Rossy Orchestra, for the yard in 1999. He was owned by my brother Sean. The first horse Derek rode that day was Tisalladream,' and Pat recollects:

He had never run before and was a trifle unlucky. He finished a close third. Derek, who even in those days showed his hunger to win, was clearly disappointed to be beaten, but he produced an ice-cool performance when guiding Rossy Orchestra to victory in the very next race.

From then on, Derek began riding in more point-to-points and he started out on his run of success that later made history. He also had rides on the track and gained valuable experience from racing against the professionals. His introduction to the sport was enviable.

Throughout his career Derek has always done plenty of schooling, and he emphasises how much he enjoys jumping young horses. 'I often rode for the Costello family, John helped me a lot, and through the late Tom snr I began schooling horses in the north of Ireland trained by Colin McKeever and owned by Wilson Dennison.' He has since ridden numerous winners for the Loughanmore yard and educated big-name horses on the point-to-point tracks. Over the years Wilson has sold many good horses, including Bindaree, Yorkhill, Bellshill and Blaklion.

As well as the scores of horses he has ridden for the Dennison academy, Derek has also been closely linked with Robert Tyner's yard in Co Cork, and after the tragic accident that befell John Thomas McNamara at Cheltenham in 2013, he went to Enda Bolger's stables in Co Limerick on several occasions and before riding horses owned by JP McManus in point-to-points and cross-country races. In February 2018, Derek demonstrated his riding ability beyond the amateur ranks when giving Edwulf a cool ride to score for JP and Joseph O'Brien in the Irish Gold Cup at Leopardstown.

At one point in his career, he had taken some time away from racing to go on an intensive jumping course with Yogi Breisner. This teacher told *The Irish Field* that 'Derek listened to and absorbed all the instructions,' adding that:

> He found it easy to adjust and improve. He has very good balance and hands, plus a natural empathy and feel for a horse. He sees a good stride and displays a soft seat into, over and after the fences. Horses respond to him in a very positive manner.

Praise indeed from an instructor who has coached Olympic event riders. If a jockey can switch off a young horse in a race and teach it to settle then it can jump with confidence. Only a few jockeys have shown this ability, but Paul Carberry, John Francome, Timmy Murphy, Davy Russell and Ruby Walsh have all demonstrated that they can do so. More than 700 of Derek's first 1,000 point-to-point winners were maidens, and they won their races by learning from their rider. 'I knew from the outset that Derek was very professional for a young lad,' says Robert Tyner, 'and riding was natural for him.' In common with AP McCoy, he has shown that he can handle pain, having broken numerous bones, but he has always been driven by the prospect of further winners. Derek O'Connor has ridden horses across the amateur-professional divide like few others, and has demonstrated to young riders the finer points of jockeyship. He has done a great service to point-to-pointing as well as to National Hunt racing. He is a family man with deep roots in the horse world.

Conor O'Dwyer

With his wonderfully cheerful countenance and infectious smile, Conor O'Dwyer is one of those people who inspires others. Having always been taught by the finest horsemen he has a great rapport with horses, and above all few jockeys can boast about winning both the Cheltenham Gold Cup and the Champion Hurdle – each on two occasions. Imperial Call won the Gold Cup in 1996 and War Of Attrition in 2006, while the Dessie Hughes-trained Hardy Eustace was victorious in the Champion Hurdle in the consecutive years of 2004 and 2005.

Yet nobody in his family bar Conor himself had any interest in horses. His mother was the matron at Wexford General Hospital and his father an accountant. But Conor was always drawn towards racing, and John Berry, a top amateur jockey and now a trainer, was his best friend at school and encouraged Conor to ride ponies, which he started doing at six. His father bought him a pony and rented a paddock with a shed close to the town. From the age of ten he hunted with the Killinick Harriers. He was light and sat well, and always wanted to be a jockey, but never rode in pony races.

Conor began riding racehorses when he was 12, at Padge Berry's yard at Blackstone in Co Wexford. Padge was an uncle of John's and an excellent trainer, who had many fine-looking National Hunt stores which he sold to England, and he trained some he had not sold. He often made them walk up and down steep sand dunes. Not only did this build up muscle but it was also excellent for a rider's balance. It was unwise to sit too far forward up the horse's neck for fear of falling off over its shoulders. Padge's horses were always superbly conditioned, and they thrived on the seaside air and walking in the saltwater.

The talented jockey Liam Codd rode out for Padge at the same time as Conor, and it was not long before the latter was advised to leave Wexford and broaden his horizons. Short of his 14th birthday, he left school for RACE, and later rode out for Frank Oakes, who trained on the Curragh. In 1983, aged 16, he rode Gayfield to win a claiming bumper at Limerick. After a few years with Frank, Conor went back to Padge, but then moved again, this time to work for Francis Flood at Grangecon. Francis was a top trainer and had been amateur champion on several occasions, during days when he rode for Paddy Sleator in the 1970s and 1980s.

Conor rode a large number of winners during his five years with Francis Flood, losing his claim after only two years, and in his second season he was the champion claimer. At that time the Irish champion, Frank Berry, was also at the yard as first jockey, and he gave Conor an enormous amount of help, especially when it came to schooling. In the young rider's opinion, Frank was 'perfection in terms of a jockey'. Conor goes on to say that he is a great person too, 'and I cannot thank him enough for all the help that he gave me'.

After spending those years at Grangecon, he then went freelance and rode out for a number of different trainers, including Mouse Morris in Co Tipperary, for whom he partnered War Of Attrition to win the Gold Cup, and Christy Roche on the Curragh. He also schooled for many smaller trainers. He often went to Pat Kelly in Galway and enjoyed riding for him. Later on, he had some great days with Arthur Moore, and spent his twilight years as a jockey as number one in Arthur's yard. Conor, who is 5ft 7in in height, could do 10st when he was riding, although his most comfortable weights were around the 10st 4lb to 10st 7lb mark. He was never champion jockey but was second on five occasions to Charlie Swan.

When he retired at the age of 41, without having had too many injuries, he was able to look back on his race-riding career with pride. He decided to call it a day in March 2008, but was persuaded to delay the announcement until the big Easter meeting at Fairyhouse a few weeks later where, much to the delight of commentator Tony O'Hehir, he won the first race on Mister Top Notch for trainer Davy Fitzgerald. It was a moving occasion.

Conor plays down his successes, and looks to the future with his training and the excitement of watching his teenage son Charlie ride the racehorses he has at home. Charlie rode his first winner at Fairyhouse in June 2019, and will hopefully follow in his father's footsteps, though for the time being is concentrating on his studies, as well as riding racehorses. He appreciates that however good you are as a jockey, qualifications are often important as well.

Jonjo O'Neill

It is hard to find adequate superlatives to describe Jonjo O'Neill's contribution to horseracing, both as a jockey and as a trainer. He will go down in history as one of the greatest jump jockeys of all time, and during his 16 years in the saddle he twice won the championship. At his zenith he captivated the hearts of the racing public and was universally admired. During the 1980s, Timeform considered him consistently the most reliable of all the National Hunt jockeys riding, and Peter Easterby, the brilliant trainer for whom Jonjo rode the iconic Sea Pigeon to win the Champion Hurdle in 1980, maintains that he was the strongest jockey he has ever seen, especially when exhibiting his ruthless determination to get a horse's head in front at the line. 'I did not give him orders. A good jockey does not need orders – it is a waste of breath. The thing about Jonjo was his will to win.'

Neither of Jonjo's parents knew anything about horses – 'my mother was terrified of them' – but his father bred and trained greyhounds as well as running the village shop. During his childhood, Jonjo earned his pocket money by delivering groceries, gas and coal from the shop. By the time he was nine he had saved up enough money to buy two piglets for £7 apiece, which he fattened up on scraps and resold for £32 each. This shrewd bit of business enabled him to buy a 14-month old pony for £27 and even get two shillings back in luck money. The filly, whom he named Dolly, eventually grew to about 13hh, and was kept in a small field behind the O'Neills' house that had been lent to them by a horse-minded neighbour.

Jonjo got help with his riding from nearby farmers, several of whom kept ponies, becoming so keen that he would 'get up on anything'. He even rode the cows and the pigs. He broke in Dolly and she became his best friend. He did as much riding as he could with her, including hunting. In the nearby village of Shanballymore, there were two brothers who kept point-to-point horses as well as their own pack

208 Starting From Scratch

of hounds, and Jonjo would ride with them across the countryside, finding his way over the banks and ditches. He also greatly enjoyed his days with the Duhallow Hunt. Often he didn't get home until after dark, but Dolly was tireless, and the jumping helped his balance. His ambition back then was to become a huntsman and wear a red coat.

As a teenager Jonjo would often attend the local point-to-points, but he never rode in one: at barely 5st he would have been far too light. But he was lucky to be growing up in the days of Pat Taaffe and Arkle, the horse who became a household name across Ireland, and gradually he became more interested in racing. In his holidays he visited Don Reid's racing yard near Mallow. Don had previously been the head lad in England to Colin Davies, the trainer of the three-time Champion Hurdle winner Persian War, and was always helpful to the enthusiastic child, indeed ultimately responsible for giving him a lift in his horsebox when driving it up-country to the Curragh to deliver a horse to Michael Connolly. This introduction to Michael saw Jonjo sign on with him as an apprentice. It was the turning point in his early life.

Jonjo had his first winner on the Curragh at 18, dead-heating on Lana, but he loved the jumping, and remembers schooling over hurdles with Bobby Beasley, the man who had been champion jockey in Ireland three times and ridden the Champion Hurdle winner, Another Flash, in 1960, as well as winning two Gold Cups on Roddy Owen in 1959 and Captain Christy in 1974 and the Grand National on Nicolaus Silver in 1961. 'I was riding a horse called Donovan and we went fast. It was an electric experience.' Before he moved to Gordon Richards' in 1972, Jonjo won a race over hurdles at Downpatrick and was victorious in a chase at Navan.

As a jockey he was a natural, but he had worked on his riding during those apprentice years by finding extra ponies and horses to practise upon during the afternoons.

I used to help with the breakers in the area. We rode them bareback. Myself and the other lads used to lunge the ponies and see which of us could stay on the longest. It was good fun. We worked hard and filled our days, but we learned so much. **9**

From 1972 until 1977 Jonjo was fortunate to receive valuable help at Greystoke in Cumbria from Gordon Richards and his jockey Ron Barry, and then he went freelance. In those days it was not easy to ride large numbers of winners in the north of England and Scotland, because there were no agents and no mobile phones, communications were slower and the competition was fierce, with trainers of the calibre of Ken Oliver, WA Stephenson, Jimmy FitzGerald, Harry Bell, Mary Reveley as well as the Easterby brothers all chasing winners.

Jonjo O'Neill was a legend of a jockey. Not only did he win a considerable number of races on the Flat, in particular when taking the Ebor at York in 1979 on Sea Pigeon, but his win on Dawn Run in the 1986 Cheltenham Gold Cup was one of the most memorable races ever witnessed at Prestbury Park. John Francome considers the successes that came Jonjo's way were 'like winning Olympic gold medals'. They were hard-fought and he had worked hard to achieve them.

The ever-modest Jonjo, who trained Don't Push It to win the 2010 Grand National and Synchronised to capture the 2012 Cheltenham Gold Cup, acknowledges that he was fortunate to have worked with top people in his formative years – people who thoroughly understood horses and racing – but his success was down in no small part to his own single-mindedness, capacity for work and determination to succeed.

'It's a very frustrating game,' he reflects. 'You can do everything right and it can still bite you. You see some real good lads in the sport and they struggle to get rides. Even though they can ride properly, they just do not get on the right horses.'

He has brought up his own sons in an admirable way, and they are repaying him by sharing his love for the National Hunt game. Jonjo jnr, in particular, is well on the way to following in his father's footsteps and could himself become a champion jockey.

Jonjo O'Neill jnr

Jonjo O'Neill jnr has had the perfect introduction to race-riding. As the son of one of the finest National Hunt jockeys ever, it is not surprising that he shows so much natural talent on a racecourse. He and his brother Anthony were surrounded by racehorses from their earliest days whilst their father trained horses at Ivy House, in Skelton Wood End near Penrith. But the young Jonjo did not begin to ride ponies until Jonjo snr moved his string down south to Jackdaws Castle, the state-of-the-art establishment near Stow-on-the-Wold.

❛ Our first pony was a 30-year old palomino Shetland called Peacock. He was naughty even in his advanced years, and when we had falls in the indoor school he would take himself off and get under the railings to escape. My second pony, Dominic, was a 13hh grey, but he too was uncooperative and did everything to get me off. Indeed, I did not like him. ❜

Fortunately, when Jonjo was eight the most wonderful dun-coloured Connemara pony came into his life. Starboy was 14.1hh and the perfect all-rounder. He was a proper boy's pony and although he was big for a young child, they were suited from the beginning. Jonjo learned a huge amount from riding Starboy in all the North Cotswold Hunt Pony Club activities, from show-jumping to hunter trials and working hunter classes. He even played in a few polo matches on this special pony. At the same time his brother Anthony, AJ, rode Playboy, a bay 13hh all-rounder who is now with Kieran and Anne-Marie McManus in Ireland. He too was a good pony, but sharper and speedier. It is so important for children to learn on the right ponies: if they enjoy riding in their early years it can lay the foundations for a career in the equestrian world. Ponies can make or break a child's nerve.

Jonjo was always interested in racing, and while at Cheltenham College where he passed his A-levels in Politics, Business Studies and Sports Science, he was already dreaming of being a jockey. He rode the racehorses at Jackdaws as well as his pony, and on finishing his full-time education spent the summer at Gordon Elliott's training yard in Co Meath, a great experience for a keen, young boy, as were his months with Enda Bolger the following year, when he did a huge amount of jumping under the trainer's watchful eye. He also spent some time at Ballydoyle with Aidan O'Brien, and rode out for Joseph O'Brien in the afternoons.

Unfortunately in October 2015 disaster struck, when the young rider returned to Co Limerick to take part in the Athlacca cross-country ride, which starts close to Enda's yard at Howardstown. It is an amazing spectacle and run over a slice of famous hunting country in order to raise money for charity. The riders negotiate numerous banks with wide ditches. At that time of year, with the leaves still on the bushes and the banks and drains overgrown, a lot of the countryside is 'blind'. Horses often mistake their footings on top of the banks, and falls on the landing side are commonplace. Jonjo was riding a cob belonging to Michael Hourigan when it stumbled into one of the ditches and crushed its rider's left leg against the far edge. The broken tibia and fibula necessitated several operations and the insertion of pins and screws, and Jonjo was out of action for three months.

The young jockey had already ridden his first winner on a racecourse in July 2015 on Temple Lord, trained by his father, in an amateur riders' hurdle at Worcester, and now he longed to resume race-riding. Yet it was not until almost a year later that he had his second winner before disaster struck again when, having spent the summer in France riding out for Guillaume Macaire, he suffered a fall on his very last day and broke his wrist.

In November 2017 Jonjo jnr turned conditional and rode for three months before a third bad fall. This time he fractured a vertebra – L5 – at the base of his back, necessitating a further eight months on the sidelines.

However, between November 2018, when he returned to race-riding, until the end of the season the following April, he rode 30 winners, which included taking the Lanzarote Hurdle at Kempton in January 2019 for Jennie Candlish on Big Time Dancer, and the Martin Pipe Conditional Jockeys' Handicap Hurdle at the 2019 Cheltenham Festival on Early Doors, trained by Joseph O'Brien. Undoubtedly an extremely promising young National Hunt jockey, Jonjo jnr has a stylish way of riding that has caught the eye of many trainers and racing experts.

Like his father, he is fiercely competitive and has already shown courage in the face of adversity. He seems to have an excellent rapport with the horses he rides and has been brought up working with, and listening to, experts. Both Jonjo snr and his mother Jacqui have educated their son supremely well. He was even taken pony racing in Northern Ireland during his days with Gordon Elliott in order to make him more streetwise against fellow riders, and his win in a pony race over there made him even hungrier for success in his chosen career as a jockey in National Hunt racing.

Lisa O'Neill

In the past, jump racing was always perceived as a male-dominated sport, but nowadays it is full of outstanding women, not only among trainers but also on the jockey lists, and Lisa O'Neill sets the standard for female riders today. Her boss, Gordon Elliott, fully appreciates that she is one of the best lady riders in the game: no other female jockey has ridden two winners of the Kerry National, which Lisa managed in 2016 and 2017, as well as memorably winning the four-mile National Hunt Chase at the Cheltenham Festival in 2017 on the diminutive Tiger Roll. Lisa says she has always felt welcomed in the sport. 'Maybe some owners would prefer a man on their horse, but I think that day has long gone, because there are so many good girls in the weighing room.'

Lisa's father Tommy had always trained around 20 horses at Garristown close to the capital, and ridden as a professional National Hunt jockey. Fortunately for her there were always several ponies in her father's yard. Her mother Margaret also likes horses and often helps out at the Tattersalls (Ireland) bloodstock sales offices in Fairyhouse, especially on sale days. Lisa's sister works for Horse Racing Ireland (HRI). As a child, Lisa rode ponies from an early age and loved taking them out hunting with the Fingal Harriers and the Ward Union Hunt, which was beneficial to her style.

Children who hunt learn to ride with longer reins and slip them on landing: if a pony's mouth is hung on to with short reins then the jumping is spoilt, and the child is often pulled over its head. Lisa loved jumping, and would build her own fences at home. Mustang Sally, who was grey and 13.2hh, became a real favourite, and when Lisa began to ride in pony races at 13, this was her preferred partner. Although she only had 20 rides she won six races, and would skip school whenever possible to go racing: 'I think my mother got sick of writing absent notes for me.'

With dreams of becoming a jockey always foremost in her mind, Lisa was sent to France when she left school to spend some months at John Hammond's yard in Chantilly. Despite missing Ireland and her home life, this was an important move towards her future race-riding career, and on returning to Ireland she followed up by taking a course at the Irish National Stud. But there was no riding and, since she desperately wanted to race-ride, she embarked upon further travels. Firstly, she went to Jonjo O'Neill at Jackdaws Castle in England, in the days of Wichita Lineman and Black Jack Ketchum, and then to the USA, where she regularly rode track work at Churchill Downs.

Encouraged by her father, Lisa took out her amateur licence at 16, but had 95 rides before finding a winner. This was on Vintage Fabric for Nigel Hawke at Newton Abbot in the summer of 2010, when as a member of the four-strong Irish team she spent a week in Britain. Lisa quickly followed up the success by winning on the Flat at the Curragh two weeks later.

Yet there were undoubtedly moments in those early days when she questioned whether she was pursuing the right career.

❛ I often thought there must be easier ways of getting through life, but I suppose my persistence, hard work and stubbornness eventually paid off – I continued to work for Dad and ride out with Jim Dreaper, who was a brilliant teacher – and I successfully rode in a number of point-to-points. ❜

In September 2012, Lisa was advised by the point-to-point expert Richard Pugh to approach Gordon Elliott. She remembers the excitement of going there, even though she broke her finger on the first day. As a 7lb claimer, she had her first winner for Gordon in a steeplechase against professionals.

Gordon Elliott and Gigginstown have since entrusted many of their rising stars to Lisa, especially in bumpers, and her links with Gordon's tremendously successful operation are strong. There is a great rapport between trainer and jockey. As well as riding out and

Richard Johnson shows Native River his appreciation after giving everything to win the 2018 Cheltenham Gold Cup

A flying dismount from an 11-year-old Jack Kennedy after pony-race success at Dingle races in 2010

Graham Lee and Amberleigh House on their way to Grand National glory in 2004

Carl Llewellyn reaches the pinnacle at Aintree. Earth Summit, successful in the 1998 Grand National, enters the old winner's enclosure

Title rivals and close friends Richard Dunwoody and Adrian Maguire arrive at Warwick together in 1994

Tony McCoy with Edredon Bleu, Terry and I after winning the 2000 Queen Mother Champion Chase, one of the all-time great races at Cheltenham

Patrick Mullins wins another Champion Bumper for his father Willie on Champagne Fever in 2012

Timmy Murphy shows his style aboard Well Chief at Aintree in 2007

Conor O'Dwyer and dual Champion Hurdle winner Hardy Eustace in the 2006 Aintree Hurdle

Jonjo O'Neill jnr and snr on the gallops at Jackdaws Castle

TOP: *Jamie Osborne and Coome Hill in the 1997 Cheltenham Gold Cup*

MIDDLE: *Dublin Flyer and Brendan Powell take off in the 1996 Cheltenham Gold Cup*

BOTTOM: *Robbie Power shows off his skills at the Hickstead Derby 2013*

The now unmistakable celebration of Davy Russell following Tiger Roll's second consecutive Grand National win

Harry Skelton shows how much Cheltenham means after winning the Mares' Hurdle aboard Roksana in 2019

JJ Slevin on his subsequent Cheltenham Festival winner Band Of Outlaws at Naas in February 2019

TOP: *The formidable partnership of Istabraq and Charlie Swan on their way to victory in the John James McManus Memorial Hurdle in October 1997*

MIDDLE: *Paul Townend struck gold in 2019 with Al Boum Photo, winning the Cheltenham Gold Cup in emphatic fashion*

BOTTOM: *Mark Walsh in the familiar colours of JP McManus is carried to victory at the Punchestown festival by flashy grey Elimay*

Ruby Walsh and Vautour flying to victory in the 2016 Ryanair Chase, one of the finest sights in racing

Norman Williamson and Monsignor in action at Ascot in the 1999 Kennel Gate Novices' Hurdle

going racing, Lisa also helps in the office. She has become a stylish rider who listens to her instructions and she uses her head in a race. Her future looks bright and she has deep roots in the sport. Opportunities have been plentiful thanks to her parents, top trainers and understanding owners. To Lisa, horses are like a drug: she lives for them and her racing results have been superb.

Denis O'Regan

Denis O'Regan was born in March 1982 in Youghal, Co Cork. His father, also called Denis, is a farmer and his mother, Geraldine, runs the Lombards pub which is 200 years old and has been in the family for many generations. From an early age Denis was extremely fortunate to have had a great understanding with the renowned horseman Michael John Desmond, who lived close to the family home and had numerous interests in country matters. Not only did he have his own pack of beagles but he also farmed cattle and produced top show horses, several of whom became champions at the RDS horse show.

Denis's father would drop off his 'pony-mad' son at Michael John's stables and leave him there for the entire day. At the age of five he was given a tough little Shetland pony called Jimmy that his dad had purchased from travellers. He was a typically naughty Shetland, and Denis rode him bareback, which was a real challenge, since good balance was paramount. Yet, despite his wicked ways, Jimmy could jump. Denis recalls many hours jumping him round the Desmonds' sandpit under the watchful eye of the expert. Working in the yard meant that Denis learned basic horse mastership from an early age. Feeding, lunging, plaiting and grooming were all on his agenda. As well, he saw how horses were broken in and taught to jump. It was a better introduction to the horse world than any Pony Club camp.

When Denis outgrew Jimmy his father found Tiger to replace him. He was a 13.2hh grey Connemara again purchased from the local gypsies. Tiger was a good pony but impossible to tie up. Denis remembers the day when he was supposedly secured to a gate, but pulled away and took the whole gate with him. He galloped for several miles down the roads, with sparks flying as the gate scraped the stones, but such is the toughness of the breed that when he was eventually stopped there was not a scratch to be seen. If Tiger had been a racehorse he would undoubtedly have been injured. After Tiger, Denis's dad was given Jessie by a neighbour. This brilliant mare lived until she was 23 and Denis did everything with her, from taking her hunting to riding her in local gymkhanas.

As Denis grew older, his ponies were kept at home, and he would ride them out every day after school even if it was dark. He would go all over the local countryside. There were no mobile phones and his parents were constantly worried as to his whereabouts, since he would jump anything in sight including cattle grids. At weekends he went hunting, and his father bought a little horsebox. On one occasion, aged 13 and crossing a river on one of the ponies, he fell into a salmon hole and was washed downstream. When he got out, soaked to the skin, his father revived him with a hot whiskey in the local pub.

Although Denis did take part in a few pony races, it was drag hunting that really gripped him, and he mastered it to a fine art. He particularly enjoyed the speed element. Many of the followers had falls and there were frequently loose ponies in the fields but Denis would catch them, jump onto them, and take them back to their owners. His companions on the drag hunts included Davy Condon, Liam Corcoran and the Keniry brothers Liam and Barry. They have become lifelong friends.

Despite enjoying the hunting and the gymkhanas, Denis dreamed of race-riding and he yearned to ride in point-to-points. His dad bought him an unbroken mare out of a field near Conna. She was well bred but covered in warts. Michael John Desmond took her into his yard and tied elastic bands around the warts so that they eventually dropped off. Once Marion's Own was old enough, Denis's father decided to train her and Denis rode her at weekends. She gave him his first ride in a point-to-point at Carrigtwohill in 1998, but he rode far too short and when she made a mistake at the first fence Denis went straight over her head, taking the bridle with him. Later, he had several placings and the mare became an excellent school mistress. She was even fifth and sixth in two bumper races.

Whilst still at school Denis spent several summer holidays with Francis Flood at Grangecon, and in 2001 the trainer gave him a bumper ride at Cork Racecourse on All Honey. He finished fifth. Three days later, at the Listowel festival, the same horse won by a short head and beat Philip Fenton's mount. This was the beginning of Denis's career as a jockey, and in the early 2000s he won plenty of bumper races.

In 2004, Denis began riding out for Noel Meade and in December he had a double at Gowran Park. A year later he rode the Dermot Weld-trained Ansar to victory in the Galway Plate. His successes in Ireland were impressive and, while based at Noel's Tu Va yard, he rode for a number of other trainers including Michael Hourigan. However, in 2007, when stable jockey Paddy Brennan moved from Howard Johnson's in County Durham to Nigel Twiston-Davies's yard, Denis was invited over to England to fill the vacancy. Yet, to start with it was not all plain sailing and like many other young Irish jockeys, he found it took him some time to settle in a different country. Being only 24 and taking on this important job had many challenging aspects. In his early twenties, Denis had a certain arrogance about him – maybe due to a lack of confidence. Despite being recognised as a good jockey and a first-class horseman, he tended to put people's backs up. At the same time Tony Dobbin had ties with Nicky Richards and Graham Lee was connected to Ferdy Murphy. Competition in the north was strong but Denis did well and remained the retained jockey to Graham Wylie for three years. He forged a great partnership with both Inglis Drever and Tidal Bay. He rode in top races and won on both horses at the Cheltenham Festival. Yet, in April 2010, Denis ended his contract with Graham Wylie and went freelance.

Nowadays, with many victories to his name, including a number of top races, Denis O'Regan continues to be regarded by trainers as a supremely talented rider. He has recently built up a good understanding with Gordon Elliott and regularly rides out at Cullentra. He has had some nice winners for the yard.

The Denis O'Regan approach to life has changed and with the

support of his wife Louise, and his young son Thomas, he is looking forward to further successes as a National Hunt jockey. Denis commands plenty of respect and is sure to continue as a prominent figure in the racing world. He is a genuine friend to those who know him well and readily gives advice to younger jockeys.

Jamie Osborne

In March 1999, with 950 National Hunt winners to his name, Jamie Osborne stunned the racing world by retiring from race-riding. He was just 31.

Jamie was a top rider and had an enviable style. His horses consistently jumped with confidence. Yet, he experienced several injuries, and reasoned that it was time to quit. Maybe more National Hunt jockeys should take a leaf out of his book since many continue when their confidence is low and they are riding on a downward curve.

During his early days as a jockey, Jamie spent several summers in France riding out for Jean Bertran de Balanda, one of the top French jumps trainers, and learned some golden rules: *keep your horse going forwards, keep it in balance and keep yourself balanced on top*. Jamie always believed in communicating with his horses, and maintains that racehorses jump through a mixture of fear and bravery. How often does a horse look to its rider for encouragement? The answer is frequently, but many National Hunt jockeys do not understand this and chase their mounts when jumping obstacles with forceful body movements and too much whip. They do not look part of the horses they ride, nor do they sit deep into them like John Francome, Davy Russell or Ruby Walsh. The top jockeys let the fences come to their horses.

Jamie's riding talents were apparent from an early age, but although he shared a brown Welsh pony with one of his sisters, his attitude to riding up until the age of ten was 'take it or leave it'. Home was close to Boston Spa in Yorkshire, and his entrepreneurial father managed a property company in Sheffield, as well as doing a small amount of farming – 'he kept pigs in the buildings and fields around the house'. Both Jamie's parents had enjoyed riding as children, and as teenagers had ridden together in a pairs class at a hunter trial. Jamie's uncle was Master of the Holderness Hunt, and Jamie would often ride the full-sized hunters. It is always exciting for a child to ride a big horse.

In those childhood days he was happy to participate at the low-key local shows, but preferred to steer the farm pick-up truck along the drive. Stable work was not for him: 'I did not like looking after the ponies, but I was happy to ride them provided everything was done for me. But I was competitive when it came to the horse shows, and I enjoyed jumping.'

At the age of 12 Jamie Osborne took his competing on working hunter ponies to a high level. He travelled all over the country and registered many wins. His parents were extremely fond of the big horse shows, and Jamie won many classes, including championships, at the top level, in particular at the Royal Show and at Peterborough. He also represented GB when a team of riders were sent to the RDS horse show. He even partnered ponies belonging to Trevor Banks, the famous Yorkshire entrepreneur who provided many well-known show-jumpers and event horses for top riders, notably the Princess Royal and Malcolm Pyrah, who rode Goodwill and Anglezarke respectively. Jamie's mother had sown the seeds for her son as she too had ridden for Trevor Banks. At the horse shows there were always more girls than boys competing but Jamie especially enjoyed this aspect of his pony days.

In his early teens Jamie bought a pony of his own for the sum of £300. It belonged to the jockey Edward Hide's wife and it was a difficult ride, but he retrained it, and it ended up as one of the best 14hh working hunter ponies in the country. Not surprisingly, with Jamie's love of wheeling and dealing, he sold it on for a large profit. This demonstrated the child rider's ability to remake a pony – riding breakers and youngsters is valuable experience for any future jockey.

Jamie Osborne was educated at the grammar school in Boston Spa and got a good education. In his spare time he watched racing and studied form. He often entered the *Pacemaker* 'Ten to Follow' competition and, despite being underage, used his pocket money to back horses. He longed to ride racehorses, and it was Trevor Banks who helped him yet again by taking him to David Nicholson's yard at Condicote in the Cotswolds when he was 13 years old.

The fortnight that Jamie spent with 'The Duke' left him hooked on National Hunt racing. Renowned for starting off and helping many top jockeys, David felt they benefited from having their first experiences on racehorses during their teenage years. 'Jamie Osborne showed no end of promise in his brief spells with me in his school holidays,' he recalled. 'Now and then you see an absolute natural, like Jamie, at an obstacle. I had high hopes for him.'

After his weeks in Gloucestershire, and intent on broadening his horizons, Jamie went to Josh Gifford's establishment at Findon in Sussex. He also continued to ride racehorses closer to home. Indeed, every day before school he would cycle the three miles to Harry Wharton's yard near Wetherby. Harry trained around 35 horses, including Amber Rambler and Phil The Fluter, and allowed Jamie to ride plenty of them on the home gallops. He also rode out at weekends for the Dickinson family near Harewood, who successfully trained some of the best jumpers in the country. During his race-riding days many referred to Jamie as 'Mrs Dickinson's darling' due to the winners he rode for her. He rode out too for Don Lee, who trained Misty Spirit to beat Dawn Run in a novice chase at Cheltenham.

On the very same day that Jamie Osborne finished his A-levels in Maths, Economics and Geography, and with his mind set on going full-time into a racing yard, he stood beside the A1 with a bag on his shoulders and a crash helmet in his hand. He had already organised his digs, and he thumbed a lift into Middleham where he began riding out for Neville Crump, Sally Hall, Chris Thornton and Jumbo Wilkinson. By then he had ridden in a few point-to-points and had a winner for Harry Wharton, but point-to-pointing was not top of his list. He reasoned that many of the maiden point-to-pointers were bad jumpers, and in those days back protectors were unheard of. He was only interested in riding horses from licensed trainers' yards.

Jamie Osborne's first winner under rules was in 1986, when Fair Bavard, trained by Harry Wharton, won a three-mile amateur riders' handicap at Southwell. It opened at 33-1 and started at 3-1. Also riding in the same race were Tarnya Davis, now married to Oliver Sherwood, and Tim Thomson Jones. In 1987, he had his first taste of the Cheltenham Festival when he rode Bally-Go for Jimmy FitzGerald to finish fifth in the Kim Muir Chase, and a 66-1 chance for Kevin Morgan in the four-mile National Hunt Chase. He finished second and a number of people took note of his riding.

Later in 1987, Jamie moved to Nicky Henderson's yard and, on the back of his wins as an amateur, took out his conditional licence. In 1988, riding on the crest of a wave, he was appointed stable jockey to Oliver Sherwood, whose brother Simon had just retired. This was in the days of Cruising Altitude, Rebel Song and The West Awake, and the new jockey had many big wins, including Aldino in the Grand Annual Chase at the 1991 Cheltenham Festival. It was the first of 11 festival wins for Jamie, who also won the Irish National for John Mulhern on Flashing Steel and the Irish Champion Hurdle on Collier Bay for Jim Old. When based with Oliver Sherwood, he won the prestigious Hennessy Gold Cup on Arctic Call in 1990, and then the same race in 1996 on Coome Hill, trained by Walter Dennis.

Jamie Osborne revelled in the big days and he enjoyed making the running on a number of his horses because he could get them into a desired rhythm. He reasoned that when in front, the majority would relax and he could ride them in the way that he liked. His quiet style was appreciated by trainers, and he was given a number of plum rides on high-class horses. Yet he was never satisfied with his performances in the saddle, and always looked to improve. He was a perfectionist and self-criticism is undoubtedly the sign of a good jockey: there is always more to learn.

During my years of training racehorses Jamie rode more than 100 winners from my yard at West Lockinge Farm, and from 1991 to 1999 I had second claim on him as a jockey. He was a big asset, and gave me my first Cheltenham Festival winner when riding Karshi to victory in the Stayers' Hurdle in 1997. It was always entertaining to have Jamie as part of our team but he never took his injuries well and he did not have the same outlook as AP McCoy or Terry Biddlecombe. 'I did not like getting hurt, not because of the pain but because I missed out on good rides and earning money. It was always a slow business getting back onto the racecourse.' He was as impatient as he was competitive.

Jamie has always liked to be different and although he currently trains Flat horses, he retains his interest in National Hunt racing. His enquiring mind, combined with his racing knowledge, means that his theories are always interesting. Given that jumping is of the utmost importance in the National Hunt game, he rues the vast amount of ignorance among trainers when it comes to educating their horses. Many have never ridden over a fence or even learned to jump on ponies. How can these trainers tell the jump jockeys how to ride? Fortunately, the leading trainers in England, Ireland and France have sound records and many of them have successfully ridden under rules themselves, but it must be hard for a young jockey to take orders from a trainer who has never participated in a race. It is why during my days as a trainer I always left Terry Biddlecombe to give the instructions.

Jamie believes that with chasers the conservation of energy is vital. He notes that many jockeys ask their horses to stand off too far at fences, and there are only a limited number of extravagant leaps any horse can comfortably execute during a race. Jumping too big is energy-sapping and detrimental to the overall finishing position. Horses need to take breathers in a race and these can only be taken when, on the take-offs, they chip in on short strides; too many long shots are wasteful. Horses who jump out of a rhythm and are economical over the obstacles are undoubtedly superior. Best Mate was the classic example – the fences came to him and he seldom met one wrong. He never wasted any energy. John Francome, Ruby Walsh and Davy Russell are prime examples of jockeys who have always encouraged their mounts to do the same. Fortunately, some of the younger jockeys of today are trying to follow in the footsteps of those riders. Let's hope they succeed.

Richard Pitman

Richard Pitman has always had a close affinity with Cheltenham racecourse. He was born at Bishop's Cleeve, a little village barely a couple of miles away. In 1974 he won the Champion Hurdle on Lanzarote.

Yet despite growing up close to the Mecca of steeplechasing, Richard did not have a family with profound horse connections, and there were certainly no links with racing. His father, a clever man, was an aircraft engineer, and though both his parents were happy hackers and enjoyed riding horses from the local riding school, it was never more than quiet rides along the lanes and across the countryside.

Richard was one of four children, and his sister Pam, who liked horses, later married Paddy Cowley, who won the Welsh Grand National twice with Motel in 1963 and Royal Toss in 1971. Richard was not interested in riding when he was young, but Pam was determined to make him learn on the 11hh pony Honeybunch that they had borrowed from a local farmer. Therefore, at 5.30am every morning, she would wake her brother and, before school, would lead him on his pony from her bicycle along the grass verges. He was barely six. The verges were rough and interspersed with drainage ditches, the riding was uncomfortable and the pony often stumbled. Richard nearly fell off many times, but when his sister found a more suitable place for cantering he was surprised by how good it felt. Jockeys often say the same thing when they ride racehorses: it is easier to canter than to trot.

Although not enjoying being forced to ride Honeybunch, Richard nevertheless developed an interest in racing, and would play truant from school any day there was a meeting at Cheltenham. He set off from home with his sandwiches in a bag, and wearing his school uniform but, instead of getting onto the double-decker that took him and his classmates to school, he would hide his school clothes in a hollow tree and change into his racing ones. Then he would walk up the hill beside the racecourse to watch the action from the fence close to the top of the hill. His mother never found out.

Richard was fascinated by what he saw, and loved hearing the noise of the horses' hooves pounding the ground. He even remembers an occasion when two top jockeys, Bryan Marshall and Arthur Thompson, were duelling for the lead in a steeplechase and one of the riders leaned over and removed the whole bridle from his opponent's horse. In the 1950s and 1960s jockeys could get away with these tricks – there were no cameras.

In his teens Richard became more interested in riding ponies, and competed at a few local shows. One summer, he remembers, winning a huge cup for the best child rider, but he says the result was a foregone conclusion because his father was the chairman of the show.

At the age of 16, having missed so many schooldays, the naughty child, who paid little attention to his book work, failed all nine of his O-levels. His parents were naturally disappointed, and his father ordered him to get a job. Due to his interest in racing and riding he was sent to work at trainer Phil Doherty's stables on Cleeve Hill, the famous backdrop to the racecourse. Photographs of his early days as a stable lad show him riding out in wellington boots with the tops turned over, a pair of tattered jeans and an old jumper. There were no crash helmets in those days.

Richard enjoyed his days with Phil Doherty and loved the sensation of speed. The trainer had a small yard of around 20 horses and was a good horseman. The racehorses were worked on the top of Cleeve Hill, which comprises 3,000 acres of grassland, but if a rider had difficulty stopping there was always the fear of going over the edge of the hill, and on foggy mornings work riding was challenging and dangerous: the marked-out gallops could not be seen. Brough Scott, who was working for trainer Frenchie Nicholson, whose horses also used Cleeve Hill, remembers Richard, completely out of control, streaking past him on a runaway black horse.

In the early 1960s, Phil Doherty lost his licence after one of his horses, Precipite, was blood-tested at Newton Abbot races. It had not run for several years, was unfancied and pulled up, but because it sweated profusely it attracted the attention of the stewards. The test was positive for a banned substance and Richard, who looked after the horse, was ordered to accompany the trainer to a hearing in London in front of the Jockey Club disciplinary board. 'It was a daunting occasion and the boss had no chance. In those days the discovery of an unlicensed substance was not just a ban for a few months, it was for life.'

After short spells with two more small trainers, John Roberts at Prestbury and AA Gilbert in Andoversford, Richard moved to Lambourn, and his life in racing took a new turn. He had been longing to have rides on the track, and the first one, Rossagio at Hereford in September 1961, came thanks to Major Champneys, by whom the keen young jockey was employed for several years.

❛ A great man, and one from the old school. His stable management was superb, and we rolled back the straw in front of the doorways every evening in order to leave a bare concrete strip, on which we would bang out the body dust from the metal curry comb to show the trainer how hard we had groomed the horse.

I learned a lot in his yard – but he was a strict taskmaster and did not suffer fools. On one occasion, on June 11, 1962, I rode in a race at Fontwell and travelled to the racecourse with the trainer. It was a day when the jockey Clive Chapman rode five winners, but I remember he hit my horse hard on its head when I drew level with him down the back straight. I lost my stirrups and my whip and nearly fell off. I ended up wobbling all over the place and slapping my horse either side of its neck with the ends of the reins. I explained what happened to Major Champneys, but all he said was, 'I don't want to hear: you've made enough of a fool of yourself for one day. Get into the car.' It was a long journey home. ❜

In 1964 Richard moved yards in Lambourn and started working for the legendary Fred Winter, who had just begun training following his brilliant years as a National Hunt jockey when he had been champion four times. Richard rode Fred's first ever runner in a chase at Ludlow but was unseated at the first fence. The horse was a strong puller and had taken charge with the inexperienced jockey. He remembers his guv'nor saying to him afterwards, 'You have to learn from these mistakes.'

After that disastrous start he had no more rides for three months, but did eventually get his first winner when Indian Spice was victorious at Fontwell on December 30, 1964. 'Strangely, I was disappointed by that win. I thought it would have been more exciting, but the horse won so easily, and by so far, that there was no contest.' Richard stayed at Uplands for the remainder of his time as a jockey, and didn't retire until 1975.

It was a long, slow road. When he first signed on with Fred Winter, Eddie Harty was the stable jockey, and then for two years Richard shared the prime position with Paul Kelleway, but when Paul moved on he was the principal jockey on his own for many years, before being joined by the ten-years-younger John Francome. Shortly after that Richard decided on retirement, having been offered a job with the BBC Racing team, which subsequently lasted for 35 years.

Over the years Richard rode some class horses for Fred Winter and, apart from Lanzarote winning the Champion Hurdle and his association with the talented Pendil, on whom he won the King George VI Chase twice, he rode the brilliant Australian chaser Crisp, whose gallant defeat by Red Rum in the 1973 Grand National has been chronicled in every racing history book. 'Riding Crisp in the 1973 Grand National was the most exhilarating experience of my life. To do what that horse did with top weight, and against the Aintree specialist Red Rum, was an incredible performance.' He rode 470 winners as a National Hunt jockey, and was a workmanlike, enthusiastic and extremely reliable pilot who listened to Fred's instructions and formed an excellent partnership with him.

Despite his lack of O-levels Richard has an excellent brain, as demonstrated by the books he has written and the many years he spent working for the BBC and the racing channels. In 2012, aged 69, he rode in the Legends Flat race at Aintree on Grand National day just ten weeks after donating a kidney, and with just 16 minutes in hand to get to his interview location for the television coverage. For many years he was married to the top trainer Jenny, and their son Mark both rode and trained winners.

Richard's philosophical approach to race-riding and way of accepting defeat were admirable, but he never had the same killer instinct as some of his contemporaries. He went out to win races, but unlike like the champions Richard Dunwoody, Richard Johnson and AP McCoy he was not driven to ride more and more winners. As his seventy-fifth birthday treat he went back to Lambourn to school over fences for the trainer Jamie Snowden – on the very ground where he had schooled for Fred Winter, 54 years earlier.

Brendan Powell

Ruby Tuesday was Brendan Powell's first pony, and he made him as a rider. Bought by his father for £20, he was originally purchased as the teaser for Waterloo Stud near Mallow, which his father managed for Liz Nelson, but he soon became surplus to requirements and was gelded. But this cracking 14.2hh bay turned out to be the best hunting pony in the vicinity.

The child adored him, and kept him with a neighbour, who fortunately had a shed beside his little cottage and a tiny field. Brendan converted the shed into a stable and made the door out of pallets. From his pocket money he bought four bales of straw each week, plus a bale of hay and a bag of hard food. He did the clipping himself, and kept the pony's mane closely hogged. Every morning he exercised Ruby before going to school, and he always rode him bareback. On hunting days with the Duhallow Hunt, where Liz Nelson was one of the masters, he would think nothing of hacking several hours to the meets and staying out with the hounds all day. He would then ride home again via the quiet back roads.

Brendan had no lights – not even a torch – and in those days there were no satnavs or mobile phones. His parents must have been extremely trusting, but the boy and the pony always ended up back at the stable, even if it was eight or nine o'clock at night. The only downside with Ruby Tuesday was that he hated show-jumping. 'But fortunately I was able to ride other people's ponies at the local shows. I loved the jumping.'

Brendan's father, Thomas Brendan Powell – known to everyone as Benny – was a prominent horseman in Ireland and greatly respected, but he always wanted his son to go into racing. One of Brendan's brothers, Leo, grew too tall to be a jockey, and is currently editor of *The Irish Field*. As Brendan hated school – never attending on a Wednesday, but going hunting instead – he left at 15 and his father sent him to the legendary PP Hogan at Rathcannon in Co Limerick.

Patt was an outstanding horseman and had a yard full of quality point-to-point horses. The top Hogan horses in those days included Underway and Any Crack, and the jockeys riding for him were John Fowler and Niall 'Boots' Madden. Patt was probably one of the greatest judges of a horse who has ever lived, and an exceptional rider to hounds. But he was tough on his horses and tough on his employees. He gave them no leeway: if he said 'jump' they jumped. Though his orders were sometimes utterly unreasonable, they had to be obeyed. PP made many top jockeys and sold some great horses. He always had the best amateurs in the county riding for him in point-to-points.

It was certainly a big shock to the young Powell boy to be delivered to this establishment and expected to settle in straight away. He had never been away from home before, and now found himself left to his own devices in one of the most spartan places in the country. His bedroom, if the tiny dark attic room could be called such, was reached by a narrow winding staircase. He had no window, and there was no heating and no electricity. The only lighting was a paraffin lamp that was lit by a match and ran off methylated spirits. Brendan remembers the rickety springs of his bed being covered by an old mattress and a horse blanket. The room was exceedingly damp, with condensation visible on the bare plastered walls. The lad never got any pay, since PP considered he was doing him a favour by having him to work there and making him into a jockey.

Brendan still remembers his first night at Rathcannon.

Dad dropped me off at four o'clock. It was cold and wet – almost dark. My bag was taken up to the attic room and I was told to come down to the kitchen and eat supper with the boss. The meal was cooked by Susan Hogan, PP's daughter. A plate of food was put in front of me on the table, but there was no cutlery.

'What are you waiting for, Mallow man?' said Patt.

'Could I have a knife and a fork?'

'No, hands were made before knives and forks were invented.

The daily work programme was tough. Brendan was woken up every morning at six o'clock and told to go into the yard where, in the dark, he climbed up an old ladder to fill 30 or 40 haynets amidst the mice in the hayloft before the rest of the staff began work at 7.30am. He was only allowed to ring home once a week on the old 'turn-a-dial' phone. The day-to-day existence was certainly austere, but it did help to make Brendan a jockey. He rode numerous young National Hunt horses and jumped countless fences. As three-year-olds, the horses were jumping banks, poles and hurdles as well as steeplechase fences. They too were given tough treatment, but it was a great experience and Brendan stayed there for seven months. Roger Hurley, one of Patt's top riders and an excellent horseman, supplied him with his lifeline of ten cigarettes a day, but he never touched alcohol, and indeed has been teetotal his entire life.

During his time with Patt Hogan, Brendan was only allowed to go home once, and that was when he broke his collarbone. He never wore a crash helmet, and back protectors were unheard of: such was the norm for young would-be National Hunt jockeys in the 1970s. Nowadays, aspiring jockeys do not realise how easy modern life has become.

Brendan did not ride in any point-to-points when he was at Patt Hogan's, but when he was 14 he had been given a couple of rides by his father at Doneraile and Kildorrery on an ex-racehorse called Buddy Overstreet. Nowadays children are not allowed to ride in point-to-points until they are 16. In 1974 Brendan weighed 7st 7lb, and used a five-stone lead cloth, since the horse he rode had to carry 12st 7lb.

After his stay in Co Limerick, Brendan went to the Curragh to work for Michael Dilger, who had a permit. He had a few unsuccessful rides in bumpers, but was at least riding out on the biggest and most famous training grounds in Ireland. Then, he remembers, one Friday afternoon he got a telephone call from his father saying that he had fixed for him to go to England to Jenny Pitman's yard. He was 18 and had never left Ireland.

Getting on a plane at Dublin and flying to Heathrow was a completely new experience, but joining a big National Hunt yard in Lambourn led to greater things, and after a year with Mrs Pitman he was promoted to head lad, which gave the aspiring young jockey an invaluable insight into the management of top jumping horses. As an amateur he had a few rides in hunter chases and hurdle races, but he did not ride his first winner until he was 22, and that was on Button Boy at Windsor for Nick Ayliffe. By this time he had become a conditional jockey, and he beat Hywel Davies in a handicap chase.

After Jenny Pitman, Brendan worked a short time for David Gandolfo near Wantage in Oxfordshire, and had a number of outside rides before moving to Stan Mellor. Once a week he would go and ride out for other trainers, one of whom was permit holder Tony Latham near Worcester. One afternoon the commentator at Worcester racecourse put out a request for any conditional jockey present to go to the weighing room, because several jockeys had been injured earlier in the day and there were now a couple of horses declared to run without riders. Brendan had no riding gear with him, but he borrowed breeches and boots, even though due to his long skinny legs it meant the boots had to be held up with elastic bands. Amazingly the ride he was given was for Les Kennard, and the horse won. The very next day he rode three more horses for Les at Ludlow and had another winner and a second.

It was the beginning of a great partnership with the West Country trainer, and with what he learned there, as well as from Captain Tim Forster, where he later became first jockey for nearly three years, he obtained an invaluable grounding.

Brendan Powell notched up some superb wins during his years of riding. In 1988 he won the Grand National on Rhyme 'N' Reason after surviving a major mid-race blunder, and he will also go down in history for the memorable partnership he forged with Dublin Flyer, a magnificent Tim Forster-trained chaser on whom Brendan won the Tripleprint Gold Cup in 1994 and the Mackeson Gold Cup in

1995, both at Cheltenham. He also won the John Hughes Memorial Trophy at Aintree over the Grand National fences in 1995.

Brendan was at his best when riding staying chasers, since he was a patient jockey who never rushed his horses at the beginning of a race. These tactics were demonstrated when he won two Scottish Grand Nationals – Roll-A-Joint (1989) and Young Kenny (1999) – and two Midlands Nationals on Another Excuse (1996) and Young Kenny again (1999). He was forced to give up race-riding in May 2000 following a series of bad falls, one of which, when he punctured his lungs at Newton Abbot, left him close to death. Despite his injuries, he retired with 603 winners to his name.

Brendan Powell has always been a notoriously hard and conscientious worker, who understands horses and knows how they should be educated, managed and prepared for racing. From 2000 until 2019 he held a trainers' licence. He had numerous winners, and his horses always looked good on the tracks. Brendan is an excellent teacher, and proud of his son of the same name who is also a National Hunt jockey and has inherited his father's natural riding ability. Nowadays, the former Grand National winner is back in his native Ireland, where he ably assists Joseph O'Brien with his vast string of racehorses in Co Kilkenny. Over the years, Brendan has made a significant impact in racing circles. Not only greatly respected, he is universally popular amongst fellow jockeys past and present. He thoroughly understands the game and had an enviable start to his chosen career.

Brendan Powell jnr

Brendan Powell jnr always wanted to be a jockey so he could follow in his father's footsteps. His mother, Rachel, also an accomplished rider, worked for Kim Bailey and led up Mr Frisk in the 1990 Grand National.

Brendan jnr was riding an old Shetland pony called Bramble when he was only four. In 2000 Brendan snr gave up his jockeys' licence to embark upon a new career as a trainer, and the family moved to Morestead Stables near Winchester. There were always plenty of ponies to be seen, and Brendan's sister, Jenny, who is three years younger, enjoyed riding as well. Their bigger pony , Snoopy, who was 11 hands, helped to educate both children.

Rachel and Sabrina Maguire, Adrian's wife, later bought their children jumping ponies from Ireland, usually from the Goresbridge Sales. Woody, a coloured 12.2hh, was extremely naughty and constantly got loose, but he had plenty of talent, and Brendan jnr jumped him in numerous shows, mostly in BSJA classes where they won many red rosettes. The young Brendan was fortunate to have a number of lessons from the top show-jumping rider, Tony Newbery, whose words of wisdom have stuck with him throughout his years of race-riding. The children had a great life, and often stayed away to compete at the horse shows. In particular, they enjoyed the Wales and West Shows at Crick, and the ones at Bicton in Somerset.

Brendan jnr's parents split up when he was 12, and for a short while the children moved to live with their mother in Jersey. When he was barely 13 years old he rode in the Jersey show-jumping team on his grey 14.2hh pony Seamus. There were some good months out there, and the children had a lot of fun. Brendan went to school in Jersey and had instruction with his riding from Rachel, who even took out a training licence herself in order to race the three horses which she owned, all of whom turned out to be winners.

After a year in Jersey, Brendan returned with his mother and sister to Britain, and he rode out for his father at Morestead as well as when he moved to Lambourn. During the summer of 2009 he went to Adrian Maguire's home in Ireland and became involved in pony racing. He lived with the Maguire family and had almost 30 rides on ponies. They were fun days and he especially liked riding in the Dingle Derby, the blue riband of the Irish pony-racing circuit. During that time spent in Ireland, young Brendan learned a great deal with regard to race-riding and he even went back for a second summer the following year. It taught him how to read a race and get competitive: the children who ride in these races are totally switched on and fend for themselves – no leeway is given to those who are indecisive. Brendan snr often went over to watch his son and was a huge support, as was Adrian, who had himself been a top pony-race rider prior to his successes as a National Hunt jockey.

Brendan jnr started his first proper job when he was 16. He went to trainer Jonjo O'Neill's yard at Jackdaws Castle in Gloucestershire. He had his amateur licence and, as well as working as a normal stable lad, he rode in more than 40 point-to-points, although he only clocked up one winner, at Godstone, for Dave Phelan. His first winner under rules came when he rode Home for his father at Southwell in February 2011. When at Jackdaws, Brendan took out his apprentice Flat licence – he was tall but very light, and in 2012 he rode a winner for the Queen on the Flat, trained by Richard Hannon, at whose stable he also rode out. It was at the July meeting in Newmarket. At 17 he began riding for Colin Tizzard and had a conditional licence, which he held alongside his Flat one. He had 50 winners from the Tizzard yard, including five victories on Native River and his first Cheltenham Festival win on Golden Chieftain in the JLT Specialty Handicap Chase in which he claimed 3lb. His second festival winner came on Present View for Jamie Snowden in the Centenary Novices' Handicap Chase in 2014 when he was 18.

Unfortunately it was at this time when Brendan jnr, riding superbly and having spent a full season as a professional, was wrongly linked, along with two other jockeys, to an alleged rape case in Lambourn. The false accusations hung over him for 18 months before the case was dismissed, but during the interim Brendan lost a number of his contacts and it has taken him a while to regain his recognition as a top rider.

Nowadays, Brendan jnr rides work at many of the leading yards, in particular for Alan King, Paul Nicholls, Olly Murphy and Neil Mulholland. Not only does he continue to ride well in races, but with his natural eye for a fence and his ability to get horses into a rhythm he is in great demand as a schooling jockey. A thoroughly likeable person with outstanding manners, all he needs now are more opportunities from top establishments. With a good racing brain and excellent style in the saddle he could still go far.

Robbie Power

Con Power, Robbie's father, was a top show-jumper, and his son grew up idolising him. In the late 1970s and early 1980s, Con was three times a member of the victorious Aga Khan Cup team at the RDS horse show, along with Eddie Macken, Paul Darragh and James Kiernan. He had the most beautiful, quiet style and he always stood out as a special rider.

Robbie's mother, Margaret, was a top event rider and competed at the Badminton Horse Trials, and she gave her son a lot of riding lessons. She comes from the renowned Latta family in Co Wexford, and over the years her relations have bred numerous top National Hunt horses and supplied many good ones to English trainers.

Unfortunately, in 1988 Con's career was cruelly cut short by a bad accident when teaching a rider in a field in a strong wind. He never heard a loose horse approaching from behind and was hit on the head either by a swinging stirrup iron or by the horse's shoe. He was hospitalised for many months and out of action for nearly three years.

Known to his friends as Puppy, Robbie was born in May 1981 and grew up in Derrypatrick, near Summerhill in Co Meath. He and his sister, Elizabeth, did plenty of show-jumping when they were children. Robbie's 12.2hh pony, Skibereen Girl, was bought for £200 and then found to be carrying a foal. After a short spell in the paddocks she won numerous competitions and was sold to a buyer in England for £25,000. The family's best 13.2hh pony, Shady Boy, joined the Power team because he used to stop in the ring, but he soon changed his ways and with his new connections became well known on the show circuit. In 1997, Puppy won the 14.2hh show-jumping championship at the RDS horse show on Radiant Kismet.

During the winter months it was hunting that got the biggest tick. The Ward Union Hunt and the Meath Hunt gave the Powers a lot of sport, and both children had super ponies. The county is renowned for its big drains (ditches), and teaches young riders balance as well as awareness. In his teenage years, Puppy was allowed to be a whipper-in with the Wards.

Robbie left school at 16 to concentrate on his riding. He had already ridden and schooled some of the horses and ponies that his mother had bought, and his show-jumping successes won him a training bursary to visit the Irish show-jumper Peter Charles who was based in England. He stayed in Britain for three years, was paid £100 a week and rode many different horses. When Peter was competing on the continent Robbie was riding the horses at home and at the big English horse shows. He received priceless instruction from a top man.

In 2001 Puppy returned to Ireland and began to ride out racehorses at Jessica Harrington's yard, where his mother had a mare in training. Initially, he rode this horse to finish unplaced in a bumper, but then on December 19, 2001, on the same mare, Younevertoldme, he won a novice hurdle at Punchestown, beating Ruby Walsh by a neck. It was his first ride over hurdles, and from that day onwards he wanted to be a jockey. His father had produced and sold several good National Hunt horses in the past, notably Toby Tobias to Jenny Pitman, and as a child Puppy had ridden his Shetland pony, Judy, around the fields at Summerhill to lead the young racehorses.

After his initial winner he started riding out for Willie Mullins as well as for Jessie. He had his first win, as a conditional jockey, at Leopardstown on Hennessy day in 2002. At the end of that year, during the Christmas period he won the Grade 2 novices' chase at Limerick on Intelligent for the Harrington yard and when riding the same horse was victorious a year later in the Midlands National at Uttoxeter. He was still claiming 5lb. In fact 2003 was an especially good year for the young jockey and in August he won the Galway Plate for Thomas Mullins on Nearly A Moose. At the end of the 2003-04 National Hunt season, Robbie Power was champion Irish conditional.

Once hooked on racing Puppy ceased show-jumping, except for a visit back to Hickstead in 2013 when he won the famous

Speed Derby on his sister's ultra-consistent three-star eventer Doonaveeragh O One. For a National Hunt jockey who had won the Grand National to return to show-jumping was unprecedented. But Robbie is an exceptional rider, as his Aintree win on Silver Birch for Gordon Elliott in 2007 had shown. Partnering Sizing John to win the Cheltenham Gold Cup in 2017 further demonstrated his superb talents.

Robbie is renowned for the way he presents horses to fences. Thanks to his show-jumping experience he can weigh up obstacles from a long way out, and he has a fine eye for a stride. The jumping side of race-riding always came easily to the jockey but switching from horse shows to the National Hunt game meant that he had to learn how to ride a race. Nowadays, his tactics are sound but unlike many of his fellow jockeys he has not benefited from the experience of the pony-racing circuit.

Robbie Power remains Jessica Harrington's number-one jockey and he rides many horses for the Potts family. On his travels to England he has forged an excellent understanding with the Tizzards, and with horses of the calibre of Lostintranslation and Reserve Tank, both of whom are based with trainer Colin, there is plenty to dream about. Further high-profile wins are likely, and the former show-jumper is firmly established as a leading National Hunt jockey. He is well supported by his wife, Hannah, and their young daughter, Emma, could well follow in her father's illustrious footsteps.

Willie Robinson

Even in his eighties, Willie Robinson is as great a character as one could ever meet, he has an extremely dry sense of humour and a twinkle in his eye. His name will forever be linked to the great steeplechaser Mill House, whom he rode so stylishly and quietly in the 1960s for those epic duels with the mighty Arkle.

Willie Robinson was born in 1934, and his father trained a small string of racehorses at Phepotstown, near Kilcock in Co Meath. 'There was a lovely grass field and an uphill gallop. No all-weather surfaces in those days.' The family always farmed, and Willie was brought up in the countryside surrounded by animals. His sister, Mary Rose, was also an accomplished rider and later married the fine horseman Seamus Hayes.

Willie and Mary Rose used to build a course of fences around the farm each year and created 'our own Grand National'. They had two exceptionally good ponies: 'the Fat Thing', who was three-parts thoroughbred, and the Black Pony, who was part Welsh and very solid. Willie particularly enjoyed hunting with the North Kildare Harriers – 'we always got a good hunt'. The children would ride many miles to the meets and stay out with the hounds all day before hacking home in the dark. If the ponies lost sight of one another they would neigh continuously, so everyone knew the whereabouts of the child riders. Their mounts were inseparable.

Willie never attended the Pony Club, because his father disapproved of the instructors. He never had lessons, and did not wear a riding hat at home – crash helmets were still to be invented. In races, the riders wore cork helmets that looked more like half boiled eggs and were easily dislodged if a horse fell. During his years as an amateur, Willie rode in several point-to-points and won five, but 'I didn't look for point-to-point rides as I knew most of the horses were badly schooled or not schooled at all, and if I rode them I'd be certain to end up on a stretcher.'

In one year, in the early 1950s, his father trained the two best bumper horses in Ireland and Willie rode them both. He also won races over the banks at Fairyhouse and Punchestown, which demonstrated his superb balance in the saddle and ability to sit in the right place on a horse – not too far forward and not too far back.

In 1956 at the age of 22, Willie Robinson became a professional jockey. There were no apprenticeships in the 1950s, and to obtain a licence all that happened was that a jockey's name was approved by two Turf Club officials. Willie was proposed by Lord Fingall and George Malcolmson. To begin with, he continued to ride for his father – and was second in both the English and Irish Derbys on Paddy's Point.

Before moving to England to ride for Fulke Walwyn in the late 1950s, Willie was retained in Ireland first by Major John Corbett in the north and then by Dan Moore. The former was from all accounts a 'very good-looking man' whom Willie reckoned 'broke more than a few hearts when he announced he was getting married'. He trained close to the beach in Tyrella, and made his training a lot of fun. Willie would drive up there and cross the border in his old Morris Minor. He was 'often lucky to make it' up the steep hills.

Yet, his luck in Northern Ireland was good, and in 1962 he won the Ulster Harp National on the Peter Cazalet-trained Laffy, who was owned by Queen Elizabeth, the Queen Mother. Laffy appeared to finish second to Connkehely, but that horse, who was running in a bitless bridle – a hackamore – swerved to miss out a fence and was subsequently disqualified.

Willie learned plenty about racing from Dan Moore, a legendary trainer in Ireland who was later responsible for L'Escargot winning the Cheltenham Gold Cup in 1970 and 1971 as well as the Aintree Grand National in 1975. Willie also rode out for Phonsie O'Brien, Vincent's brother, and Charlie Rogers. He had winners for both.

This stylish rider then moved to Lambourn.

On arriving in England I wanted to find the police station to register my car and hand over some documents, so I asked for the Guards' Barracks, which is what police stations were called in Ireland. The lady I asked looked extremely surprised and said, 'There are no army barracks here. Lambourn is not a training area for soldiers.' I think she thought I was half mad. **❜**

Willie was retained by Fulke Walwyn as stable jockey for nine years and his days yielded many wins. It was a great partnership. He was the only jockey to win the Hennessy Gold Cup three times, riding Mandarin, Mill House and Man Of The West, and, besides winning the Cheltenham Gold Cup on 'the Big Horse' Mill House in 1963, he also won the Champion Hurdle on Anzio in 1962 and on Kirriemuir in 1965. He partnered Team Spirit to victory in the Grand National in 1964.

That horse was the perfect model of a racehorse – barely 15.2hh and by Vulgan. Big horses are not necessarily the best types for Aintree: the stallion Battleship, trained by Reg Hobbs, was 15.1hh and he carried the 6ft 2in amateur Bruce Hobbs to victory in 1938. Tiger Roll, who won with Davy Russell in 2018 and 2019, is 15.3hh. Big, long-striding horses often find it more difficult to shorten up and take that extra stride in front of a fence; shorter-striding, compact individuals are often more cat-like. Neither Red Rum nor Gay Trip were big horses, and they too won Grand Nationals.

Despite the many times Pat Taaffe beat Willie in the Arkle/Mill House days, they were the greatest of friends and lived close to each other in Ireland. They opposed each other in a number of epic races, but, even when beaten by him, Willie never felt bitterness towards his rival jockey. They rode two outstanding horses, and the public took both to their hearts.

Willie Robinson was always a natural in the saddle. Jockeys can improve their style and their balance, but a lot is inherited and Willie sat correctly on a horse from day one and was always positioned in the centre of balance. He barely ever moved over an obstacle.

When he stopped riding Willie trained a few horses himself, and King's Company, ridden by Freddy Head, beat Sparkler and Lester

Piggott in the 1971 Irish 2,000 Guineas. Throughout his racing career he was backed up by his knowledgeable and supportive wife Susan, an excellent rider herself whose father, Major Cyril Hall, managed the Irish National Stud in the days when the great stallion Tulyar stood there.

Willie Robinson remains unique in his achievements – he won a Grand National and almost won a Derby as well. He had that enviable unflappable magic touch with horses, and seemed to instinctively know how a racehorse should jump and gallop. Horses always went sweetly for Willie, and he was always loved by his public despite being a tough professional. His eyes light up at the mention of Mill House: he 'was the easiest horse I ever had to ride', he says, 'except that he was quite strong'.

Davy Russell

Davy – David Niall – Russell, who was born in June 1979, is an exceptional rider and a great jockey to watch in a race. He has had an amazing career, and his two Grand National wins on Tiger Roll in 2018 and 2019 will go down in all the history books. Yes, the horse was a star, but Davy's riding was outstanding.

Davy's father was originally a mechanic at the petrol station in Youghal in Co Cork. He never rode, but owned a few racehorses and bought 100 acres of land on the edge of town. He enjoyed farming and milked around 80 cows. Davy was one of six children, all of whom shared the same 12.2hh pony that had been bought unbroken at Tallow Horse Fair for £375.

The Russell children enjoyed their riding, but it was Davy who had the greatest enthusiasm, and he grew up with some good ponies. One of them, Vixen, who was 14.2hh and chestnut, did everything. She was hunted with the United and West Waterford Hounds, ridden in team chases, show-jumped and pony-raced. On one occasion, Davy recalls, she won a 'flapping' race on the Saturday and a significant show-jumping competition on the Sunday. She ended up being sold abroad.' He especially enjoyed the team chases because they were all about speed. His teammates were the Keniry brothers, Barry and Liam, as well as Colin Motherway. They had many successes.

Davy did not take part in many pony races and whilst acknowledging that they provide a great start for young would-be jockeys, he also believes that they encourage children to get into bad habits. 'They ride in a sloppy fashion and have no style. Their leathers are too short and they rely too much upon their whips.' He thinks children should sit into their ponies more and ride with a longer length of leg.

During those childhood days, Davy was already determined to become a jockey, and would often walk around the house and yard dressed in his father's racing colours – black with yellow diamond, the symbol for the Renault cars he used to sell. While still at school Davy spent his summer holidays in trainers' yards. He went to Frank O'Brien in Piltown when he was barely 13 and learned proper stable management as well as riding out racehorses. At the weekends he kept his eye in for jumping by competing on his JA pony at local shows and at 15 he spent his summer with Jim Bolger where he was proud to be given the sole responsibility of looking after a barn of nine horses. Davy also spent time with trainer Dermot Weld on the Curragh.

During one summer he spent a few weeks in England together with his friend, the prolific point-to-point rider James Sheehan. The boys lodged at West Lockinge Farm, where they had lessons on the schooling ground from my husband Terry Biddlecombe. 'Sit still,' Terry used to say to the jockeys, 'stay behind the horse's shoulders and let the fences come to you.' By all accounts the former champion jockey was extremely impressed by Davy's natural ability and told him that he could easily grow up to be the next Richard Dunwoody.

At 16, Davy had his first ride in a point-to-point, his father having bought him a mare as a schoolmaster. Davy used to ride her around the fields in order to get her fit before he went to school. Yet, the first outing at the Skibbereen point-to-point was unsuccessful, and Whitebarn Cailin did not provide the young jockey with a fairy-tale win. 'I'd never been so fast,' he recollects. 'It was a real shock to my system.' Davy also had a ride in a bumper for Pat Budds on a horse called Percy Hannon, but was only fourth.

Davy Russell left school at 17 and spent a year at Kildalton Agricultural College in Piltown, which was extremely convenient as he could ride out for Aidan O'Brien on the Hill at Owning and in those days the champion Flat trainer was training jumpers. After his college days Davy was determined to make his career in the racing world and spent invaluable time with Eugene O'Sullivan at Lombardstown near Mallow. Eugene would assign a horse to every young jockey who worked for him, and Davy was given the rides on Nearly A Hand and gained plenty of experience in handicap chases around the country.

Derek O'Connor, Brendan O'Sullivan and Martin Ferris were also at the yard, with William O'Sullivan the stable's amateur. They were great days with a lot of fun thrown in.

During the winter of 1996-97 Davy would ride almost every weekend in a point-to-point, but still no winner. He had to wait until 1999 to pick up a spare ride for Jimmy Mangan at Tallow on Spanish Castle. After which the winners came thick and fast.

Although he had a slow start, Davy Russell's years in point-to-pointing were ultimately extremely successful. He rode for top yards, notably for Liam Burke, Robert Tyner and Pat Doyle, and had nearly 300 winners in total. In the 1998-99 season he was novice rider champion, tying with Simon McGonagle.

In the spring of 2002, when Davy was walking the track at Ballynoe point-to-point, he started chatting with Tom O'Mahony, who was renowned for placing jockeys in English training yards. After their conversation, Davy moved to Ferdy Murphy in Middleham. He still remembers getting into his car and driving to Yorkshire, knowing nothing about handicaps, ratings or dealing with owners. It was an alien world and he had no idea where he was going.

His first win as a professional was on Inn Antique in a novice hurdle at Sedgefield on November 12, 2002. He spent two years with Ferdy and had many high-profile riding successes, winning the Peter Marsh Chase on Truckers Tavern in 2003 and finishing second to Best Mate in the Cheltenham Gold Cup on the same horse, but he missed Ireland and hated the cold winters. It was good experience for a young jockey, but despite riding winners he couldn't wait to return home.

Back in Ireland he spent a year with Edward O'Grady and then went freelance, riding out regularly for Mick O'Brien, Charles Byrnes, Robert Tyner and Arthur Moore. He won lots of races. The Railway Man – trained by Arthur – was his first Grade 1 winner.

It was at this time that Davy was offered the job with Gigginstown to ride the O'Leary horses and he had plenty of successes before being fired – a move that surprised everybody in National Hunt racing.

Since then, however, he has been invited back to ride their horses on countless occasions and been associated with many of their stars, notably Tiger Roll. The wheel appears to have done a complete turn.

Over the years Davy has registered many big successes, not least the Cheltenham Gold Cup on Lord Windermere in 2014. In 2018 he was leading jockey at the Cheltenham Festival. The top horses he has ridden include Weapon's Amnesty, War Of Attrition, Solwhit, Forpadydeplasterer, Presenting Percy and Back In Front, and he has been Irish champion jockey three times: 2011-12, 2012-13 and 2017-18.

These days Davy Russell is the senior statesman in the weighing room, and sets a great example to the younger generation. Davy studies the way in which less experienced jockeys ride and is always happy to analyse their weaknesses and offer advice. He maintains that children do not spend enough time riding ponies and he believes that all aspiring jockeys should know how to break in a horse and ride one from the start. Breakers provide the best form of education for any rider. They turn jockeys into horsemen.

The young jockeys of today do not sit into their horses and ride them from behind, which is particularly noticeable when they race around bends. Fifty yards from a bend a rider should be taught to set his horse up and balance it in readiness for making up ground after the corner. It is all about riding too short and bumping up and down on the horses' backs. It is the fault of the system: from the beginning young jockeys are not taught in the right way. They are not horsemen, just passengers who ride with their whips and are perched on top of their mounts. It is an unattractive way in which to ride a horse, and far less effective than the old, well-tested system.

Davy does not like overuse of the whip in races. 'It is used far too much and in place of the rider's legs and body. If a horse does not go for three cracks it will not go for ten.' Terry Biddlecombe had exactly the same philosophy. Admittedly whips have changed, and the current ones are less likely to mark horses, but Davy still deplores their excessive use.

Davy Russell will go down in history as one of jump racing's finest jockeys. The public admire him for his courage and unruffled countenance. Not only does he ride high-profile winners in Ireland and England but also in the USA and France. As one of his fans said after the 2019 Grand National, 'That jockey's bloody brilliant!' Few horsemen can handle the pressure of the big days like Davy Russell and he is an outstanding horseman with balance and style. He is also extremely knowledgeable on pedigrees of National Hunt horses. He enjoys producing youngstock from the family home in Youghal, and is developing an enviable nursery for future stars. He is likely to be deeply involved in the sport for many years.

Peter Scudamore MBE

The Scudamores have been prominent in the racing world for seven decades, and the present generations continue to demonstrate the closeness of the family.

Peter Scudamore's father, Michael, was a special man who, as well as winning the Grand National on Oxo in 1959 and the Cheltenham Gold Cup on Linwell in 1957, was respected and admired by all who knew him. The young riders of his day looked up to him for advice. A kinder and more understanding man would have been hard to find. Yet he was also tough and courageous.

His son Peter was determined not to let his father down, and by taking eight National Hunt jockeys' championships he ensured that Michael and his mother Mary were able to see that the support they had given him in his childhood had borne fruit. In winning two Champion Hurdles, four Welsh Nationals, two Scottish Nationals and a Champion Chase, Peter (Scu) demonstrated that he could ride any horse over any distance.

Peter grew up on the 150-acre family farm at Prothither in Hoarwithy, nine miles from Hereford, and racehorses, as well as cattle and sheep, were seen around the house. He had a wonderfully happy childhood. 'I learned, when riding out with Dad, all the old-fashioned ways of looking after horses – he gave them oats, cider vinegar, mashes and good hay. When getting them fit, we walked for ages on the roads before doing long, slow canters.' When Peter was very young, his father was still riding as a jockey, but serious injuries from a bad fall in 1966 ended his career. It was then that he took out a trainers' licence.

It was the Biddlecombe family who got Peter into ponies.

I remember going to a show at Ross-on-Wye, and the man on the loudspeaker introduced me as Peter Scudamore, the son of the famous jockey, Michael. It was a show-jumping class, and my pony refused three times at the first jump. It was highly embarrassing and I was naturally very upset.

It was after this that Dad took me to Walter Biddlecombe's farm near Upleadon. Walter was Terry's father and an amazing rider. His horse knowledge was second to none. He even put the shoes on his own horses, but he was a dealer at heart, and always had lots of ponies for sale. After our visit we came home with Black Opal, who was only 12.2hh but an incredible jumper. So much so that he would jump out of any stable we put him in. If we closed the top door, he would smash the windows, and if we put him in the fields – even with company – he would regularly jump the paddock railings and be found on a different part of the farm or in the village. In the end, we kept him in a high-fenced cattle yard and he settled. 〗

Despite these antics, Black Opal was, from all accounts, the perfect pony for Peter. He was a brilliant hunter as well as performing well in the show-jumping ring and taking in numerous hunter trials. 'He would jump anything, and he taught me so much.'

School days for Peter were at the Catholic school Belmont Abbey in Hereford, run by monks. Being a full-time boarder, he was taught independence and it weaned him off his idyllic home life, though his school friends never understood why he wanted to be a jockey. Scu rode out on racehorses from the age of 12, and he worked them around the water meadows beside the River Wye which were owned by Venetia Williams and used by Michael as gallops. He was often run away with but learned a vast amount and was never scared. Back at home under the watchful eye of his father he schooled numerous horses over chase fences. He was a supremely fit child, as not only did he ride the horses but he also helped on the farm. He has especially happy memories of the hay-making days, when bales were thrown up onto the trailers as the farmhands drove around the fields on the tractors. It was hard work but rewarding and Scu thrived on his country upbringing.

As he grew up, Peter was given rides in point-to-points which was the family tradition – his grandfather had regularly judged at the tracks and his sister Nicola rode a winner for the Twiston-Davies family. Scu's first winner between the flags was at the Belmont point-to-point when he was just 17 – he actually finished second to a horse of Bill Bryan's, but was awarded the race when Bill's jockey weighed in light. He proved to be a capable young jockey and he was mad keen. He ended up with six wins. The point-to-points provided the perfect springboard for his race-riding career.

On leaving school with good academic results, Peter was sent to Willie Stephenson's yard at Royston in Hertfordshire. The trainer had been responsible for Oxo for his father's Grand National win in 1959, and he had also trained Arctic Prince to win the Derby in 1951. Indeed, he was the only man in the 20th century to have saddled the winner of both these prestigious races.

However, Willie was a hard taskmaster and, although he knew that Scu wanted to ride in races, he told him, 'You'll never make a jockey – you're not hard enough. You should be an estate agent.' Indeed, Willie went on to line him up for a job with the agents Bernard Thorpe. Fortunately, when Scu entered their branch at Stow-on-the-Wold, he discovered it was close to David Nicholson's training establishment at Condicote. He started riding out there every day before work and then, with his amateur licence, rode nine winners in his first season under rules. His first winner was for Toby Balding when, at just 19, he partnered Rolyat to win an amateur riders' hurdle at Exeter. Peter certainly learned the finer points of race-riding when attached to David Nicholson's yard, and always remained loyal to him, even riding The Duke's first ever Cheltenham Festival winner when successfully taking the 1986 Triumph Hurdle on Solar Cloud.

However, it was Peter's association with Fred Winter that really put him on the map, and he ended up by winning the Champion Hurdle for Fred in 1988 on Celtic Shot, an extremely poignant occasion as the champion trainer was not present to see his winner having had a fall downstairs which was then followed by a stroke. After Fred's accident, Scu moved to Martin Pipe's yard and his appointment as stable jockey took his race-riding to a new level. He had 792 winners for the Nicholashayne champion trainer who famously declared that 'all I required was a jockey who wanted to win'. Peter was certainly a fine judge of pace, and on the Pipe horses he often led all the way. 'He went out,' says Pipe, 'knowing the horses would jump and he got them jumping and running. He used to ride the racecourses the proper way, the same as AP McCoy – both jockeys knew where the wet ground was and they rode accordingly.' Throughout his days as a jockey, Scu was renowned for his will to win and it hurt him to lose. 'I was probably at my best when I was young because I was full of confidence and never believed I would get hurt. My enthusiasm pushed danger to the side. Lester Piggott was my hero.'

Peter Scudamore sets a fine example to today's young jockeys, and emphasises the value of a close-knit family upbringing, but it saddens him to see how few of the current riders are coming into racing from upbringings within village communities. Standards have undoubtedly slipped with regard to basic horsemanship skills, and he feels that the emphasis is now upon 'doing everything as quickly as you can in order to get a ride on a racecourse. Everyday life moves in the fast lane, aided by mobile phones and the internet. Social media has taken over jockeys' lives.'

When Peter Scudamore retired at the age of 34, he wanted to put back into racing his knowledge of the sport that he valued, hence his work with the BBC and writing for the racing pages of the *Daily Mail*, which gave the public many insights into the game. His views have always been interesting and sound.

Nowadays, whilst assisting his partner Lucinda Russell with her training in Scotland, he is a wonderful teacher for the young enthusiasts who come to the yard. However, despite the current fashion for equicizers he believes that there is no substitute for riding a horse. Practical experience and watching others on the gallops or schooling grounds count far more than 20 minutes perched on a man-made machine. Feel and the human eye are of vital importance and confidence is everything.

It is not surprising that Scu was such a fantastic jockey. 'My father set such an example of toughness that I had to show a similar toughness' – indeed Peter became almost blinkered in his attempt to ride winners. He now realises there are other things to life and, while understanding that young jockeys are hungry for success, he never forgets his father's words. 'Dad maintained that there were three important things in life – to sleep with a woman, jump Becher's at Aintree and jump out of a plane with a parachute.' Scu has certainly ticked off the first two, but has said no to the final one, despite once jumping off a mountain in the Swiss Alps.

The Scudamore dynasty is unique, running through the last 60 years of jump racing 'like a golden thread in a rich tapestry'. It could never be repeated. Scu's son Tom represents the third generation, and has already ridden many good winners under National Hunt rules – notably Thistlecrack for Colin Tizzard as well as Dynaste and Vieux Lion Rouge for David Pipe – but, unlike his father, can also claim to have parachuted out of an aeroplane. Scu's other son Michael is now successfully training close to the family home in Herefordshire and has already had a winner at the Cheltenham Festival.

Peter Scudamore thoroughly deserves his MBE for his services to the sport, and I feel honoured that he rode winners from my yard. He has done a vast amount for National Hunt racing and his career as a jockey was outstanding. Happily, he retains his enthusiasm for the game and continues to help others.

Gavin Sheehan

When Gavin Sheehan was ten he liked the idea of having a pony, so he asked Santa Claus for a rocking horse.

Father Christmas did not come up trumps, but Gavin's mother read her son's letter and bought him a real 13hh pony who was black with a big white star. He was no beauty – scruffy and long-haired with no mouth and scant manners – but, kept in a neighbour's field, he gave Gavin his first riding experiences. The young boy taught himself to ride, but Star was not always co-operative and the child had plenty of falls. He rode his friend's donkey as well and even took part in a few donkey races, which were very popular in the Cork area where he grew up.

When one of the stallion donkeys, the Captain, sired some foals, Gavin saved up his pocket money and bought Sergeant Darko for €100. He was six months old, but as the years went by Gavin broke in this donkey and rode him.

❝ I had no idea how to teach a donkey to be ridden, but I was told that I should use a straight-bar bit and tie horse hair round it to make him mouth. I did this, but the bit was way too wide and he had a tiny muzzle. I drove him with long reins, but he always had a dreadful mouth and he dragged me everywhere. I rode Darko in a few donkey Derbies, and my grandmother made my colours. ❞

The desire for a rocking horse came about through going with his friends to watch the local 'flapping' and trotting races. Gavin had not grown up in a family that rode horses, although his mother always liked the idea of them. He did spend his childhood surrounded by stunning countryside, however, and is pleased to have been able to enjoy all the sports offered to him at school – Gaelic football and hurling being his favourites. The closest he came to racing was watching it on television. To that extent his rise to become one of the stable jockeys to Warren Greatrex has been an unusual one.

When he was 12, Gavin was taken to Co Tipperary during the summer holidays to trainer Pat Carey's yard near Thurles. His friend John Paul Williamson, who had a few point-to-point horses and worked for Pat, taught him to sit up on the racehorses. He also learned how to muck out stables and groom the horses. At 13, even though he had still not mastered the art of doing a rising trot, he cantered a horse round the perimeter track on Thurles racecourse – fortunately it was a schoolmaster and did not pull – and Gavin got a real buzz from the experience. From that day he decided he would like to be a jockey.

Back in Co Cork, the O'Donovan family owned a yard from which Davy Keane trained good racing ponies for Castle Racing, and one of the Sheehans' neighbours was a member of the well-known Castle Racing syndicate, which owned a number of top racing ponies. One of the syndicate's older ponies, Gypsy Blaze, a black 12.2hh pony who boasted many wins, having been ridden during her brilliant past by jockeys such as Chris Hayes, Davy Condon and Paul Townend, had been semi-retired and was living in a field. Gavin began riding her and learned how to properly rise at the trot by taking her onto the horse walker and turning up the speed dial. He also rode her with Stephen O'Donovan's string of horses, which meant learning to negotiate the rough tracks and bends in the local forests. Once a week he cantered Gypsy on Eamonn Fehily's gallop, but he rode with long stirrups and did not look like a jockey.

When he rode in his first pony race at Ballybunion in August 2006, Gavin noticed the other riders had very short stirrups, so he pulled up his leathers to copy them. Unfortunately, he was totally at sea and even cantering to the start could barely steer his pony. During the race he hit an upright post, resulting in a heavy fall and a broken wrist. It was a humiliating first venture into racing and it made him question whether a career as a jockey was really for him. Was he too light – even with his boots, breeches and colours he weighed only 6 stone – and would he ever be able to ride with short stirrups?

Luckily for Gavin he quickly gained further experience by riding some top ponies at the yard, and in the middle of the 2006 season was handed the ride on Night Owl, who had been ridden to many victories by Paul Townend. A liver chestnut with a white face, he always wore a blue bridle with a sheepskin noseband. Gavin rode him on the beach track at Inchydoney and duly won.

Night Owl had a fantastic record on that sand course, and the victory changed Gavin's life. He ended up winning more than 100 races on the pony circuit at a time when his fellow riders included Adrian Heskin and Danny Mullins. He soon became the first jockey for Castle Racing and was the champion pony rider in 2007 and 2008. He had ten winners at the famous Dingle meeting in Co Kerry. These 'flapping' races are called pony races, but many of them are for horses – nearly always thoroughbreds, and ones who may or may not have previously run under rules. Gavin's best horse was Cheguevara, who was 16.1 hands high. An ex-racehorse can take part in pony races but, once it has done so, it cannot go back onto the track. Since in 'flapping' races horses' names are changed, this has, in the past, opened the door for the running of ringers – horses who may well not be ones they are said to be – but nowadays with microchipping it is almost impossible for the horses to get mixed up.

In 2009, Gavin Sheehan went to Michael Hourigan's stables in Co Limerick, having decided to pursue a career in race-riding. Adrian Heskin took the same route. Gavin had hardly done any jumping, even though he had ridden out with the point-to-point trainer Gerry Cully. He did plenty of jumping at Lisaleen and was integrated into Michael Hourigan's system for breaking in young horses, who are taught to accept their riders in a very short space of time. It was completely different to what Gavin had done with his unbroken donkey.

Whilst at the Hourigan establishment he acquired a number of point-to-point rides from local yards as well as riding in several bumper races for his boss and for Adrian Maguire but his sole win was on Old Wigmore at Rathcannon in 2009. Many of the horses he partnered were poor jumpers and he had a high number of falls. When he handed in his notice at the end of January 2011 he found himself to be at a crossroads, and remembers questioning his desire to continue as a jockey.

Before returning to Co Cork, Gavin went to Enda Bolger's yard near Kilmallock. He was at a low ebb and needed a boost for his confidence. The days he spent with Enda, he declares, were 'the best two weeks of my life'. Enda is a brilliant teacher, who gets a rider to trust the horses he rides and sit in the correct place, in the centre of balance, when they are jumping. Negotiating the banks and cross-country fences at Howardstown, as well as accompanying Enda on his famous rides across the neighbours' fields, gives jockeys priceless experience and confidence. John Francome still remembers a day spent with Enda when the pair of them went out for a bit of fun. 'We rode for many hours and began by jumping a hedge out of the yard. This was followed by stone walls, banks, barbed-wire fences and even cattle grids. Enda is fearless.'

Back in Cork, Gavin spent time with John Joseph Murphy at Highfort near Upton, where he did more jumping – John had always been connected to the show-jumping world – and in February 2010 Gavin rode a winner for him, What's A Billion, at Thurles. He also had a point-to-point win for Robert Tyner, but then broke his shoulder in a fall from one of Eamonn Fehily's horses.

Convalescing gave him time for thought, and when he started riding again it was through the Fehily brothers that he moved to England in August 2011 and became Charlie Mann's conditional jockey. In his first season for Charlie he had seven winners, followed by 21 winners in the second one. At the end of the 2013-14 National Hunt season he was the champion conditional jockey with 50 winners, and it was then he moved across the road to Uplands in Lambourn to ride for Warren Greatrex, for whom he won the World Hurdle at the 2015 Cheltenham Festival on Cole Harden.

For a jump jockey who comes from a non-equine background to be given a top position in a leading National Hunt yard is a significant achievement. It is not essential to be born with horse connections; if you are willing to learn and are prepared to work, anything is possible.

Harry Skelton

Harry Skelton has had a remarkable tally of winners over recent seasons, almost exclusively for his brother Dan, who trains at Lodge Hill in Warwickshire. From the beginning of the 2015 season until April 2019 the tally stood at 511. Harry has in recent seasons finished high up in the jockeys' championship lists, and could end up as champion one day. So where did it all begin?

Harry was brought up partly in Shropshire by his mother, who had separated from his illustrious show-jumping father Nick, and partly in Warwickshire, where his father lived. He was sitting on ponies at his father's yard as far back as he can remember, and had some outstanding show-jumping ponies. Oxo, a 12hh Welsh-New Forest cross, was his first pony, but then came his jumping ponies, and most of them were top performers, with Skibbereen Girl, Welsh Wonder and Fontmail Rasputin rating high on his list of favourites. Harry often missed school on a Friday to prepare for the big shows on Saturday, jumping at all of them, including Hickstead, and winning many classes. His father is a great teacher.

In 2000, Nick Skelton had a bad fall at the Essex County Show and was out of action for a number of months. The following year Harry spent his school holidays at trainer Reg Hollinshead's yard in Staffordshire where he started riding racehorses. He loved the change from ponies, but continued to ride his show-jumpers at the top shows until he was no longer eligible. At 16 he rode in a couple of point-to-points, which he enjoyed but he did not have a winner. Yet because he was light he became hooked on the idea of race-riding, and spent valuable months at Richard Hannon's yard in Wiltshire.

He liked the idea of riding on the Flat, but his brother Dan was assistant to champion trainer Paul Nicholls, so he moved to Somerset, where he remained an amateur for ten months and rode his first winner for Jimmy Frost on October 1, 2007, on Temper Lad in a conditional jockeys' selling hurdle at Exeter.

Harry stayed with Paul Nicholls until April 2012, but the rides had dried up, so when Dan began training in Warwickshire he moved back with him and in the 2012-13 season rode eight winners. He had undoubtedly gained invaluable experience at Ditcheat and ridden class horses, but he was never going to have many winners from the champion trainer's yard.

With a star show-jump rider for a father – who won the individual Olympic gold medal in Rio 2016 with Big Star – Harry could have gone a long way with show-jumpers but it was racing that he preferred and he is just as dedicated as his father. His wife Bridget Andrews is herself an accomplished jockey under rules and, like his brother, Harry is driven by the prospect of more winners.

Harry is a great asset to the Skelton team at Lodge Hill, where there are superb facilities for jumping, and he does plenty of schooling. If determination and a competitive streak are the ingredients for top honours then Harry possesses both. He has an excellent manner with owners and the racing public, and is popular with his weighing-room colleagues. Currently his obsession with winners rules his life, but winning is not everything in racing, and with time Harry will probably get the whole game into perspective, though not before he has put all his energy into taking a jockeys' championship. He has already had three Cheltenham Festival winners, and is sure to add to that tally, but he and Dan still need their shop-window horse who returns season after season. There is every reason to believe this will happen.

JJ Slevin

JJ Slevin was brought up surrounded by horses. He had his own pony from the age of three. Buttons was about ten hands high and well over 20 years old. He would wander loose around the yard and provided JJ could tempt him with some food which he emptied out onto the ground, he could then climb onto him by standing on a bucket. However, the pony got wise to his efforts and the little boy was often to be seen walking round and round the yard with his bucket but no pony.

James Joseph Slevin's mother is Aidan O'Brien's sister, and his father, Shay, holds a training licence and breeds National Hunt horses as well. He used to work for the trainers PJ Finn and Jim Bolger, after which he moved to Ballydoyle and became Aidan O'Brien's head lad. JJ's grandfather Denis O'Brien always lived in Wexford, and trained more than 140 point-to-point winners. Aidan received his early lessons from him.

JJ always rode his ponies bareback, which taught him about balance and grip from the start. He enjoyed hunting with the Bree Foxhounds, and his father would go to the marts and buy youngsters for him to break in and educate before selling them on. The fairs at Ballinasloe, Clifden and Maam Cross were a particular haunt, and the Slevins would cram their unbroken purchases, many of them Connemaras, into an old horsebox. With his older brother Mark – now a vet – he competed at the local shows and enjoyed show-jumping.

At school JJ was a good pupil with a sharp brain who found the lessons easy, but it was riding ponies that he enjoyed most. At 13 he began pony racing, and a few of the Slevin ponies were taken to 'flapping' tracks. He had a good 14hh pony, but it was not a thoroughbred and could not match the speed of the blood ponies. He thoroughly enjoyed those days, and rode against embryo jockeys like Kielan Woods and Keith Donoghue. 'The starts were very important, and the races toughened us up.'

After getting his Leaving Certificate, JJ went to Griffith College in Dublin to spend three years studying journalism. During that time he rode out for John Robinson near the Curragh and Ross O'Sullivan, who trains near Naas and is married to Katie Walsh. He had taken out an amateur licence while still at school, and he rode in several bumper races as well as point-to-points, with his first win coming in 2009 when, at 17, he rode Here Comes The Rain to victory for his father in the six-year-old maiden race at Ballydarragh in Wexford. Aidan O'Brien had won a bumper on the horse's dam. JJ ended up with 35 point-to-point wins. His earliest efforts under rules were nowhere near so successful, and he had 110 rides before scoring on Chapel Garden in 2013 for John Clifford in a bumper race at Thurles.

After getting his degree, JJ spent a year with Aidan at Ballydoyle, followed by a year in England with Nigel Twiston-Davies. He found the English system to be noticeably different to the Irish, but learned a great deal from his time in the Cotswolds. JJ's father currently stands two National Hunt stallions by Galileo, El Salvador and Centurion, and JJ takes plenty of interest in the stud work. In his spare time he still enjoys helping with the breakers.

Nowadays, JJ rides out regularly for his cousin Joseph O'Brien and is a great help to him with the daily training programme. The two of them have forged an excellent partnership which looks certain to last many years. JJ has ridden plenty of winners for the Carriganog Hill yard. In 2017 he won the Martin Pipe Conditional Jockeys' Handicap Hurdle at the Cheltenham Festival on Champagne Classic, trained by Gordon Elliott, and in 2019 Band Of Outlaws, trained by Joseph, won the Fred Winter Juvenile Handicap Hurdle. He loves Cheltenham and has had some good rides there. He has a bright future as a National Hunt jockey.

Bill Smith

The turning point in Bill Smith's life was probably his meeting with Kiwi Kingston, the New Zealand heavyweight wrestling champion. The sportsman was close on 18st and imported large German-bred show-jumpers which he took to the local shows.

The Smith family lived at Hayling Island in Hampshire, where Bill kept guinea pigs, rabbits and cats. He enjoyed being in the countryside and was promised a pony by his father when he passed his 11+ exam. At his secondary school he joined the Horse Rangers of the Commonwealth Riding Club – one of only three boys among 200 girls. 'We wore a special uniform with a beret hat and we spent time marching as well as riding. It was great fun.' At the weekends he attended the local shows, which is where he met Kiwi.

The wrestler lived in Horsham, and in the winter months invited the young lad to see his show-jumping yard. From then on, whenever he was not at school, Bill went to the stables, which were part of a 40-acre farm. He was allowed to take his own pony with him, and in return for work was given a few lessons, but he learned even more from watching. Although the boxes were basic and there was no electricity, it was a fantastic experience for a child and he enjoyed every minute of the time he spent there.

There were precious few horse connections in Bill's family. He is an only child, and was born in London, where his father, another Bill, had a cycle shop in Chiswick. Bill snr enjoyed cycle racing, and once rode from York to London in such good time that he reached the capital before a letter which he had posted in York arrived. During Bill's childhood, however, the cycle business gradually went downhill and, despite opening two new shops in Surrey, the family decided to move to Hampshire.

Bill remembers the day he left school, when he was 14 years old.

It was 3pm, and I went straight to the station and got on a train to Horsham. The show-jumping yard was one and a half hours away from home, but that didn't worry me – all I wanted to do was ride, and I got the leg-up on a lot of naughty ponies. I successfully show-jumped a few of them for the boss and his wife. My parents used to come to the shows, and I became very competitive, but I used to sulk if things did not go right. One day a pony stopped three times at the first fence, and I was furious. I was in a proper mood and because I sulked in the car I was not allowed any lunch as a punishment for my behaviour! **9**

This streak in Bill's make-up stayed with him: when he was racing he hated losing any race that he expected to win.

As a child Bill was very light, and weighed less than 7st. He was a shy boy and embarrassed about being 'small and puny'. However, everybody told him he should be a jockey. Thus, towards the end of his 15th year he went on a month's trial to Fred Rimell's famous training yard in Worcestershire.

6 I was paid five shillings a week and picked stones off the gallops. One of the horses in training was Spartan General, and I got to stroke his tongue while his lad groomed him, because he was keen on biting and kicking, but with his tongue in my hand he was a gentleman. But I did not enjoy my time there and could not wait to leave. There was no excitement and I decided that racing was not for me. **9**

After his unsuccessful introduction to racing, Bill Smith spent time at Moss Bros in Portsmouth. It was mostly hire work – morning suits and hats for weddings, shoes, shirts, collars and ties. He was paid one shilling and ninepence an hour, and he got commission if he managed to get people to hire out extras like stiff-collar shirts, gloves and special shoes. 'I would measure up clients with a tape measure and advise them what to buy or hire.' He spent 18 months at Moss Bros but, despite being kept busy, he was at the bottom of the pile as another senior assistant took 'the cream of the clients under his wing'. However, there was another man working there who had a friend with racehorses and ponies. It was through this owner that Bill had his first ride in a point-to-point.

In 1966 he rode a horse for Donald Underwood at the Cowdray point-to-point. He had never jumped a steeplechase fence before, nor been on gallops – 'the only galloping I'd done was up Midhurst high street. I was left at the start and, despite the horse running well, I fell off two fences out. Mr Underwood was furious.' However, Bill continued to work for the owner, and many years later rode his good racehorse, Mon Plaisir. On his second point-to-point ride, at Hackwood Park near Basingstoke, in a two-horse members' race on Bob Rutter, he managed to win, but the rest of his point-to-pointing career was inconsistent, and Bill clearly had a great deal more to learn about jockeyship. Thus, when permit holder John Blake, a tipster, asked him to ride his horse, Silver Meade, in a hurdle race, he was delighted and in 1968 it was his first winner under rules.

John Blake, as well as preparing horses at home, also had horses in training with Bill Marshall, who at that time was looking for a 7lb claimer. In 1969 Bill Smith joined the professional ranks and had a number of successes, including Harlech Lad, who won five races on the trot. Bill's riding was on the upgrade but there was minimal footage to be found of any of the races in the 1970s and jockeys could not study their riding style. They used to rely on what trainers or fellow jockeys told them. Nor were there any jockey coaches. It was hard for riders to improve their techniques, which they only did with plenty of practice and copying others.

When Bill's race-riding career snowballed, in 1972, on the advice of Terry Biddlecombe, he returned to Fred Rimell's establishment. He rode a number of winners from the Kinnersley yard including taking the 1973 Champion Hurdle on Comedy Of Errors. He also rode for trainer Edward Courage and won several races on the hugely popular Spanish Steps, as well as registering two wins in the Champion Chase at Cheltenham on Royal Relief in 1972 and 1974.

Bill Smith had many high-profile years as a National Hunt jockey, and ended up with 501 winners. He completed the course eight times in 11 Grand Nationals, but he also had his share of injuries and broke numerous bones. The months on the sidelines hit him hard. 'I was 35 when I retired in 1983, and I could not wait to give up. I was no longer enjoying riding in races, plus the wear and tear that my body had endured was beginning to take its toll.'

He had been bitten by the racing bug and experienced a number of memorable days in the saddle. When he stopped race-riding he successfully trained Arab-racing ponies for Sheikh Mohammed and spent time on the horseshow circuit, where he owned numerous good hunters produced by David Tatlow. Bill Smith is a good talker and a dapper dresser; he can always be singled out in a crowd and continues to enjoy the racecourse atmosphere, especially at the major meetings.

Charlie Swan

The Swan family home is Modreeny House, near Nenagh in Co Tipperary. It overlooks acres of picturesque parkland and the magnificent trees on the avenue are edged by a gently flowing stream. The approach to the house presents a classical picture-postcard view. Charlie's father Donald, who was in the British Army, and had served in the Queen's Dragoon Guards, bought Modreeny together with its 25 acres in 1965 for £30,000. It had not been lived in for 12 years, and a local farmer had been using it for his sheep and chickens.

When he moved to Ireland, Donald trained racehorses on his land, having previously spent time in England with trainer Toby Balding. He successfully turned out a string of winners. However, there are not many racing connections in the Swan family, except on Donald's mother's side. Her great-grandfather, Tom Chaloner, had been a Flat-race jockey in the 1860s and had partnered Macaroni to win the 1863 Derby. Don enjoyed his years as a trainer and at the same time became master and huntsman of the Ormond Hounds. He has always been a tremendous sportsman and tells some good stories.

Charlie Swan considers that the start he was given at home paved the way for his career as a jockey. From an early age he helped his father with the racehorses and spent time with the breakers. He was small and light, which meant he was in demand when it came to backing the racehorses. He did 'loads of hunting' and had some really good ponies. His 13.2hh pony, Lightning, was bought for £200 from Miley Cash, who was a horse dealer and Walter Swinburn's uncle. Two pounds was given back for luck. Lightning was well known in the area and a great jumper, and Charlie did everything with her including pony racing, even though she did not truly stay the distances.

The young jockey did well on the pony racing circuit.

❜ Pony racing is very good for teaching one about a start. The start in any race is one of the most important aspects. A jockey needs to be alert and have his wits about him – many valuable lengths can be lost if you get a bad start. Even if a horse needs to win its race from behind, it is better to be jumped out at the start and then dropped in to settle. ❜

Charlie won his first pony race when he was 12 years old at Ballinasloe in Co Galway.

❜ I started riding when I was four and to begin with I used to ride my sisters' ponies. I wanted to be a show-jumper. It was Jack Cavanagh, the farrier, who got me into pony racing. As well as ponies he raced a number of small thoroughbreds, on whom a whole string of Irish jockeys first experienced the thrills of race-riding. ❜

Lester Piggott was Charlie's hero: he used to watch him as many times as he could on the television and tried to copy him – 'even the way he held and waved his whip'.

The young rider's first winner at a racecourse was at Naas in March 1983, on a two-year-old trained by his father called Final Assault. It was also Charlie's first ever ride. He was still at school and just 15. He had broken in this youngster himself and, since he had been riding the horse at home, his father offered him the leg-up for his first racecourse appearance. The result was unexpected and a surprise to everybody. It won by six lengths. 'In addition to the boy's lack of experience,' reported Tony Power in the press the next day, 'he had a stone of lead under a 7lb saddle and, judging by his cool handling of Final Assault, he will be a very useful rider.' How true these words were to prove.

Charlie left school at 16 – 'I was never much good at lessons, even though I liked maths' – but he had managed to ride his first three winners whilst in full-time education. He never had problems with his weight, and at 16 he weighed out on one occasion at 7st 2lb. With his apprentice licence, Charlie spent a short time with trainer Dermot Weld before moving on to Kevin Prendergast, where he rode a good few winners. 'I went there because I knew that he only had one apprentice. However, that rider was Kieren Fallon, but I was not to know then how good he was going to be as a jockey.' Kevin Prendergast has always been a great producer of jockeys, and gave Charlie an enormous amount of advice. But when his weight started to rise, the teenager moved to Dessie Hughes's yard. He too was a well-known source of good riders. 'Basically, I was self-taught, but if I wanted advice Dessie was tremendously helpful. I used to watch a lot of videos, in particular the ones of John Francome. One learns so much from watching the styles of experts.'

Charlie Swan was extremely successful when he started riding as a jump jockey and during his busiest National Hunt days, Charlie became first jockey to Mouse Morris and then to Noel Meade. He also partnered a lot of winners for Edward O'Grady, from whose yard he rode horses for JP McManus, who also had them with Aidan O'Brien. 'Aidan and I always got on well. We were on the same wavelength, and we liked horses to be ridden the same way.' Charlie rode many winners for Aidan, and his association with Istabraq, who won three Champion Hurdles, is legendary. The trainer maintains Charlie was one of the best jockeys that he ever used: 'I always knew where Charlie would be in a race and he always obeyed instructions' – indeed in that first race at Naas his father had told him to stick to his outside draw and stay where the going was better, and his son had obeyed his orders to the letter. During his racing days he walked all the courses beforehand.

Charlie Swan ended up with 1,188 winners over jumps in Ireland. In 1995 he rode 150 winners in his native land. He was nine-times Irish champion jockey and captured his first championship in the 1989-90 season. He was victorious on 17 occasions at the Cheltenham Festival and in addition to his wins in the Champion Hurdle, he won the Champion Chase on Viking Flagship in 1995.

In 1998, during his last year as champion jockey, he took out his training licence.

The wheel had turned full circle and Charlie followed in his father's footsteps by training his horses from the stables at Modreeny. Apart from installing several all-weather gallops – a woodchip uphill gallop and a round sand one – there were only a few changes since Donald held the reins. Though Charlie only trained for a limited number of years, the gallops are still used by Denis Hogan.

Charlie Swan was a top-class jockey and had many significant wins under National Hunt rules. He was always popular with the racing public and extremely consistent. His style was admirable and his tactics were hard to fault. Charlie's eldest son Harry, as well as being the silver medallist in the Junior European Eventing Championships in 2018, is already riding winners in bumper races. Maybe he too will follow in his father's illustrious footsteps. As Charlie demonstrated there is no substitute for family backing if you wish to pursue a career in racing. The champion jockey had a dream start to his favourite sport and his childhood riding days were invaluable.

Graham Thorner

Graham Thorner was among the top National Hunt jockeys of the 1960s and 1970s. In the 1970-71 season he won the jockeys' championship. He was a tough competitor with a strong will to win, and his style, while not in the classical mould of John Francome or Ruby Walsh, was unique to him and extremely effective.

He came up through the old school, when life was tougher for young jockeys, and it was hard work to make your way to the top of the tree. Graham started out as a stable lad to Captain Tim Forster, a 'guv'nor' of impenetrable countenance whose standards and beliefs, that included consistency and honesty, were notoriously set in stone. The Captain would tell his jockeys they were merely paid servants who were fortunate to be employed by him. Graham seldom travelled to the races in the same car as his boss, and only on rare occasions did jockeys darken the doors of the Old Manor House at Letcombe Bassett. Graham never had a choice of horses he would like to ride: he was just told which ones he would partner. There was one set of rules for the trainer and his owners, and another for the staff.

> We never really had a chat or a conversation. That's how it was. The Captain did not want his jockeys to get close to him. Nowadays nobody would work for a trainer who lived like that – he used to say, 'I pay you a retainer, it's my privilege to do what I like.'

But the Forster factor was based upon loyalty, and gradually, despite early spells of bullying, Graham grew to accept the Captain's work ethic, to the extent that he stayed at Letcombe for his entire career. He became the Captain's stable jockey and rode around 650 winners, including Well To Do to victory in the 1972 Grand National. He went there in 1964 at 15, and did not leave until his retirement in 1979.

Graham grew up in Somerset, where his father farmed 80 acres near Axbridge. He fully supported his son, who had a passion for riding ponies. On his 14.2hh JA ponies, all good buys, Graham jumped successfully on the West Country circuit, collecting numerous prizes and developing a good eye for a fence and a stride. Those were the days when Marion Coakes (now Mould) was competing on the legendary Stroller, and competition was rife.

Graham always wanted to be a jockey, and he got a taste for racing by helping out at Herbie Payne's yard. He would avidly watch the racing on television – all black and white – and often put an old racing saddle on one of his ponies to practise his style. By chance, Graham's uncle Jim worked in Gloucestershire for Mrs Henriques, one of Tim Forster's principal owners, and it was through her that he was accepted, once he had finished school, to be a stable lad.

Life was certainly tough for stable staff back then. There were no creature comforts, indeed there was little contact with the outside world. A new member of staff was put to live in the hostel, where bunk beds and old grey army blankets were the norm. Young boys were given a rough time by the older lads:

There were many times when I was really scared, and I used to walk away from the hostel and cry my eyes out. The lads would sleep in the afternoons and drink heavily at nights; they would pick on the young kids and bully them. My balls were blackened twice with shoe polish and hoof oil. Cold baths were common, and the duckings were scary – especially when my head was held under.

In many racing stables in the 1960s and 1970s jealousy was rife, especially if a young jockey was getting rides in races and the older lads were staying at home, but looking back at the treatment I received I should say that, although it appeared barbaric, it toughened me up, made me streetwise. But at least the lads loved their horses and looked after them really well.

The standards of horsemanship were high in Tim Forster's yard, and the routine was always the same. Every summer the stables were emptied and disinfected. Then they were freshly painted. The Captain used to say: 'It's such a pity that the horses have got to use them again and spoil them.' A tidier and better-run yard would have been hard to find.

In his first season for the Captain, Graham rode as an amateur and had three wins, as well as numerous outside rides. His first win as a professional was on Sandy Saddler at Plumpton in 1967. Graham says he never had any lessons all the time that he was at the Forster establishment. His guv'nor gave him no tips on riding – 'the Captain only said "Well done" to me on three occasions during the 17 years I rode for him, although apparently he did say positive things about me to other people. But Ron Vibert, from whom Graham took over as first jockey, was extremely helpful, as was Brough Scott, who sometimes rode out at the yard.' Basically, Graham developed his own style of riding.

Graham Thorner was successful in many top races. As well as winning the Grand National he took the Hennessy Gold Cup in 1974 on Royal Marshall II and the King George VI Chase in 1976 on the same horse. He won the coveted Arkle Chase at Cheltenham twice, once on Denys Adventure (1973) and then on Alverton (1978).

He was certainly an extremely brave jockey, who got every ounce out of the horses he rode. His whip style, however – with his arm held high above his shoulder – got him the nickname 'Whanger', and would certainly be unacceptable to the stewards of today. Though he hit a horse hard – which he often did, and far back close to its tail – he seldom ever marked it and most of the Captain's string had long careers, often racing until their ages were into double figures.

Despite the unusual trainer-jockey relationship between Tim Forster and Graham Thorner, the Captain did stand up at the rider's farewell dinner in London and say,

I know Graham was irritated that I didn't give him more chances at the beginning, but I was very clever. I waited and let him make his mistakes on other people's horses, but it was perfectly obvious from the start that he was going to be a fine rider, due to his natural abilities and horsemanship. He had a racing brain and a will to win.

After retiring from the saddle Graham trained for a while, but found it difficult to delegate, and was probably too pernickety and kind to his horses. When Edredon Bleu died in 2018, having been in retirement at the Thorner farm for 14 years, he shed many tears. A lot of the toughest jockeys have a soft streak. But he has a good eye for horses, and a number of his purchases have gone on to win good races.

'Captain Forster didn't give a shit how he treated his employees,' reflects Graham, 'but if anybody knocked him I would say, "Shut up: he's my guv'nor."' Loyalty rated very high, and Graham had huge respect for his boss. It was a partnership that stood the test of time and it worked. Yet it could never be replicated. Today's aspiring jockeys would do well to read about the former champion's early years in the game. Graham considers many of them are spoilt, and rely too heavily on mobile phones, the internet and their agents. They don't have the basic riding skills, nor do they care about stable management.

They think they are jockeys but they cannot ride: they bump up and down in the saddle without using their legs. In my day we were closer to our horses, and many of us had been riding from an early age. There were no shortcuts. But today everything is done in a hurry.

Andrew Thornton

In June 2018, Andrew Thornton decided to call time on his years as a National Hunt jockey. He was nearly 45, and had become the senior statesman in the weighing room. He had bounced back on numerous occasions after crippling injuries, and was always a fighter with a determined streak. One of very few jockeys who wore contact lenses while riding, he acquired the nickname of 'Lensio'. To retire with 1,007 career wins was a tremendous feat, and he had some notable successes to his name: not only the 1998 Cheltenham Gold Cup on Cool Dawn, but also the Royal and Sun Alliance Novices' Hurdle at Cheltenham with French Holly, the 1997 King George VI Chase with See More Business, and both the Scottish and Welsh Nationals with Gingembre (2001) and Miko De Beauchene (2007) respectively. Gingembre also won the prestigious Hennessy Gold Cup in 2002.

Andrew's family always had racing interests. His grandfather had more than 78 winners as a Flat owner, with the good handicapper Grey Steel one of his better horses, and Denys Smith, Jimmy Etherington and Neville Crump were his trainers. Andrew's father David always farmed in County Durham and, although there were some beef cattle, the land was mostly arable. His mother, Jean, had show-jumping on her side of the family.

When he was almost six, Andrew's father bought him a black Shetland-cross pony called Tiger. He was a real character and would always try his hardest to unship his rider.

One day I was attempting to ride Tiger in the farmyard, but he whipped round on the concrete, virtually fell over and then bolted down the 600-yard driveway. I fell off almost immediately, but I was more determined than ever to get the better of him. I remember Dad saying that I would not be a proper jockey until I'd fallen off ten times.

Tiger refused to jump, but Andrew soon had some good jumping ponies to ride, in particular Flicker One. His sister Victoria had Flicker Two, both were 12.2hh, but strangely they were not related. On one occasion Flicker One jumped a five-bar gate. Andrew loved going hunting with the Hurworth Hunt, where he continued to jump gates as well as big hedges, but the master, Reg Dennis, told him, 'If you break a gate you will have to pay £52 to have it replaced or mended.' Andrew thoroughly enjoyed his days in the Pony Club, taking part in show-jumping competitions and the Prince Philip Cup gymkhana games. Often he rode bareback.

Andrew Thornton went to Barnard Castle School as a boarder, where he was in the first team in rugby and enjoyed athletics, squash and cricket as well as cross-country running. In the holidays he would ride out for WA Stephenson, the outstanding trainer from Crawleas, near Bishop Auckland, who could be counted upon to turn out in excess of a hundred winners every season. He was 14 when he started there, and Chris Grant, who proved to be an enormous help to Andrew, was the main jockey. The late Alan Merrigan also gave Andrew plenty of advice.

The enthusiastic teenager was allowed to look after a couple of horses, and River House, owned by WA's nephew Peter Cheeseborough, was his favourite. 'I knew when he was right because he would goose-step when he walked!' Also in training at that time were Blazing Walker, The Thinker, Durham Edition, One Man, Killone Abbey and Stay On Tracks – brilliant horses and brilliant years. The full-time lads looked after four horses each and would get a £10 note from the owners if their horse won a race. WA was a shrewd man. 'He knew his horses like the back of his hand,' says Andrew, 'and I got on really well with him. Every day he asked us how our horses were – in particular, "Has he eaten up?" If the horse had not licked out its pot it would be given a quiet day.'

Andrew Thornton left school at 16 to work full-time at Crawleas. It was a great opportunity for any aspiring jockey. He was paid £33 per week after the deduction for his board and lodgings, which were in an old converted pub close to the yard. It was a tough life but rewarding, and riding so many different horses under the watchful eye of the maestro was the making of the young rider. Andrew also fed all the horses in the fields and helped harrow the gallop.

At Kelso in November 1990, having taken out his amateur licence the previous month, he had his first ride for the trainer. The horse started at 20-1, but unfortunately broke its hind leg up the run-in. His second ride came ten days later on The Laughing Lord at Sedgefield, but there were no more for six months until he finished second on Sunny Mount at Hexham and received a lecture for going too wide. His first winner was on Wrekin Hill at Sedgefield in November 1991 in a three-mile amateur riders' handicap chase, where the horse carried 11st 7lb.

Andrew worked for WA Stephenson until the trainer died in December 1992, but he had written down the names of a dozen trainers in the south of England whom he had planned to contact when the famous stables closed down. These included Kim Bailey, Josh Gifford and Martin Pipe. He settled on Bailey and moved to Lambourn, but

I was nearly sacked after 18 months as Mr Bailey told me that I rode too long and I kept falling off. Admittedly I was not riding well, and Norman Williamson was also attached to the yard, and he rode very short. I had some much-needed lessons from Yogi Breisner, who put me back on track and helped with my weaknesses. He discovered my centre of gravity, which meant dropping my irons four inches.

It was never easy for Andrew Thornton to ride short, because he was a tall man – 5ft 11in – and liked to ride with a length of leg to properly sit into his horses.

Andrew rode a variety of winners for Captain Tim Forster, and then started riding for Robert Alner, for whom he had a total of 209 winners, and for Seamus Mullins. A number of the Alner horses, strong chasing types and great jumpers, came from the Costello family in Co Clare, as had many of the WA Stephenson inmates. Indeed, when Andrew won the 1998 Cheltenham Gold Cup on Cool Dawn, he was riding a former Costello horse.

He may not have been the most stylish jockey to watch, but he was extremely effective and kept his horses well balanced. He gave them plenty of confidence. His style was inimitable, and Andrew could be spotted from a long way off: he was never a man to ride with his 'toes in the irons', as is the fashion among a number of today's National Hunt jockeys. Even the children who go pony racing, Andrew complains, are told to put their stirrups onto the toes of their feet. It would be far more helpful, he thinks, if they rode bareback and did more hunting: in that way they would learn proper horsemanship, and establish the correct balance without relying solely on their hands. He believes that too much emphasis is placed on health and safety and jockeys 'looking pretty', as opposed to simple common sense.

Highly intelligent, and well informed on all racing matters, Andrew was known to study the form meticulously when he was riding, and his knowledge shines through in his new media work, especially when he is commentating for Radio 5 Live and ITV. He has a big future in that field and will certainly stay involved in the racing game for many years to come.

Paul Townend

When Ruby Walsh announced his retirement at the Punchestown festival in April 2019, the champion trainer Willie Mullins promoted Paul Townend to his number-one spot in the finest jump yard in Ireland. He is a leading National Hunt jockey and has twice been Irish champion, first in the 2010-11 season and then in 2018-19.

Paul's father Timmy is an extremely knowledgeable horseman who has always owned and bred horses, primarily point-to-pointers, and is a popular figure in the locality near Midleton in Co Cork. From a young age Paul would ride ponies and help his father around the yard. Tragically his mother died of cancer when he was 15, but even when she was very sick she would still go and watch her son on the pony-racing circuit. Paul has two sisters: Jody, who successfully rides as an amateur in National Hunt races, and Caroline who works for Horse Racing Ireland (HRI).

School for the Townend boy was at Ballincurrig, a little village close to his home that has been put on the racing map by the successful exploits of Michael Moore at all the major National Hunt bloodstock sales. As a child Paul did plenty of show-jumping and used to jump at the shows in Lismore every Friday night. To begin with he rode a 12hh pony called Homer, who was an excellent all-rounder and carried him out hunting as well. The second pony, Bob, was nearer to 13.2hh but, although he was a brilliant jumper, he was very free – 'he ran away with me every day.'

From the start of his race-riding days, Paul modelled himself on Paul Carberry and Richard Hughes. When he was 12 his first cousin, Davy Condon, persuaded him to try pony racing, and at the age of 13 he was allowed to take part, and the new venture was an immediate success. Paul's father drove him to the races, and his son began by riding ponies for Pat and Joan Griffin at Glenbeigh, with Night Owl being one of his star rides. Afterwards he rode for the Castle Racing Syndicate, whose ponies were trained by Davy Keane in West Cork, and he won the Dingle Derby for them on Tony B. Paul considers the best pony was The Pie, who was 13.2hh, but he only rode him a few times as he was the principal mount of Emmet McNamara. 'Emmet was always beating me,' he remembers, 'but we were the best of friends.'

Paul ended up with more than 200 wins on the 'flapping' tracks, and gained plenty of race-riding experience in these tough, 'give-way-to-no-one' contests. He rode mostly in the southern counties of Ireland, rarely in the north or the midlands. As well as riding ponies he was very good on the thoroughbred rejects from the tracks, most of whom measured over 15hh. They were sharp as well as fast.

After passing his Junior Certificate, Paul gave up his education at the age of 15 to spend a year with Willie Mullins, and has stayed there ever since. Closutton has become his second home. Paul began as an apprentice and never rode in point-to-points but he did plenty of schooling – although the Mullins' yard is not renowned for its regular jumping. He had several winners on the Flat when he was just 16 in 2006. The Chip Chopman provided him with his first winner in an apprentice race at Limerick racecourse in 2007.

Thereafter, the young jockey began riding in hurdle races and steeplechases, and he rapidly lost his claim. Willie believed in him from the very beginning and even entrusted him to ride Hurricane Fly on his first venture into Grade 1 company in Ireland. Another trainer who quickly spotted the young jockey's talents was John Kiely, who allowed him to partner the strongly fancied Indian Pace in the Galway Hurdle when he was barely 17 and had barely had a handful of rides over hurdles.

Paul Townend has now had a number of high-profile successes, including the 2019 Cheltenham Gold Cup on Al Boum Photo, which provided his trainer with his first ever win in the blue riband of National Hunt racing. Paul has also experienced Grade 1 wins on the brilliant chaser Un De Sceaux. The horse is the racing public's darling, and at Punchestown in 2019 he won the BoyleSports Champion Chase. This followed on from his win in the Clarence House Chase at Ascot in 2018. Besides the Gold Cup, Paul Townend's two wins at the Cheltenham Festival on Penhill – Albert Bartlett Hurdle in 2017 and Stayers' Hurdle in 2018 – are memorable, and in 2019 he won the Racing Post Arkle Chase on Duc Des Genievres.

The champion Irish National Hunt jockey has risen up through the ranks with rapidity, without having done a huge amount of schooling on the racehorses he has ridden. But jumping comes naturally to Paul and he has a lovely way with horses. His outgoing, verging on cheeky, character means that the jockey rides in a relaxed manner and he appears to transmit his confidence to the horses. It is good to watch him in a race, and he is extremely ambitious. He was competitive from an early age, and with so many lovely horses at his disposal he looks like staying at the top of the National Hunt tree for many years to come.

Sam Twiston-Davies

It is refreshing to be able to point to a National Hunt jockey who is 100 per cent enthusiastic about his career. Sam Twiston-Davies has always been a winner, right from the days when he rode ponies in the Shetland Grand Nationals at shows like Olympia. His love of race-riding is infectious. He has an excellent way with the press, owners and the public, and his articles in the *Racing Post* are full of common sense.

His father Nigel is one of the top National Hunt trainers in Britain, and has always supported his son in his career. Although Sam's father and his mother Cathy went their separate ways they only moved a few hundred yards apart, thus both parents were always at hand to watch over their boys – Sam is two years older than brother Willy. There is a lovely atmosphere at Grange Hill Farm, and it is quickly sensed by humans and horses alike.

The two boys grew up together, and were from all accounts extremely naughty and impossible to control, but they loved riding their ponies. Sam's pony, Chester, was brown and white, about 13hh and conveniently versatile. Both children were members of the Heythrop Pony Club, and hunted regularly as well as enjoying hunter trials and show-jumping competitions. Sam then won plenty of pony races but 'because I was a fat child, I did not like going on the scales'. He also took part in a few tetrathlons – running, riding, shooting and swimming – which he found challenging.

Having grown up in a racing environment, where swear words are as common as discussions about girls, there was certainly never any need for sex education lessons when the boys went to Cotswold Comprehensive School at Bourton-on-the-Water, but they did learn manners and how to behave when going racing with their father. They tolerated school because as soon as they got home they could ride, and at 12, Sam was allowed to sit on the racehorses at Grange Hill Farm.

At 16 years of age, Sam was presented with his amateur licence and he then rode in several point-to-points. His first win was in 2008 on Grenfell at Cottenham. He also had a few rides in hunter chases, and was second in his first ever ride on Baby Run at Bangor. He then won a hunter chase on the same horse at Ludlow, and finished third in the Foxhunter Chase at Cheltenham behind Cappa Bleu – some achievement for such a young rider.

Having left school, Sam worked for his father and rode out for him on a daily basis and in 2010 he took out his conditional jockeys' licence. He had plenty of successes and in the 2010-11 season he won the conditional jockeys' championship. Whilst he continued to ride primarily for Nigel, he then spread his wings and during the 2013-14 season, with his stable jockey Daryl Jacob on the sidelines, Sam rode a few horses – and winners – for Paul Nicholls.

In 2015 Sam Twiston-Davies became the Ditcheat stable jockey and he had a good innings, with a number of big-race wins including the 2015 Queen Mother Champion Chase on Dodging Bullets. That prime position lasted until the end of the 2017-18 season when, on account of more jockeys coming into the fold at Paul's establishment, in particular Harry Cobden and Bryony Frost, Sam agreed that the time was right to end his first-jockey contract. Thus, he went freelance.

Sam enjoys his freedom, and nowadays rides a lot more for his father as well as for Dr Richard Newland, but he had some great days on the Ditcheat horses, notching seven Cheltenham Festival winners, although The New One (Neptune) and Ballyandy (Champion Bumper), as well as Baby Run (Foxhunter), were trained by his father. Sam's name will always be linked with The New One, a prolific winner of 20 races, as well as with the handsome grey Politologue.

The prominent jockey has undoubtedly inherited many of his father's characteristics, in particular Nigel's competitive streak and will to win, although, in everyday life, he would appear steadier than reports of the trainer in his youth. He is totally focused and takes life seriously. His riding style, with his waving lower leg, may not be to everybody's liking, but it is effective and horses respond well. There is no reason why Sam should not go further as he is driven to ride as many winners as possible and will travel the length and breadth of the country if the prospects look promising. He is a hard worker and is dedicated to fulfilling the opportunities offered to him in his chosen career.

Katie Walsh

Katie Walsh announced her retirement from race-riding after her win on Antey at the Punchestown festival in 2018. An exceptional horsewoman, she set high standards on the racecourse, not only for female riders but also for amateurs, riding many superlative races, including when she finished third on Seabass in the 2012 Grand National and was victorious three times at the Cheltenham Festival. She also took the 2015 Irish National on Thunder And Roses. Like many of the top Irish amateur riders, Katie was superior to many of her professional counterparts.

The Walsh family lives and breathes horseracing. She is the daughter of the trainer Ted Walsh, himself a fine amateur rider in his day, and she is the sister of the multiple champion jockey Ruby. Her other brother, Ted, is married to Nina Carberry, and her elder sister, Jennifer, spent many years as Ruby's agent.

There were always ponies at the family home in Kill, Co Kildare, and Katie had a lot of fun with the white-faced chestnut Flash, as well as with Princess. They were 13hh and 14hh respectively and both outstanding hunters, as well as being good pony-club all-rounders. Katie hunted regularly with the South County Dublin Foxhounds and, unlike Ruby, enjoyed local shows and Pony Club camps. She also took part in Mounted Games competitions and tetrathlons.

As she grew up Katie was lent the Connemara pony Anois Is Aris, known as Tony The Pony. He was a JA show-jumper. Together they took part in many Pony Club team competitions and represented Ireland at the Pony Club event championships in Britain. When she was 16 Katie evented a second pony, Tell Me More, and was picked for the European Championships in Germany. To complete those eventing days she rode a 16.2hh homebred horse called Stoneybrook, in the Young Riders' team in Poland as well as at Blair Castle in Scotland, and in the Bramham Three-Day Event in Yorkshire. Her mother, Helen, went everywhere with her daughter, and they had some memorable days. The lessons that Katie was given for show-jumping and dressage proved invaluable for race-riding. She always had good hands as well as a deep independent seat, and a finely trained eye for judging strides into fences.

At the same time as her eventing Katie was also riding racehorses at home under the watchful eye of her father, and at 17 she took out an amateur licence. Her first ride was for Ted at Leopardstown in June 2001 on Total Success, and her first winner was Hannon in an amateur Flat race at Gowran Park in 2003. He was also trained by her father.

Having developed a taste for race-riding, Katie Walsh hung up her eventing boots and concentrated on her new interest. She was given some fine opportunities, and even rode Commanche Court in a couple of hurdle races for experience. She rode out for Willie Mullins as well, and after having several bumper winners for the champion trainer she graduated to being one of his regular jockeys. Fittingly, it was for Willie that she rode her final winner in 2018.

At Cheltenham in 2010 Katie partnered Poker De Sivola to win the National Hunt Chase, as well as Thousand Stars to take the County Hurdle. In 2018 she won the Champion Bumper on Relegate. It was her final visit as a rider to Prestbury Park. In July 2013 Katie married her long-time partner Ross O'Sullivan, who is also a trainer, and it was for him she rode Baie Des Iles into twelfth place during her last Grand National in 2018. In total she rode 181 winners in Ireland, as well as eight in Britain, three in Australia and one in France.

Katie Walsh was an exceptional National Hunt jockey, and young jockeys of today should take note of her fine riding style. She continues her involvement with the sport through her media work. She is both eloquent and knowledgeable on camera. She also prepares future Flat-race winners at the breeze-up sales, and is heavily involved in the bloodstock world.

'I've had a marvellous career,' says Katie, 'and I have unbelievable memories.' The profile of female jockeys is growing fast, and Katie

Walsh, together with Rachael Blackmore, Nina Carberry, Bryony Frost, Lizzie Kelly and Lisa O'Neill, has undoubtedly championed their cause. With female jockeys winning prestigious races at all the major National Hunt festivals, it cannot be long before Aintree's showpiece is taken by a member of the fairer sex.

Mark Walsh

Mark Walsh, who is no relation to Katie or Ruby, has had a meteoric rise from lowly origins. When he was growing up his father was involved in the fruit and vegetable markets at Smithfield in Dublin. He does not have connections in the horse world but behind the family home was an acre of land. Ponies were soon to be seen for Mark, his brother and two sisters to ride.

As he grew up, Mark Walsh spent a considerable amount of time with Charlie O'Neill, the huntsman to the North Kildare Farmers hunt. He would ride Charlie's hunters and sit on some of the point-to-point horses kept in the yard. Charlie taught him a vast amount. Taking part in hunter trials helped his jumping style and eye for a fence, but it was pony racing that he enjoyed most, and it convinced him that he wanted to be a jockey. During his school holidays he rode out for Peter McCreery, who trained Son Of War to win the Irish National in 1994. This gave him a taste for riding thoroughbreds.

After leaving his school in Clane at the age of 15, Mark joined the renowned trainer Christy Roche on the Curragh. Christy, who had been champion jockey on the Flat many times and had won three Irish Derbys, was known to be a brilliant teacher. Mark took out his apprentice licence, and then at 16 a jump jockeys' licence. He remained at the Curragh yard for five years and rode in a number of races over jumps as well as on the Flat. His first winner was in a handicap hurdle at Punchestown in 2002 for Marcus Callaghan on Shrug. His second winner, later the same year, was for Christy when, claiming 7lb, he rode Allofasudden, also at Punchestown, in another handicap hurdle. His only Flat winner was in 2010 when he went to Australia on a jockeys' exchange with fellow Irish jockeys Paul Townend, Davy Condon and Stephen Gray.

Mark gained more opportunities and rides from JP McManus, receiving invaluable help from Frank Berry, McManus's racing manager, and also rode horses for Enda Bolger, another superb teacher. Mark was victorious on several occasions in cross-country races on horses trained by the renowned Co Limerick trainer. Indeed, he has won cross-country races at Cheltenham, as well as the La Touche Cup at the Punchestown festival. His quiet and unassuming manner made him a popular choice with JP's trainers, and when an owner believes in a jockey and gives him plum rides it inspires confidence and Mark's belief in himself grew.

In 2016 Mark Walsh won the Irish Gold Cup at Leopardstown on Carlingford Lough, and from then on his career took off. His first Cheltenham Festival winner came on Bleu Berry in the Coral Cup in 2018, and he then had two more in 2019, which included riding Espoir D'Allen to success in the Champion Hurdle. Yet an unfortunate accident at Punchestown a month later, when a kick from a fallen horse broke the jockey's leg badly, meant he missed the next three months of race-riding.

Mark Walsh has a pleasing position on a horse and he does not override his mounts. Like the best jockeys he waits for the fences to come to him, and allows the horses to build up a good rhythm to their strides. Level-headed and modest, Mark knows that a jump jockey's life can be dangerous and that injuries are widespread, but he is always looking to the future. He is extremely ambitious and a hard worker, and he could easily reach the very top. He thoroughly deserves all the success that comes his way.

Ruby Walsh

It is no overstatement to say that as a National Hunt jockey, Ruby Walsh was probably one of the greatest of all time, anywhere in the world. In Ireland he is the most successful rider in history, with 1,980 successes, and with a further 776 winners in Britain he has an enviable total of 2,756 winners to his name.

He also won the Australian Grand National in 2015 on Bashboy, the French Champion Hurdle in 2012 on Thousand Stars, and the Nakayama Grand Jump in Japan in 2013 on Blackstairmountain – with the purse for the last race of £850,000 making it the most valuable race that he ever won. To have risen to such heights despite having broken 67 bones is an incredible achievement.

It was Ruby's brilliance as a rider, coupled with his philosophical approach to life and exceptional work ethic, that enabled him to overcome the countless adversities and still leave National Hunt racing at the top of his game. When he won his final race at Punchestown on Kemboy on May 1, 2019, it was a ride that epitomised the qualities that have made him such a legend. It was the perfect way to say goodbye.

Coming from a family with strong horse connections, Ruby, like his jockey sister Katie, never remembers a time when he was not surrounded by horses and ponies. The only member of the Walsh family not to have come from a horse background is his mother Helen, whose father was a sergeant in the Garda. His grandfather, after whom the bank at Punchestown racecourse, Ruby's Double, was named, was a horse dealer by trade. He originated from Kildorrery, between Mitchelstown and Mallow in Co Cork, and the family business was buying and selling every type of horse from troopers to pointers. After travelling to America he moved back to Ireland and trained at Phoenix Park, before moving his horses to Kill in Co Kildare, which is where Ruby and his father Ted were brought up. Grandfather Ruby would go to fairs and sales all over the country in an attempt to turn his horses into money, and even when he was training his horses were always for sale.

Ted, Ruby's father, has likewise always been closely involved with horses, and won many races as an amateur jockey. He trained Papillon, ridden by Ruby, to win the 2000 Grand National. For good measure, Ruby then won a second Grand National in 2005 on Hedgehunter for Willie Mullins. Ted still sends out winners.

When Ruby was old enough, he began to ride ponies, and at the age of seven was given Pebbles on his birthday, but he never got on with him, since he was 'stubborn to ride and refused to jump anything'. However, everything changed when Flash arrived at the yard. He was about 13hh, and chestnut, with a white face and a flaxen mane and tail. Ted bought him from the Delaneys near Fethard in Co Tipperary and he cost £1,000; even in those days it was a good price for a pony. All the Walsh children rode Flash, and he was the perfect schoolmaster.

The same could not be said about Dessie, the grey 14.2hh pony that followed Flash. He was hot-headed and had a poor mouth, but he taught Ruby how to hold a puller, and he could jump. Both Ruby and his good friend Alan Fleming, who was later to train racehorses in Surrey but in those days worked in the yard for Ted, had plenty of fun jumping hedges in the fields as well as riding over the cross-country course that belonged to the local equestrian centre adjoining the Walsh land. They were educational days, even though on one occasion Ruby had a bad fall and ended up in Naas hospital with concussion. However, he has no recollection of the fall and it never affected his nerve. It was the first of many falls he would suffer during his race-riding days.

Ruby always wanted to be a jockey and, despite enjoying his days out hunting with the South County Dublin Hunt and the Kildare Hunt, it was always racing he had on his mind. He tolerated school, but hated studying, even though he was a bright pupil. To placate his mother he stayed on at secondary school until he passed his Leaving Certificate, but was regularly riding his father's racehorses. To keep up his interest during his schooldays he played Gaelic football, hurling and soccer, as well as being an active member of the Naas Rugby Club.

In his final year at school he was confronted by a careers' guidance teacher, who asked all the pupils for their plans when they left Rathcoole. She was not amused when he told her he was going to be a jockey. 'The school head, Gerry Keirnan, kept me back after class one day and told me that he wanted to see my parents. "This racing lark will have to stop," he exclaimed. "It is the most important year of your life." But he was not talking about my attempt to be champion amateur.'

In May 1995, when he was 16, Ruby rode in his first race and partnered Wild Irish in a bumper at Leopardstown. He was unplaced, but in July he rode his first winner when Siren Song won a similar race at Gowran Park. Both horses were trained by his father, Ted. Such were his successes as an amateur rider that at the end of the 1996-97 season he was champion, and again in the 1997-98 season. Already looking stylish on a racehorse, he had been well taught by his father. He learned to do everything in the right way from the start.

Ruby also benefited from school holidays spent with trainers, in particular Noel Meade at Castletown in Co Meath and in the summer of 1995, with Aidan O'Brien at Ballydoyle. He learned to ride a variety of different horses on the gallops, but was always a natural horseman and had already helped educate plenty of young horses in the fields around his father's yard.

After leaving school he began riding out for Willie Mullins, and when that astute man hung up his own boots as a jockey at the end of the 1995-96 National Hunt season he started to give Ruby, as a claiming amateur, plenty of rides on horses from his yard. Apart from spells in England partnering top-class horses like Kauto Star and Master Minded for Paul Nicholls, Ruby stayed with Mullins' Closutton yard for the rest of his career.

Ruby Walsh was champion National Hunt jockey in Ireland no fewer than 12 times, and in his native land will always be remembered for brilliant wins on Hurricane Fly, Faugheen, Douvan, Un De Sceaux, Annie Power, Quevega and Vautour to name but a few.

His riding style was unique: 'perched over his horses', as Alastair Down said in the *Racing Post*, 'he was like some cross between a question mark and a half-crooked pistol. He stood out in a race like a banana laid on a bucket of coal – unmistakable and inimitable.' Ruby's horses jumped out of their strides, and he was always positioned in the centre of balance. He kept horses relaxed and he liked them to gallop in a good rhythm.

In the past there have been a number of top National Hunt jockeys, including some fine champions, but it is never easy to compare them, and it is unfair to do so. The riders develop their own styles and individual approaches to race-riding. Richard Dunwoody, John Francome and AP McCoy were household names and simply brilliant riders. But throw in Ruby Walsh and the final verdict on who was best is impossible. Ruby was outstanding in the saddle and, at his very best, a joy to watch. Everything came naturally to him – we will never see another of Ruby's calibre.

Norman Williamson

A gifted and natural horseman, as a jockey Norman Williamson had that 'will-to-win' drive. 'Stormin' Norman', as he became known, was greatly admired, not only by trainers and fellow jockeys but also by the racing public. His style was enviable: he showed that balance and confidence are needed to ask horses to go forwards – none of the modern-day bumping about on the back of the saddle and on horses' loins. Norman was a neat rider who sat in the right place, using the strength in his legs to get forward impulsion. His career total of 1,168 winners sums up his talent. His famous double at the Cheltenham Festival in 1995, when he landed the Gold Cup (Master Oats) and Champion Hurdle (Alderbrook), both trained by Kim Bailey, will go down in racing history as a fantastic achievement.

He was not from an established horse family. Norman's father was a farmer who had plenty of cattle but no horses, although he did have a donkey. Norman's elder brother went on to become a successful farrier who has 'an amazing eye for assessing horses' feet'.

Norman was born in 1969 at Bandon in Co Cork but in 1978 the Williamson family moved to Ballyhooley near Mallow, and from there the child's passion for riding grew – indeed, when the weaned cattle were in the crush he would even climb onto their backs. When he was seven his father bought him a 12.2hh pony from a local horse fair. It was unhandled, and it was found tied to a telegraph pole. Fortunately, the Lombard family, who lived nearby, agreed to take on this wild pony and broke it in. Little Boy Blue, as he was named, turned out to be a real star: not only was he a brilliant jumper, but he also doubled up as a racing pony.

Norman learned to ride on Little Boy Blue and won many classes at the local shows. One week they won a Grade-A show-jumping qualifier on the Thursday and on the Sunday were victorious in a pony race. This was some achievement, since show-jumping and racing are two totally different disciplines. Norman loved going hunting with the Avondhu Foxhounds. 'Out hunting one learns to be aware of situations. A rider has to be awake crossing the country, and jumping the many different obstacles really helps one's balance. On one occasion, when I was 11 years old, I remember hunting all day bareback because my saddle was broken.'

In no time at all there were a number of good ponies at Ballyhooley as well as Little Boy Blue – Harry Williamson had a good eye for picking them. He was a renowned stockman and showed many Hereford cattle. His expertise paid off when he selected ponies for his son and he became ultra-competitive at the horse shows.

Once Norman started competing in the pony races he became hooked on race-riding, and he was an immediate success, chalking up 64 winners in one season alone, a record at the time that stood for many years afterwards. One day at Banteer in Co Cork there were seven races and Norman rode six of the winners. At a mere 6st he had the ideal physique, and he was tough with it. The Tyner family from Kinsale, in particular Eric Tyner and his son Robert, were a great help to Norman when he began.

His idol was Philip Fenton, who was older and rode the larger ponies. Norman mostly stuck to the smaller ones, in particular those in the 12.2hh category. 'One had to be awake at the start, and the races instilled a real determination to win. If one took the inside track it was tough and rough, and the rider would more than likely be put through the ropes. Only the children who were streetwise and tough were winners.' Often the meetings were held on indifferent surfaces that were far from level, and the ponies needed frost nails and calkins to stop them slipping on the bends.

❝ We even raced on beaches, and on one particular day in Co Kerry the timings were wrong and the tide came in. It was chaos. Everybody was upside down, and both jockeys and ponies were swimming. The only downside of the pony-racing circuit was that we were all too much stick-happy. ❞

Norman's successes did not go unnoticed, and many people talked about the natural talents of this young Cork boy. He was champion three times, and won more than 200 races.

By the time he left school Norman's weight had risen to 8st, but he was more determined than ever to become a jockey, and he was sent to Dermot Weld's famous establishment on the Curragh. He wanted his licence, and served his three-year apprenticeship despite being extremely homesick. He remembers lodging for £15 a week with a lovely family in Newbridge, where he was given 'two slices of bread and a cheese sandwich every single day'. Norman gained a lot of experience with Dermot Weld, and had two rides on the Flat in amateur races. He sometimes rode work with Mick Kinane, who taught him a great deal, in particular how to get horses to settle and switch off. He remembers once riding the lead horse for Lester Piggott when the legendary jockey made one of his rare visits to the Weld yard.

As he grew heavier, however, it was clear that Norman Williamson was not going to make a Flat-race jockey, and so on Dermot Weld's advice he moved down to Co Limerick to PP Hogan's point-to-point yard. He was often shouted at by the boss, but remembers having a lesson on his style from the champion jockey Martin Molony, while the schooling over the banks that he did on PP's young horses was a priceless education for any jockey.

Despite riding a winner for Patt Hogan – Give Me A Break – he was sacked by the Limerick maestro as a result of some unjust accusations made by older members of staff, who were jealous of the young rider. With Patt, everything was either black or white. He would come to a decision very quickly, often without any evidence to back it up, and if he took against someone he was unforgiving. All the same, he was an amazing man: probably the best judge of a racehorse there has ever been.

Thus Norman was forced to move on, and he returned to his birth town of Bandon where he began working for Gerald O'Donovan, who had a number of point-to-point horses and stood the stallion Arapaho on his stud farm. He bred many good horses, and even sold some of his homebreds to the Costello family in Co Clare. Norman's first winner under National Hunt rules was Jack And Jill in a novice chase at Clonmel in 1988. Two weeks later he rode a double at Tramore.

After the promising start to his racing career he was offered a job by English trainer John Edwards at his Herefordshire yard, but Norman did not want to leave Ireland, although he did have some rides in Britain for the Edwards yard, including a second placing on Charter Hardware in the Kim Muir Chase at the Cheltenham Festival, and a second in the Scottish Grand National to the Brendan Powell-ridden Roll-A-Joint.

Eventually Norman did move to Britain, where he not only rode winners for John Edwards but also for Charlie Egerton, for whom he finished second on Mely Moss in the Grand National in 2000. He also had a number of rides for Venetia Williams (Lady Rebecca and Teeton Mill), as well as for Kim Bailey (Master Oats and Alderbrook) and Howard Johnson. In particular he forged a great partnership with Howard's Direct Route, who was beaten only the shortest of heads by Edredon Bleu in the epic 2000 Queen Mother Champion Chase. The following year Norman rode Edredon Bleu to win the Peterborough Chase at Huntingdon. He also rode for PP Hogan's nephew Edward O'Grady, who had some excellent horses in his care.

Norman Williamson retired from race-riding in 2003 at the age of 34 after several bad falls but, having bought Oak Tree Farm in Co Meath and married Tim Hyde's daughter, Janet, he could see that there was a busy life ahead of him in the bloodstock world. Norman has since done extremely well with his breeze-up horses. He is also Joint Master of the Meath Foxhounds, and his son Josh, who rides well, could easily follow in his father's footsteps and become a jockey.

When race-riding, Norman always believed in his own ability and rode with supreme confidence. He may have been opinionated and strong-willed, but he was extremely engaging to the owners. He always gave thought to his race-riding and was destined to be successful right from the start. He never disappointed his supporters.

Francis Woods

Francis (Frannie) Woods has a link to the greatest steeplechaser of all time. His father Paddy was senior stable lad to Tom Dreaper and rode the legendary Arkle in all his work, as well as partnering him to an early victory on the track. Later, when Paddy Woods embarked on his training career in Co Meath, it was at a yard close to Tom Dreaper. It was the ideal place for Frannie to begin riding. Not all his six siblings shared his passion, although his brother Eddie rode for Fred Rimell and is now a prominent breeze-up consignor in Florida.

As a child Frannie had an old 13hh pony named Snowy whom he rode regularly, often bareback, and took to all the local Pony Club fun days, including camps. However, his father was not keen on pony racing. When Frannie left school at the earliest possible opportunity – he didn't even wait to see his Junior Certificate results – he went to work for the trainer Con Collins on the Curragh. He spent two years with Con, who at that time was training See You Then, with whom Nicky Henderson famously managed to win three Champion Hurdles. He remembers the horse as being extremely savage. It exhibited the same traits in Lambourn.

After spending time with Con Collins, Frannie returned to his father's establishment. He then weighed around 9st 7lb, and as a conditional jockey he had his first winner in 1987 in a conditions hurdle at Down Royal when he partnered Show M How for Pat Martin. Later on, he had days out hunting with the Ward Union Hunt, at the same time as Paul Carberry and Charlie Swan, and had some great days. He was also invited by Charlie to have days with the Tipperary Hunt, alongside jockeys Brendan Sheridan and Ken Morgan.

In 1994 Frannie joined up with trainer Arthur Moore, and he was given a number of good rides, in particular Klairon Davis, on whom he won the Arkle Chase in 1995 and the Queen Mother Champion Chase in 1996. Frannie also twice won the Irish Grand National, on Son Of War in 1994 and Feathered Gale in 1996, which was like history repeating itself, since his father had also won two Irish Nationals, in 1963 on Last Link and in 1965 on Splash.

Arthur Moore is always full of praise for Frannie's handling of Klairon Davis, and says that his superior horsemanship saw the horse go better for him than for anybody else. Frannie recalls his favourite horse as having been a short-coupled individual without a lot of rein – length of neck – on whom a jockey needed to be light-handed.

In 1997, having amassed nearly 300 winners, Frannie suffered severe injuries in a near-fatal car crash. His left shoulder was badly damaged, and some important nerves severed. After discussions with his doctor, in February 1998 he announced his retirement. The racing world was saddened when he hung up his boots, but Frannie says it may have been time for him to stop anyway.

❝ I was not riding as well as I used to. I was minding myself, and my nerve was not as good as it used to be. I was partnering lesser horses and plenty of novices. I had been spoiled by the good ones I'd ridden previously, and I was no longer enjoying race-riding. ❞

It's always difficult for jockeys to admit they are no longer riding with their previous dash, and a pity more do not retire when the enjoyment has gone. When jockeys ride with the handbrake on and prevent their mounts from going forward in a positive way, the falls are more likely. Horses are extremely sensitive animals, and seem to know when a rider is anxious and the confidence has gone. Now Frannie is married to Niamh Cashman, whose father Liam founded the famous studs at Rathbarry and Glenview in Co Cork, he can continue to enjoy National Hunt racing by buying, selling and breeding top jumping horses.

Index

Photo acknowledgements

Plates section 1
Page 1 (top) Alec Russell/Mirrorpix, (bottom) Patrick McCann/
Racing Post
Page 2 (top) Edward Whitaker/Racing Post, (bottom) Patrick
McCann/Racing Post
Page 3 (top) Patrick McCann/Racing Post, (bottom left) Alan
Crowhurst/Getty Images, (bottom right) Edward Whitaker/Racing
Post
Page 4 (top) Edward Whitaker/Racing Post, (bottom) Julian
Herbert/Getty Images
Page 5 (top) Edward Whitaker/Racing Post, (bottom) Ed Lacey/
Popperfoto via Getty Images
Page 6 (top) Edward Whitaker/Racing Post, (bottom)
cranhamphoto.com
Page 7 (top) Mirrorpix, (bottom left) Edward Whitaker/Racing Post,
(bottom right) Patrick McCann/Racing Post
Page 8 (top left) Gerry Cranham, (top right and bottom right)
Edward Whitaker/Racing Post, (bottom left) Split Seconds/Alamy

Plates section 2
Page 1 (top) Patrick McCann/Racing Post, (bottom) Healy Racing/
Racingfotos.com
Page 2 (top) John Grossick, (bottom left) Dan Abraham, (bottom
right) Sporting Life
Page 3 (top) Edward Whitaker/Racing Post, (bottom) Alan
Crowhurst/Getty Images
Page 4 (top, bottom left and right) Edward Whitaker/Racing Post
Page 5 (top) Martin Lynch, (middle) Healy Racing, (bottom)
Samantha Lamb

Page 6 (top and bottom left) Alan Crowhurst/Getty Images, (bottom right) Patrick McCann/Racing Post
Page 7 (top) Caroline Norris, (middle) Michael Steele/Getty Images, (bottom) Patrick McCann/Racing Post
Page 8 (top) Edward Whitaker/Racing Post, (bottom) Ed Byrne